A WAY OF LIFE

by D. E. Pohren

University of Hertfordshire Press

First published in Spain by The Society of Spanish Studies 1979

This edition published 1999 in Great Britain by
University of Hertfordshire Press
Learning and Information Services
College Lane
Hatfield
Hertfordshire AL10 9AB

Published in the United States by The Bold Strummer, Ltd.

Other books by the author:

The Art of Flamenco
Lives and Legends of Flamenco
Adventures in taste: the wines and folk foods of Spain
Paco de Lucia and family

ISBN 1-902806-03-4

Printed in Great Britain by J. W. Arrowsmith Ltd.

INTRODUCTION BY THE PUBLISHER

From the Introduction to the revised Spanish edition of *A way of life* published by The Foundation Fernando Villalón in 1998:

"This book is the first of a collection that we are calling, simply, Morón. In my opinion we could not have a better initial work than this, the 'fascinating' and 'delicious' unofficial history of Morón as lived by Donn E. Pohren for nearly two decades, a period during which flamenco was alive and part of daily life. In this work the author does not offer an objective study, but rather a faithful description of 'his unique personal experiences'. In these pages appear situations, anecdotes and characters which enable us to relive those years in which Pohren 'el americano', or, as his friends from hereabouts knew him, 'Pore', was our most remarkable neighbour, a person capable of leaving a comfortable position for the romantically audacious adventure of discovering the essence of the art to which he decided to dedicate his life. We are only now beginning to appreciate the importance of the time he spent amongst us.

This book, written with a style and brilliance that can only evoke emotion, gives us the opportunity to recover those days just before 'progress', for better or worse, began transforming our customs, enthusiasms, our very sense of identity".

Diego Fernández González
Vice President, Fundación Fernando Villalón[1]

Donn Pohren was born in Minneapolis in 1929 of Scandinavian and German descent. He was still in his teens when he was introduced to flamenco by Spanish expatriates in Mexico in 1947. After two years at the University of Minnesota and two years in the army as a draftee he returned to Mexico under the GI Bill to study at Mexico City College (now the University of the Americas). During this period he commuted between Mexico and Spain where he attended the University of Madrid and got deeply into flamenco.

1. Fernando Villalón (1881-1930) was Morón's most famous son. An eminent poet, he was a member of the cultural generation of 1898, and as such a colleague and good friend of Federico Garcia Lorca, Juan Ramón Jiménez, and the others. He was also a bullbreeder with revolutionary ideas that eventually lead to his financial ruin. In addition, he was an avid flamenco aficionado and as such a friend and admirer of Morón's promising young guitarist of that day, Diego del Gastor.

On completing his BA at Mexico in 1957 he moved with his Spanish flamenco dancing wife, Luisa Maravilla, to San Francisco where they taught and performed flamenco dance and guitar and opened a tablao. Homesickness led to them setting up home in Spain in 1959.

Since, as he puts it, "no one understood beans about flamenco" he began to write his four books on flamenco, all widely translated and recognised as classics by lovers of real flamenco. *The Art of Flamenco* (1962) was followed by *Lives and Legends of Flamenco* (1964) and, after a long gap, *A way of life* (1980). *Paco de Lucia and Family* followed in 1992. He has also written a respected guide to another of his passions, the wines and foods of Spain (*Adventures in Taste: the wines and folk foods of Spain,* 1972).

A way of life is principally based on his eight years running a flamenco centre at Morón in Andalusia, "the wildest years of my life which I barely survived". This experience of flamenco and its mainly Gypsy singers, dancers and guitarists makes this book a vivid and unforgettable picture of flamenco at a time when it was still entirely genuine and a part of everyday life. Long out of print, this revised edition will introduce a new generation of enthusiasts for flamenco to the spirit of flamenco and the huge contribution made to it by the Gypsies of Andalusia.

Donn Pohren ran his flamenco centre in Moron from 1966 - 73 but when the flamenco life style disappeared he closed the centre and settled with his wife and daughter in Madrid. They continued to demonstrate and lecture about flamenco, mostly in American universities and colleges. In 1970 he became the only foreigner to be awarded the national flamenco prize by the Cátedra de Flamencologia in Jerez de la Frontera.

CONTENTS

To my departed friends

Manolito de Maria
Diego del Gastor
Fernandillo de Morón
Pepe, of Casa Pepe
Enrique Méndez

All of whom made flamenco,
and my life, far richer.

PREFACE

Long ago I proposed a trilogy on flamenco, quickly turned out the first two volumes, and then lapsed into silence. I was simply not prepared for the third.

The philosophy, general knowledge, and technicalities of the subject were tackled in 1962 in my first effort, "The Art of Flamenco" (revised sixth edition now in preparation, 1999). This was followed in 1964 by "Lives and Legends of Flamenco: a biographical history," which, as the title suggests, attempted to portray flamenco's history, above all the past two centuries, through biographies of flamenco's greatest remembered artists (presently out-of-print but third revised edition in preparation).

And now, finally, this third tome of the trilogy, which endeavours to describe as vividly as possible what is perhaps flamenco's most important component - its life style - and how this extremely colourful way of life fits into, and is affected by, Andalusian (and world) culture and progress. This material took far longer to glean and absorb than that of its antecedents, for it was not a matter of normal research and intellectual exercise. The flamenco life style as well as its Andalusian framework had to be experienced at firsthand and given time to jell. This book is the fruit of twenty-five years of doing just that. It has been a fascinating and delicious period, and in my opinion adds up to a result that may well interest even the reader who has had no previous knowledge of, or interest in, flamenco and/or Andalusia.

We might begin this study by exploding the popular myth that flamenco is the tragic expression of an oppressed people, moving blackly across life's stage amidst great wailing and gnashing of teeth. Poets and other tragedians have successfully presented flamenco in this light, but the fact is that nothing could be further from the truth. I would estimate that within the realm of true flamenco as lived by its exponents in Andalusia (this excludes all types of commercial staging), light-heartedness is the name of the mood about ninety-nine percent of the time, not only in the art, but in the life style as well. The flamencos are traditionally a happy-go-lucky bunch, tireless and inventive in their oftentimes daffy efforts to make their existence an enjoyable one.

9

And this they manage to do regardless of the equally as traditional poverty in which they exist. Or perhaps because of it, for today's affluent times are showing us that as the flamenco's material well-being increases, they seem proportionately to lose their ability to abandon themselves to living for the moment. The philosophy involved, I believe, is that when one has nothing to start with and no hope of improving this condition, one sucks each ounce of pleasure and adventure from every possible situation right now. In today's newfound prosperity, however, the flamenco trend is to hold down steady work, acquire material goods, fatten savings accounts, square away one's life before stepping out: in short, follow in the footsteps of industrialized citizens everywhere. This, of course, is thoroughly understandable, but deadly to the way of life herein described.

The few technical terms used in this book are explained either in the text, or the glossary. Footnotes have been placed in a special appendix at the end of the book. I recommend you read them. They contain much pertinent information that will provide a greater grasp of the material as a whole. Regarding the common practice of printing all non-English words in italics, in this book there are so many such words, and some repeated so often, that for the sake of reading fluidity we have used italics for these words the first time they appear only.

PART I

SETTING THE SCENE

SETTING THE SCENE

My first experiences with flamenco and its way of life date back to Andalusia in 1954. At that time flamenco was a largely unwanted fringe art, above all the more raucous gypsy variety; this was directly reflected by the dire poverty in which the gypsy flamencos lived. To be sure, the non-gypsy flamencos were not much better off, but there was always something of a demand for the non-gypsy flamenco forms and these artists could normally maintain a somewhat higher standard of living. Of course, by Western industrial standards, both gypsy and payo (non-gypsy) flamencos lived in miserable conditions, and only by comparison would the westerner have been able to discern that poverty is indeed relative.

I remember clearly my early probes into the flamenco life of Andalusia. The first experiences of note were in the old Malaga neighborhood marked by the streets De Los Negros and Cruz Verde, where most of the city's flamencos lived at that time. At best the payos crowded into small one or two room apartments in the disappearing *casas de vecinos*. These "houses of neighbors" were two-story buildings generally built around large, unroofed cobblestone courtyards onto which all rooms converged. The courtyards played an extremely important role in communal life, serving as common area for cooking, laundry, children, gossip, card and domino playing, bullfight and soccer training and, not infrequently, screaming fights between neighbors living in too close proximity. The buildings shared vastly inadequate sanitary, laundry and kitchen facilities. Long lines before the toilets were normal (one to a floor), as they were before the kitchens (usually two, on opposite sides of the courtyard, each consisting of one or two charcoal burners and a sink with a cold water faucet) when it came time to prepare the morning chicory or cook the day's sole meal (midday). It was invariably necessary, in fact, for several housewives to get together and prepare communal dishes, nearly always bean and/or potato stews containing a few scraps from the cheaper cuts of pork, a little blood sausage, and a large chunk of salted pork fat. The tenants who could afford electricity lighted their rooms with dim, bare bulbs hanging forlornly from the ceil-

13

ing. The others, over half, I would estimate, used candles, or smelly old-fashioned oil-burning contraptions. The furnishings were minimal – two or three straight-backed pine chairs, a bed or two, a table – and the decorations consisted of a crucifix, religious prints and calendars, and wedding photos of the inhabitants and of their parents, all looking scared stiff, and perhaps a photo of the parents with their children. And the odor: such places always stank of poverty, of lack of water and stopped-up toilets and dirty clothes they didn't dare wash anymore because they were already in tatters and were all they had.

Nonetheless, the casas de vecinos were quite picturesque, visually saved from slum category by the Andalusian penchant for flowers and greenery. The women grew multitudes of carnations, geraniums, mint and other plants in pots, tin cans of all sizes, wooden crates, whatever would hold dirt and moisture, and placed and hung them around the front of their respective abodes as well as on and about all pillars, the fringes of the courtyard, the second story railing, everywhere. It is amazing how this horticultural inclination mitigates the condition of poverty to an enormous extent throughout all of Andalusia. There are splashes of color on every house front and hanging from each balcony, and entering anyone's interior patio or courtyard is invariably a lush and pleasing experience. The fact that this custom is respected and appreciated by the Andalusian populace as a whole reflects, in my mind, an advanced level of civilization only too rarely found among the world's underprivileged.

As poor as the casas de vecinos sound, however, they were sheer luxury compared to the quarters of many other flamencos I came into contact with at that time throughout Andalusia, including the gypsies of this same neighborhood. These gypsies encamped in a large open courtyard, the walls of which, together with wooden pillars, supported narrow spans of roofing, wall-less on three sides, under which they slept and huddled together for protection against the elements. Cooking was done over open wood fires in the middle of the courtyard. There was no water; it had to be carried in from a fountain some blocks distant. Toilet facilities were, of course, non-existent, as they were throughout most of poorer Andalusia at that time; nearby vacant lots were utilized. Furniture was out of the question. Electricity likewise. Even candles and oil lamps were considered an unnecessary expense; the sole night lighting was firelight. Such living was not too bad – perhaps even romantic – for a time during nice weather, but left much to be desired during the winter and rainy months.

We used to visit the neighborhood flamenco bar, a little

hole-in-the-wall owned by the son of a well-known flamenco singer and replete with an impressive collection of flamenco records. Once we were known as aficionados and good for a few drinks, all we had to do was start sipping the first wine or two and the flamencos would begin asppearing like magic. We would provide wine and corresponding *tapas* (tasty little dishes of food) for all, and the flamenco would soon issue forth without any urging on our part. The ringleader and one of the most colorful of these flamencos was a *payo* called "El Poeta", who would entertain endlessly with poems of the flamenco poets interspersed with uproarious stories of his life and adventures. Then there was La Paula, a middle-aged gypsy woman who had once danced in Carmen Amaya's troupe and who commanded considerable respect thereabouts. And many others. And these impromptu *juergas* (flamenco jam sessions) would soon be going full blast and would last until the wine ran dry, which means to say until our funds ran out because in those days bars in Spain were allowed to stay open all night if they so chose. Everyone drank common bulk wine, and considering that in the mid-fifties one could supply four or five liters of such wine, with corresponding tapas, in a bar of this type for the equivalent of about one dollar, these memorable experiences were absurdly economical and often did go on and on.

Not all flamenco in those days was on such a non-professional and economical level. A sprinkling of flamencos in each large town or city made their living, or attempted to, through their art, as has always been the case. During the period 1850 through 1959, Sevilla was the city par excellence for this type of professional flamenco activity. Flamencos from all over Andalusia would journey to Sevilla and try make a go of it in the *cafés cantantes* and private juergas for which the city was famous. It was not easy, however, and most would end up returning to their pueblos and resuming their former lives.

We hit the tail end of this activity in 1956, when we moved to Sevilla for several months. We entered right into the thick of things by taking a room with the famous Pavón family in their three-story house in the Plaza de la Mata, my wife, Luisa, to polish up her dancing with Carmen and Eloisa Albéniz and Arturo Pavón Jr., I to study the guitar and dance accompaniment. Eloisa's husband, Arturo (Sr.), was still alive then, and I shall always remember him singing softly to himself by the hour as he whiled away his last years seated in his chair by the open front door. His far more famous brother, Tomás Pavón, had recently died, while his renowned sister, la Niña de los Peines, still had another decade or so to go.

15

In 1956 the flamenco scene in Sevilla was still in full bloom, an all night and often round-the-clock affair. A stroll along the Alameda de Hércules and the *calle* Feria about two or three in the morning would reveal countless sidewalk cafes overflowing with flamenco artists waiting to be hired for juergas. And the whores, a most complete line-up of whores of all ages and dimensions, also looking to be hired, for in the flamenco juergas in those days flamencos and prostitutes usually went hand-in-hand. Sevilla had fame of being a wide-open city and attracted wealthy *señoritos* from all over Spain and from the farthest reaches of Europe, and such lively aficionados demanded, and got, the *complete* juerga treatment.

Each cafe in this most flamenco part of town had *apartados* — private rooms reserved exclusively for juergas - and nightly they would fill up with flamencos, whores, and the paying señoritos. And they threw money around, stacks and stacks of it, and we quickly learned that our limited budget would not go nearly so far in Sevilla as it had in Malaga. So in Sevilla we became bystanders, lingering in the cafes outside the juerga-room doors, hoping to be invited in or at least to glean a bit of the art of these artists, for some were outstanding in their fields. (It was in this fashion that I first heard the fabulous guitarist Manolo de Huelva, and the singing and playing of many other artists of the day.)

Around dawn the juergas would usually break up, the artists were paid, and the señoritos would go off to bed down their hired ladies. That was when things really got going; the flamencos with money in their pockets and a full head of steam would repair to one or another bar in the area and blast off. Here they would drink and frolic and perform for each other, often taking along some of the unhired girls and setting them up with drinks and getting them to dance and sing (usually well!). The girls, after a goodly quantity of booze, often became quite affectionate and would alternate with the flamencos of their choice in some solitary part of the establishment. What are friends for, after all! And things would surge on and on, and they would move on to other bars and would often end up spending every penny they made the night before, much to the dismay of the families of those who were married. I knew one guitarist with a multitude of kids who often carried on in this fashion, and his wife had no choice but to send the kids out to beg. That was the main shame of the wide-open flamenco scene of those years: perhaps marriage should not have entered the picture until after these irresponsible artists were too tired, old or fed up to continue carrying on.

This colorful life roared ahead until 1959, by which time it had become entirely too scandalous for the Church, staunchly backed on this issue by the respectable women of Spain. For it was not only Sevilla, but cities and towns all over Spain that happily took advantage of the bars being open all night long and the liberated life this generated. But the Church alone probably could not have done much had it not been for a government move, somewhat in desperation, to attempt to increase Spain's efficiency. How, the government asked (reluctantly, for government officials enjoyed the night life as much as anyone else), could a country expect to be reasonably competent if a goodly share of its working population was out carousing all night and did not make it to work the next day, or at very best arrived at work sloshed? By now Spain was enjoying political and commercial ties with Europe and the United States, and Spain's blatant inefficiency was most embarrassing and, worse, was losing Spain a lot of money. So laws were passed closing all bars at 12:30 a.m., which effectively killed most juerga action because juergas rarely began until after that hour, and prohibiting street walkers. Flan᠈nco in Sevilla was paralyzed overnight, although there were loopholes. Outlying country inns were permitted to remain open until 3 a.m., and some flamencos took to frequenting them, but it was not the same. Most of the moneyed hell-raisers lost interest, and the flamencos had no choice but to find jobs in the new *tablaos* (commercial flamenco establishments) that were just then beginning to flourish in the cities with the advent of significant tourism in Spain, or return to their villages. The tablaos, in their appeal to tourists and Spanish high society, hired the young and good-looking, and the veteran artists of true worth had no choice but to frequent the country inns or go home. Most went home.

Obviously, the next move on our part was to follow them back to their villages, and that, as it turned out, was a highly fortuitous turn of events, for the flamenco of the villages was of a most pure variety, untainted by big city pollution, and the delightful flamenco way of life held strong, immune so far to progress and change.

There were many visits to Alcalá de Guadaira, a town on the Guadaira river some seventeen kilometers from Sevilla, to be with Manolito de María ("el de la María"), a great gypsy singer and fine, if somewhat unorthodox, person. "To be" with Manolito meant to search him out in Alcalá, first trying his cave, a little one room grotto just at the base of the Roman castle overlooking the river. Manolito's was one of the many caves in the neighborhood, dug into the hillside at various levels. The area was actually quite colorful, once you got used to the odor of animal and human waste (no sewage disposal of any kind, of course, and the only water supply was the fountain up on the main castle road) and the fact that the precarious path leading to his cave might have been washed away in spots during the rainy season. If Manolito was not in his cave, which was usually the case, then one began the round of his favorite bars (those extending him credit at that particular moment), which in itself was often quite an experience. One or another of his flamenco friends could always be found in each bar, and of course a drink would be had with each and they in turn would tag along and join in the search. By the time Manolito was found we were often quite a tipsy little bunch, and would include all the makings of a fine flamenco session. Manolo el Poeta was a regular, with his recitations of the flamenco and bullfight poets sparked by moments of inspired dancing. "Barcelona" would always show up, tall, well-dressed, putting on the con by trying to intrigue us with the "rare" song forms of which he was *the* expert and which we could hear for only one hundred pesetas (his singing was considerably worse than mine – and I don't sing – as was his knowledge of those rare forms). And there was Algodón, and occasionally Enrique, gypsy son of Joaquín de la Paula, legendary singer from Alcalá into whose shoes his cousin, Manolito de María, had stepped upon Joaquín's death.

And thus it would start, to end God-only-knew when.

But all the visits to Alcalá were not so lively. Other times I would find Manolito sober in his cave, playing with his grandchildren or talking to his wife or daughter. Then we usually went down to the bar by the river and relaxed and talked over coffee and aguardiente or a bottle of red, and I came to know Manolito quite intimately. Other than being the outstanding singer of the style of *soleares* and *bulerías* from his town and area, he was a sheep shearer by trade, and actually did put in the month or so work a year this entailed. Other than that, his daughter worked in the local olive factory and supported the entire family. Manolito did make some money singing in paid juergas, but it was invariably spent by the time he reached home. He could not hang onto money, and would scatter it wildly whenever he came into contact with it, as if it were contaminated.

There was one occasion, however, when Manolito did come home with money in his pocket, although through no fault of his own. In 1964 I organized and managed a private flamenco club in Madrid, and I hired Manolito to sing in it for a few weeks. He arrived in Madrid on a bitter cold winter night in shirt sleeves – it had not occurred to me that he had no clothes for such a sojourn. This was quickly solved by the generosity of some of the club members, together with a few of the local gypsies. A heavy turtleneck sweater was donated by one aficionado, an overcoat

18

by another, and so forth, until Manolito was quite bundled up and prepared for the Madrid winter. At any rate, during Manolito's stay in Madrid I paid him just enough to cover his expenses and a reasonable amount of spending money, and kept the rest for him so he could present it to his family upon arrival back in Alcalá.

And what a great day it was! One would have thought God had returned. All the neighbors flocked to his cave to look at his big city clothes, by now relatively formal wear, and hear him tell his adventures in the grand manner. And what happiness when he showed his family his Madrid savings – some four thousand pesetas, quite a sum in those days for a family I am sure had never seen more than a thousand pesetas at a time – with which he bought them all new shoes and clothing. The money was soon gone, but the members of Manolito's family were certainly the best dressed paupers in the cave area that year!

At age fifty-eight Manolito was still quite the woman's man. When we would saunter through his neighborhood, an astonishing number of females of all ages would greet him in a most affectionate manner, and Manolito would have a few playful words and perhaps a promise or pinch for each of them. In addition to his way with women, Manolito had a quick intellect and flashing wit which, combined with his flamenco talent, kept him in command of his band of flamenco cohorts and on top of his life in general. He could be extremely funny when drinking, and possessed to an amazing degree the gypsy capacity for creating colorful and unusual situations than can have only colorful and unusual outcomes. Life was rarely dull around most of the flamenco characters depicted in this book, and never dull around Manolito. Fortunately, he was also a gentle and understanding person, and used his wit to make people laugh, not to attack. Such as when he would come home reeling and broke after two or three days away, feeling a bit apprehensive about what the *"foca negra"* might say or do ("black seal," his term of endearment for his obese, nearly black gypsy wife). So he would throw his hat through the cave entrance, explaining that if it flew out again he wouldn't go in there for love or money. I never saw the hat fly out. His wife would smile and welcome him back, asking no questions (at least, in my presence).

One day while having a few Manolito suggested we visit his cousins over in Utrera, a town, he explained, loaded with excellent flamencos but highlighted by two sisters, la Fernanda and la Bernarda. We quickly covered the twenty-one kilometers to Utrera, and another important door was opened into this fabulous world of village flamenco.

This was some years before Fernanda and Bernarda became nationally, and then internationally famous, and they still considered themselves just good aficionadas, living the flamenco life to the hilt. Their situation was quite different in one respect from that of most of the other flamenco artists of those economically difficult times: their father had been a butcher, a common trade for the few hard-working gypsies in Andalusia, and had accumulated a certain amount of wealth and possessions. For instance, a large house that virtually vibrated with juerga at nearly all hours, as I was to find out on subsequent visits to Utrera.

Artistically, these sisters were, and are, unique. Bernarda sings some of the wildest and most driving bulerías that can be heard, and is also quite excellent in several of the other *cantes*. She is, however, overshadowed by Fernanda, whose unbelievably moving soleares make her queen of that serious and basic form. As a matter of fact, no other singer that I have heard, male or female, injects such emotion into any cante as Fernanda, with one exception: Manolito de María himself. This was amply demonstrated toward dawn the following morning, when Fernanda and Manolito broke the emotion barrier. The highly demonstrative gypsies wept openly as the singing of these two peeled away layer after layer of deceptive covering to reveal life's hypocrisy, selfishness, brutality, and , ultimately, futility. Even I, normally undemonstrative, found myself being plunged with the rest into the well of depression.

But before that memorable climax the night was filled with gaiety. We entered with armsful of bottles. Fernanda embraced, both of us, and Bernarda embraced Manolito and shook hands with me, which pretty well describes the difference in character of the sisters. Fernanda is exceedingly warm and open with everyone, to the extent that her rather indelicate and primitive features seem to blend into a certain radiant beauty, causing many aficionados of both sexes to be uncommonly attracted to her. (I know of three foreign aficionados, all young enough to be her sons, who have proposed seriously to Fernanda, and several normally heterosexual female aficionadas who claim they would have liked nothing better than to have an affair with her.) On the other hand, Bernarda is reticent and retiring until drink brings her out of it, and then it is fifty-fifty whether she becomes charming or aggressive. And when Bernarda gets aggressive, everyone scatters.

Before long Perrate and Gaspar dropped in, with Manolo el Camarero and other of the local flamencos, not to mention Fernanda's never-ending immediate family of nieces, nephews, sisters, and so forth. During the night everyone danced and sang.

Manolito was in his glory and at his funniest, full of frolic and horseplay. Some serious cantes were sung by those specialists who excel in them, and they were received with *olés* and enthusiasm, but by no means with seriousness or sadness, for the true sadness that may be generated by these forlorn forms normally will arrive only when wine and fatigue combine to lower the exhilarating gaiety of the group and make it susceptible to sadness. Then and only then will a melancholy verse truly be melancholy, when it causes life's misfortunes and tragedies to surge forth in magnified form. This moment may not arrive during a juerga, no matter how long it lasts. On this first night in Utrera it arrived at dawn and lasted perhaps an hour, an unforgettable hour during which Fernanda and Manolito mourned our very existence.

One might think that the juerga would break up after such an experience, but oh no, not these flamencos. In such situations the flamencos usually quickly recoup their good spirits, and the juerga continues. But what, I thought, could follow such a rare occurrence? Simple – a change of scene. Whenever the flame of a juerga flickers low, the flamencos are expert at perking it up again. Common methods are to visit an assortment of bars, where new blood will join in with fresh pranks and artistry, or, more exciting if there is transportation available, run over to some nearby town and roust out the local flamencos. And this sometimes goes on and on, causing one truly to marvel at the boundless energy of the flamencos. In fact, even the flamencos marvel at it.

Up to this point I had noted that the villages seemed to have a vital lack of guitarists available, for all the experiences to date had been without guitarists, excepting myself. I accompanied them occasionally, when they particularly insisted, but knew that unless the singers and dancers were completely at ease with the guitarist the juergas developed far better without the guitar. In the case of these unworldly artists, whose flamenco experience at that time was limited to their own small geographic area, to be at artistic ease meant being raised together with the same flamenco forms until even the finest subtleties became second nature.

They were simply not used to singing with the guitar, and were only at ease doing so with the rare exceptional guitarist from their area. I had determined to find such a guitarist, and upon asking the flamencos who their preferred guitarist was invariably received the same emphatic answer: Diego del Gastor, from the nearby town of Morón de la Frontera.

Diego, it was said, was the best guitarist of them all, above all in his specialty, accompanying the cante. He also had quite a reputation as an eccentric, and possessed a trait much admired by the gypsies at that time: a complete disregard, even scorn, for money and material possessions. Stories were abundant about his turning down lucrative juerga offers from wealthy señoritos whose snobbish or condescending manner he could not tolerate, or of walking pay-less out of juergas he had deigned to accept because he did not like the attitude of those present. I liked what I heard and was about to seek Diego out, when chance did the job for me. A gypsy friend dropped by our place in Sevilla one night and told us to get cracking, there was a gypsy get-together out in Utrera that night which promised to be exciting. Featured artists were to be Fernanda and Bernarda, Juan Talega, the old singing maestro from Dos Hermanas whom we had also taken to visiting at that time, Antonio Mairena, and many others, and included as sole guitarist none other than Diego del Gastor. If my memory is correct this was in 1960 and was either the first or second *"Potage"* (garbanzo bean stew) *de* Utrera, an annual fund raising juerga organized by the local brotherhood of the gypsies. (The Potage has since grown out of all proportion and today is valid only for making money. In 1960 some one hundred souls attended, nearly all gypsies, and it was held in an old dirt-floored warehouse on the outskirts of Utrera. In 1976 a noisy mob of fifteen hundred attended, paying outlandish prices and getting served very poor "potage" and even worse artistry.)

Utrera, 1960. The artists for the night sat along the far side of a long table facing a semi-circle of tables for the public. The gathering was relatively intimate, and the warehouse turned out to be fine acoustically; no sound equipment was needed. The artists were an imposing bunch, among the most famous in the flamenco world, with their corresponding over-sized egos (a normal and seemingly helpful, even necessary, asset in any of the performing arts). Even in such a group, however, Diego del Gastor was unquestionably the foremost figure at that table. Not at first glance, I should add, for septuagenarian Juan Talega, with his rugged, nearly black face contrasting sharply with his thick mane of white hair, his solid body appearing as powerful as his deep, profound voice, sat looking every inch the godfather. Diego's prominence was of a more subtle nature. Refinement is the key word. Although product of a roughhewn community, born in 1908 of a relatively wealthy gypsy cattle dealer and gypsy mother who weaned him on the soleares of his birth place, the mountains of Ronda, Diego exuded an aristocratic air that was in no way put on. Why this was so I have never been able completely to figure out. True, Diego did receive some formal schooling as a youth, an unheard-of procedure among gypsies at that time and still rare even today. He was, in fact, one of a very few gypsies in the gathering that night who had learned to read. And read he did, voraciously (especially when recovering from juerga excesses), everything he could get his hands on, from poetry to newspapers to political essays to translated Zane Grey and Pearl S. Buck and Tolstoy. There was no doubt that education, combined with his very quick and curious intellect, certainly accounted for part of his refinement, but by no means all, for Diego's very appearance was aristocratic. With his nearly white face and white hair combed carefully to one side to cover a balding spot, Diego looked far more like Spain's ambassador to England than a gypsy guitarist, regardless of his otherwise distinct gypsy features. His demeanor followed suit. Diego was extremely courteous and thoughtful of others, and had the gifts of putting people at ease and bolstering their self-impression in a most easy and natural manner. His air of refinement was so great, in fact, that one was apt to forget that Diego was, after all, from a primitive and crude ambiance, and that during the course of a juerga he might drop ashes or cigarette butts or spittle on your living room floor, that he didn't know how to manipulate a seat toilet and was not too good with silverware. Although his father had been considered well-to-do, none of the family, friends, relatives or acquaintances of his youth had the vaguest notion of such things. All were illiterate. Meals were spooned from the communal stew pot, fingers were used for eating whenever possible. Bathroom facilities did not exist, nor running water. Floors were usually dirt or cobblestone. Entire weeks were spent driving cattle from one village to another, selling them, returning home, sleeping under the stars en route. But there was also leisure, when Diego and three of his brothers learned to play the guitar. This was a most unusual accomplishment in those days, when normally not one soul in those backward villages could afford guitar lessons, even if an instructor could be found, much less the instrument. Except, of course, the village elite, consisting of the priest, pharmacist, doctor, if the town was large enough to support one, and two or three wealthy landowners, none of whom normally would bother with the guitar at any rate.

Diego was extremely shy by nature. This night in Utrera he began cautiously, pleasant enough although not at all at ease. But as the juerga progressed and empty wine bottles began filling the long table he was enveloped by an air of decisiveness. His accompanying became more assertive as the wine flowed until finally he became one with each singer or dancer, while still retaining his individuality as a guitarist. He gave a remarkable lesson in the art of accompanying that night, proving himself even superior to his legend.

Two days later I was off to Morón de la Frontera in search of Diego, in a meeting that was seriously to affect the course of my life, and of course that of my family, for the next fifteen years. Following Diego's instructions, I arrived at the Plaza San Miguel, a quite lovely square situated in the upper part of Morón, about mid-morning. Three factors made this plaza significant: it offered an excellent view of Morón's twelfth century Moorish castle, perched high on a wooded hill overlooking the plaza; it was dominated by the majestic Church of San Miguel, with its cracked steeple that at any moment threatened to topple down and bring with it its nest of storks; and it was the home of Casa Pepe, a bar that for years had served as headquarters for Morón's flamenco element. As I entered Casa Pepe I immediately spotted Diego, standing at the bar reciting poetry in a rather raucous manner, his hair disheveled, face unshaven, eyes gleaming, gesticulating wildly...

> *"Echa vino montañés,*
> *que lo paga Luis de Vargas,*
> *el que a los pobres socorre*
> *y a los ricos avasalla..."*

> *"Pour me some highland wine,*
> *Luis de Vargas is paying,*
> *he who helps the poor*
> *and tramples the rich..."*

Diego finished this dream of poor people everywhere, written by the late poet Fernando Villalón, a marquis and, ironically, one of Morón's richer citizens in his day, and began expounding on its merits and on those of the poet, who had been a good friend of his and "who was not at all like most of the rest of the rich sons-of-bitches in Andalusia." He suddenly spotted me and called *"Hola,* come have a drink." We had only talked briefly in Utrera and I was afraid he wouldn't remember me, but he did, seemingly because there were very few foreigners interested in flamenco in 1960, and apparently none who had made his way to Morón and to Diego.

He could not have been more cordial, introducing me around, making me feel completely at ease. It turns out I had arrived at an excellent time, for Diego was still going strong from the Utrera gathering of two nights earlier and had just arrived back in Morón himself that morning. He had stayed in Utrera with Fernanda and

24

company playing, drinking and generally carrying on, and had not eaten or slept in the interim. (This was not unusual for Diego; if things were interesting enough he could go on indefinitely. When in his prime, he used to take the six day Sevilla fair in stride without even seeing a bed. The last time he did this, when no longer in his prime, he suffered a stroke.) I say this was an excellent time to arrive because it was after two or three days of juerga that Diego's playing would reach its peak, when his guitar would come alive with expression in a manner I have never heard equalled.

I had to marvel that anyone can even play the guitar after two or three sleepless days and nights of drinking, much less play it better than when fresh, but in time came to learn the formula. First of all, one must possess an extraordinary capacity for alcohol and an extremely low-level need for sleep and food, achieved by Diego and others like him through many years of living the flamenco life style. Secondly, Diego and most others in the flamenco world had learned to pace themselves. At the beginning they keep up with everyone else, perhaps surpass them due to their enormous capacities, but when each one's moment of uncertainly arrives he slacks off and sips for a time while munching on a few tapas, until he feels his head clear a bit. He can then drink steadily again for some time, slack off again, and so forth, for hours and days. But what about sleep? That is the third point. The flamencos learn to nap at every desired opportunity, and the most minimal nap of perhaps fifteen or twenty minutes goes a long way with them. I have seen Diego nap in a chair in the corner of Casa Pepe when I thought he was surely too far gone to continue, only to have him bound up after a half-hour ready for another twenty-four. Also, while in juerga and pretty far gone, they take utmost advantage of any traveling, passing out immediately and awakening fresh at the destination. In fact, they prefer such naps to a full night's sleep because naps avoid, or at least postpone, hangovers. They know through experience that as long as a certain alcoholic level is maintained, hangovers stay in the background. As a matter of fact, the avoidance of hangovers is an important factor in the prolongation of juergas. But when the juerga *was* definitely over, for it had to end sometime, Diego used to taper off slowly, switching gradually to milk and fruits and catnapping in chairs and other such uncomfortable contrivances until he thought he had the hangover licked and he could afford to go to bed. This plan worked well throughout most of his lifetime. Only towards the end was he plagued with the most horrible hangovers, that caused him time and again to swear never again.

Another way flamenco guitarists keep going, giving them a definite advantage over the others, is that when performing their drinking is cut far down. A guitarist cannot play and drink at the same time, and he is playing most of the time. Dancers also have an advantage, as they sweat out a lot of the alcohol. With singers, however, it is another story. They are neither busy most of the time, nor do they sweat it out, and thus they simply must exercise more control.

At any rate, that morning in Casa Pepe several rounds of wine were consumed while Diego and his frinds took turns reciting the "flamenco" poets: Villalón, García Lorca, Antonio and Manuel Machado, José Carlos de Luna, others. Several times following recitations Diego launched into erudite but not pedantic explanations of the poems if he thought them unclear or confusing, above all with those of García Lorca, many of whose poems are open to manifold interpetations. Diego seemed to know Lorca well, and his interpretations were often brilliant, setting off a round of exclamations and discussion as these new nuances became understood. This was a new experience for me, for here united were a flamenco guitarist, a butcher, a pastry-maker, a shoemaker, an office clerk, a retired cabbie, a barber, and two temporarily unemployed construction laborers reciting from memory and intelligently discussing the poetry created by some of Spain's finest minds. A few of these people were illiterate or nearly so, others had only the most basic education, they had rarely left the immediate area, and yet they were enthralled by complicated symbolism and imagery that appeal only to the most highly educated minorities in other countries.

Another phenomenon I had never seen, and rarely have since, was that Diego seemed completely integrated with this group of friends, all of whom were Spanish non-gypsies. Here truly was a miracle, for the norm is for the gypsies to hold every non-gypsy in some degree of contempt, and vice versa; gypsies led their lives, Spanish *payos* theirs, in an atmosphere of mutual tolerance, but they rarely mingled in this friendly, disinterested fashion. As I was to find out, Diego was above prejudice. He harbored personal likes and dislikes, of course, but had an open mind about all groups, races, creeds. This is extraordinary for anyone, but above all coming from a background like Diego's (it has been my experience that the uneducated classes usually are prejudiced about nearly everything and everyone). Diego's group of non-gypsy friends, on the other hand, considered Diego an exception to the rule. They distrusted, and felt ill-at-ease with, nearly all other gypsies.

After awhile the poetry started wearing thin and they

26

switched to singing humorous songs, rapping out the beat on the heavy wooden bar. First Enrique Méndez, drinking buddy par excellence of Diego and wonderful old-time flamenco. His favorite verse, when in a playful mood, imitated a distraught wife fed up with her husband:

"Ay va, que barbaridad, que harta estoy de marido..." (Good grief, my goodness, I'm up to my ears with my husband...)

Then Bernabé Coronado, butcher by trade, always full of hell and outlandish pranks, singing and dancing his droll rendition of one of the cornier popular songs of some years back:

"Isabel, tú eres la flor más perfumada..." (Isabel, you are the most perfumed flower...)

After a while, Diego got going on certain unique pre-civil war *tanguillos,* some political in nature, others quite spiced up. Many were very clever and had the group cracking up. Others caused his friends to shuffle uneasily and glance about, for they reeked of anti-regime, and secret police were everywhere in Spain at that time. However, I came to find out the danger was not great in this case, for everyone in town knew who the secret police were. Besides, by 1960 the police had become quite tolerant at village level; one really had to go out of his way to incur their wrath. (1) In Diego's case, even more so. He was respected as an artist and gentleman, and the police knew that when he was drinking this normally apolitical person might start blurting out *"barbaridades."* They either ignored him, or secretly chuckled along with him. They knew he was harmless, anything but an active revolutionary.

Fresh friends arrived at the bar throughout the afternoon, had their flurry of mood-making drinks, and joined us. Gregorio, the big peaceful mason who had spent fifteen years in prison after the war, who could drink impossible quantities and was not truly drunk until he started roaring his sole *soleá,* his eyes not quite focusing, an impish grin on his face. And Fernandillo, a nearly black gypsy destined to become a close friend, who at that time made his living partly by unloading trucks but basically by the con, illiterate but with a razor-sharp mind that, fortunately, was usually directed at conjuring up unique ways of having a good time. Once he saw that flamenco was catching on, in the mid-sixties, he quickly developed his own style of dance and song which, combined with his inventiveness, perfect sense of rhythm, and incredible sense of fun made him the spark plug of juergas in the years to come, a *fiestero* without equal.

Two o'clock rolled around and Pepe, owner of the bar, had to close up (closing hours in the villages were a bit more flexible than in the cities). Pepe played, and plays, a unique role in the flamenco life of Morón, and his story, therefore, is of special

27

interest. He began as a farm laborer who, through industry and intelligence, worked his way up to foreman. But Pepe recognized that even as a foreman, farming harbored no future for him, and when he was offered a job dispensing wine in a large wine *bodega* (part winery, part bar) in Morón, he jumped at it, with the idea in mind of saving his earnings and opening a bar of his own one day. According to plan, after a number of years Pepe had accumulated the money and indeed did open his bar.

Now new bars in small towns are very risky business, above all for outsiders (Pepe is from Huelva province, Morón is in Sevilla province). tradition almost invariably dictates where a fellow hangs out, for bars in such towns are more like clubs than mere drinking spots. If you want to find someone in a small town you never think of going to his home, but always to his bar. If he is not there, you leave a note for him that you'll be back at such and such an hour. thus village men are very reluctant to change bars for it signifies leaving their social friends behind, as well as a goodly number of business contacts. If the newcomer attempts to sidestep this problem by buying an existent bar, counting on the bars habitual clientele, he may still be in for a shock. The loss of the old owner, who for years has served not only as bartender but as friend, banker and confessor to the bars habitués, is one of the few things that will cause a man to change to another bar. Another is an exaggerated rise of prices.

Pepe knew all of this, of course but had two things going for him that gave him confidence. While working at the wine bodega he had made friends with many of the cement factory workers, who he was sure would frequent his bar at least enough to keep him in business. And he had also become friendly with some of the gypsy flamencos, above all Diego, and decided to encourage their patronage. The word quickly spread that Pepe was the only bar owner in this town of forty thousand inhabitants and two hundred odd bars who was crazy enough to extend credit on a regular basis to the gypsy flamencos. The flamencos, of course, moved right in and began running up credit as fast as they could. On the face of it, this was not a very wise course, given the dual facts that the gypsies were poverty stricken at that time and that even if not their credit rating was, with complete reason, below zero. Pepe, however, had thought it all out and had come up with the following: he knew that Diego had the very ungypsy-like quality of paying his debts, and being the undisputed leader of the gypsy flamencos in Morón could exert considerable pressure to get the rest to pay up; secondly, although flamenco was decidedly not popular at that time, there did exist a more or less affluent nucleus of aficionados who would follow

Diego to the Casa Pepe and spend goodly sums; finally, he had another lever; after any particular gypsy had reached a certain amount of credit, Pepe would cut him off from the bar until he paid up. Pepe knew that no ıflamenco could be apart from his fellow gypsies and, above all, outside the action for long; eventually they would beg, borrow or con the money to pay Pepe. Nonetheless, it was not always so clear, and more than once Pepe wondered what the hell he had gotten into, but yes, he did well in the long run, and Casa Pepe certainly dominated the Morón flamenco scene.

But back to my first visit to Casa Pepe. No one wanted to break up the gathering at a mere two in the morning, and at Diego's suggestion we loaded up a few bottles of wine and a case of beer and followed him out into the summer night. We did not go far, moving down a street lighted only by the moon and through a large, barely discernable doorway to the right. After stumbling over the cobblestone flooring of an intensely black hallway for a considerable distance, we emerged into a large, walled-in court that shone blindingly in the moonlight. Dark, low buildings rimmed the court on two sides which, I was told, housed a goodly percentage of Morón's gypsy population. Three of Diego's five sisters lived here with their families, as did Diego's sole remaining brother, Mellizo, and his elderly mother, quite senile at the time and confined to a wheel chair. Diego's sisters claimed they lived there with Diego in order to "take care of him", but of course in reality it was the other way around. During those hard years Diego was the only one in the clan who regularly brought in money (through paid juergas), and was in large part responsible for supporting the entire family.

Diego was in the mood to play, and one of his nephews brought him a chair and his guitar. The rest of us settled down on the ground, distributed the wine and beer, and waited. Diego, his hair silver in the moonlight, his nose gypsy-beaked in silhouette, began playing. It took only a moment to realize that this was like nothing I had ever heard. It was not even like the Diego of the Utrera gathering, the excellent and moving accompanist. This was a mystic Diego, opening his soul for his friends in this moonlit courtyard. No technical frills marred the pure emotion; each note was significant. The music broke forth, ebbed, surged again, like some magic surf. Extremely forceful phrases were followed by passages of utmost delicacy; long silences heightened and dramatized this tapestry of feeling and beauty into which each of us was being woven. I was spellbound. I had heard much music in my thirty-one years, but none

29

anywhere near so moving as this.

Diego played on for perhaps thirty minutes. Not a sound, not even an olé, was heard. When the last notes were carried away on the warm summer air the silence continued for a few moments longer, and then all hell broke loose. Fernandillo, sitting next to me, commenced tearing his shirt off his back, then into shreds, then hurling them to the ground and stomping on them. A roar of DIEGO and OLE engulfed the courtyard, and everyone was embracing Diego, or each other if they couldn't get at Diego. The place was complete bedlam. Diego's entire family had also heard, and were also demonstrating excitedly. This could only lead to one thing: great merrymaking for at least the rest of the night. Everyone sang and danced, Diego's young nephew, Paquito, played, as did Diego's brother, Mellizo. Pepe of Casa Pepe was awakened and more wine and beer purchased. Sometime during the night a pair of municipal policemen dropped by to see what all the ruckus was about, had a wine or two, told us to try hold it down a bit, and departed, shaking their heads and grinning.

About seven in the morning we went down to the Bar Nuevo Pasaje (Pepe didn't open until nine) for coffee spotted with brandy or *aguardiente*. I felt at peace with the world after the twenty-some hours of juerga, not particularly tired, nor exhilarated, but instead feeling like something worthwhile had taken place during those hours, something that was truly worth pursuing. These people, I felt, had the answer, or at least were far closer to it than we in our punch-in world of nine-to-five-and-get-drunk-on-Saturday-night. I could not put my finger on anything we had truly accomplished or created (Diego, yes, had created), nothing that would move worlds, or make any difference to anyone tomorrow. Perhaps the answer is that we had *lived* those hours; ambitions, daily bread, schedules, pressures, mores and standards had been forgotten, time had been erased. Perhaps for the first time I began fully to understand just what the flamenco life style represented. I liked what I felt.

Diego and Fernandillo were talking about running out to the Peñón for the day. It would be warm and beautiful, and the Peñón was a glorious place, they explained, to nap on the sunny sand and hear the waterfalls play. We'd pack some beer and wine on ice, take some vegetables and meat and make a *guiso* (stew). This fetching plan snapped me back to reality.

"My god." I told them, "my wife was expecting me last night for dinner!"

"Hombre," one of the married in the group answered casually, "so were ours. If you do everything your wife wants, you don't live!"

30

They all grinned and awaited my reaction. It was not long in coming.

"At least I'll call her and let her know what's happening." After all, I rationalized, I was researching flamenco. How could I write a book about it if I hid from such opportunities. Fortunately, Luisa understood, once over her initial worry at my not showing up all night, but such situations were often to prove a cross for her to bear. Flamenco was strongly masculine in those days, above all in the villages. Women, of course, were perfectly accepted at flamenco get-togthers in private homes or in commercial establishments, but the flamenco life in the bars, where most of it was centered, was something else. Respectable women did not frequent bars, with the exception of one or two establishments in each town that were considered "family-style" and where women could go accompanied by their husbands. Being well-bred Spanish, my wife was only too aware of such unwritten rules, and always felt ill-at-ease invading these masculine domains. She well understood the Spanish patterns of thought, and knew that at the very best she was unwelcome by many of the men in the bars (like British women in their men's clubs), and at worst was automatically considered something of a prostitute, fair game if they could only get rid of the big American with her. (Village women were even more vehement about this point than their men; any woman who entered such a bar was a whore, and that was all there was to it!) Thus a woman's presence in the flamenco bars was not only demeaning for her, it made everyone involved uncomfortable and interferred with the fluidity of the proceedings. Women were, therefore, fated to be left out of much of the flamenco life of Andalusia, which most understood and accepted and, in fact, often preferred, for the countless hours of standing around in such smoky and noisy places is not generally a woman's idea of heaven.

Although my wife understood her limited role in this adopted life style, and my enthusiasm for it, it could not help putting a strain on our relationship. That she weathered those years is something of a miracle, achieved through an admirable display of self-control and patience.

So the picnic was on. Diego talked a cab driver into taking the day off and coming with us, carrying half the group in exchange for his food, wine and gasoline for the day. I took the other half. (In 1960 only the wealthy, cabbies and foreigners could afford cars; not one of the flamenco aficionados I knew throughout Andalusia owned a car, not even those considered well-heeled.) We purchased the wine and beer from Pepe and also borrowed his huge stew pan, got the food and ice at the marketplace, and were soon bumping due south over a terrible dirt road. This was the first time I had traveled south from Morón, and just that day realized that the town is situated on the extreme southeastern edge of the vast Sevilla plain, where the foothills of the Sierra de Ronda begin. The drive that warm morning through the low mountains was winding, lovely and leisurely. "Leisurely," actually, is an understatement; it was impossible to go over ten miles an hour on that road, and of course we had to have animated rest stops at each country inn we passed. After taking nearly two hours to cover some twelve miles, we finally turned off the road onto, of all things, an abandoned railway line that shot straight into a mountain wilderness. Diego explained that this line had been constructed by Primo de Rivera back in the 1920's, as part of his plan to provide work for everyone who wanted to work. The line was complete with now-deteriorating stations and a series of impressive tunnels and magnificent bridges, and was to have been the only direct link across Andalusia connecting the Atlantic (Jerez de la Frontera) with the Mediterranean (Málaga). It was a fine idea, but alas, Primo de Rivera was ousted from power shortly before the line was completed, and the new government decided to abandon it. Fortunately, neither the tracks nor ties had been laid, leaving it accessible to automobiles if anyone was insane enough to try it; far more common users were herds of goats, sheep and brave bulls. Yes, brave bulls; this isolated back country was ideal for bull ranches, some of which were apparently not well fenced, for the bulls seemed to roam this country more or less at will, as we found out on several subsequent visits. (2) This particular day, however, we traversed the few miles to the Peñón without incident, and in fact at a faster pace than on the main road.

After perhaps half-an-hour on the line we passed a lonely station on our left, and shortly after arrived at a towering railroad bridge that spanned a deep divide, at the bottom of which ran the River Guadalmanil. Nearby, to the south, the river cut between high cliffs, spreading into a tranquil lagoon between the cliffs and spotted on one side with a small, white sand beach. At the far end of the lagoon tumbled a most inviting waterfall, high enough to stand under and let the water beat on one's body. The river was also graced by a series of smaller waterfalls and sand beaches as it emerged from between the cliffs and came towards where we stood. High on the cliffs lived hundreds of birds of all sizes — cawing crows, sparrows, hawks, vultures, eagles — and at any one time anywhere from two dozen to two hundred birds would be gliding high overhead, searching for prey and no doubt curiously observing their rare visitors.

32

The trip had been well worth it. The spot was spectacular! And here we spent the day, swimming, napping, drinking, a little singing and guitar playing, but mostly relaxing and regaining strength. The food prepared was memorable; memorably good if you had an excellent digestive system, memorably bad if not. The salad of tomatoes, green pepper, garlic, onion, black pepper corns, oil and vinegar, all in considerable abundance, was delicious, as was the stew of pork, potatoes and vegetables if one could handle the effects of the handful of hot red pepper that Fernandillo so casually tossed in. Fernandillo maintained that he was not only the best, but the best looking chef south of Paris, and these were his specialties, explosively succulent as we spooned them from the communal salad bowl and stew pan.

On the way back to Morón we stopped off in Coripe, a spotlessly clean little town so remotely located that many of its citizens at that time had not been as far afield as Morón. But Diego had been to Coripe many times during juerga excursions, and seemed to know half the town. The first task was to attempt to quench our ravenous thirst, caused by the excessive garlic, onions, hot pepper, wine, water and sun, with goodly quantities of the most refreshing ice cold beer I can remember. The beer revived us instantly, and Diego decided to break out his guitar. The locals were delighted. Flamenco with the guitar was a rare event in this isolated village, and in this case was even more notable because the great and eccentric Diego del Gastor was playing. The locals drank, sang and danced with Diego; the event was surely the highlight of their season.

Meantime, the day was sinking fast. It was nearly 10 p.m., and I could see that the group was getting revved up again and that the juerga could go on indefinitely. Which was well and good, except that I had a wife and child at home who were used to some measure of stability and consideration. I began suggesting I had to leave, but everyone was having far too much fun to consider the idea. I insisted, however, and finally two of the group who had to work next morning decided to depart with me, leaving the rest to pack into the taxi when the Coripe bar closed.

An hour later we arrived at Casa Pepe. Innocently, I intended to drop my two new friends off and head straight back to Sevilla, but to no avail. My friends insisted on inviting me to the *"penúltima"* (next-to-the-last, for Andalusian folklore has it that the last arrives only with death), nearly carrying me by force into Casa Pepe. And guess what? A most lively session was in progress, involving most of Diego's young nephews, four of whom – Paquito, Juanito, Agustín and Dieguito – were up-and-coming guitarists a la Diego. Another, Andorrano, was a singer-dancer; his dancing, above all, was unique and inspired. Since it was Sunday, everyone in Casa Pepe had been drinking all day and was by now literally aglow, taking turns dancing, singing, inventing crazy antics. My good intentions dissolved, and closing time found me happily drinking and enjoying life.

By now it had dawned on me that to break from these people you could not indulge in formal goodbyes. There is always somewhere else to go, something to do, and they will never let you go unless you are most determined and willful which, I must confess, I rarely was. I have always believed that life is too short to avoid good times. Within reason, of course. This particular night, for instance, they wanted to continue over in the gypsy courtyard, as we had the previous night, and I finally had to achieve the first in a long series of effortless outs; merely disappearing into the night. I was later to learn that this is precisely what they all did on the rare occasions they decided to go home.

On the way back to Sevilla that night I reflected on the flamenco life in Morón, and decided that it was definitely for me. But on a permanent basis, not just hit-and-run like this time. True, we could have moved to Morón during my three year civilian stint at the nearby American air base, but the road between Morón and the base, although only seventeen kilometers, was so terrible it would have ended up destroying both my nerves and the car if I had to cover it twice a day. Besides, Morón would be no place to live for one who held an eight to five job. I knew myself; I would never have made it. Either the job or my health would have had to go.

No, if we moved to Morón it would have to be on the basis of somehow making a living within the flamenco way of life. But how? The answer was not long in coming. Obviously there must be many aficionados like myself who would be enchanted with Morón and everything it had to offer but who would not have the time, opportunity or energy to do it on their own. And even if they did want to do it on their own, Morón had only the most primitive lodging and food to offer in its two *fondas* which would not appeal to most people, no matter how hardy. In short, what was needed was some kind of nicely-appointed establishment that could offer aficionados room and board as well as lessons, juergas, the flamenco experience in general. In this manner I could not only make my living in Morón and within the world of flamenco I so longed to experience to its fullest, but also attempt to show the world that flamenco is not composed solely of the garbage that is nearly always offered in commercial establishments and shows everywhere, including Spain. My first enthusiasm dimmed a bit when I thought of the financing, organization and enterprise this would entail, but the idea lodged itself firmly in the back of my mind.

As it turned out, five long years were to pass before the Morón idea became reality. In the interim, three years were spent living in Sevilla's Barrio de Santa Cruz while I worked as a civilian accountant (a practical trade I picked up when on the GI bill at Mexico City College while learning to play the guitar) at the air base near Morón. Such bases of operation gave me ample time to continue in the flamenco world, and also to produce my first book on flamenco, "The Art of Flamenco" (1962), and research the second, "Lives and Legends of Flamenco" (1964). When the first book proved successful, I was able to leave my job at the air base and turn more seriously to my full-scale aspirations and dreams within the flamenco world.

For starters, a group of aficionados in Madrid wondered if I would be interested in organizing and managing a private flamenco club, for members only. I was delighted and threw myself into it, and there went 1964 and part of 1965. The club was a worthy effort, and did fulfill a double need in the Madrid flamenco world: commercial *tablaos* were starting to prosper at that time, and aficionados were beginning to get desperate for a touch of the pure. The club provided that. The tablaos gave employment to many flamencos, but rarely to the less saleable (the old, those too pure to adapt, and/or those who would not lower themselves to perform in tablaos). We, on the other hand, organized our thrice weekly juergas exlusively with those pure and proud artists, with exciting results. The trouble was, in Madrid there were not enough pure artists available to sustain the interest of the club members for a long period of time. We were badly lacking in variety, and besides, there was very little flamenco ambiance in Madrid (although much more than now), and after some months I was dying to return to Andalusia. So I kept trying to convince the club financiers that Morón, not Madrid, was the place in which to perpetuate not only the pure art of flamenco, but equally as important, the flamenco life style. The combination of my constant cajoling and the club's difficulties finally convinced the financiers that perhaps Morón was, after all, the most feasible answer.

Thus it came to pass that in the wee months of 1965 Diego was contacted in Morón about a possible site for a flamenco center, necessarily outside of town so that we would be free from neighbors' complaints, the curious, and, in general, the uninvited. As fate would have it, he happened to know of a *finca* (ranch, or estate, with small acreage) for sale that indeed would serve for such an endeavor. Negotiations were quickly

35

completed after a visit of inspection, and by autumn of 1965 I was in Morón on a permanent basis, with just six months in which to prepare the finca for its first guests.

PART II

MORON AND THE FINCA

PERIOD OF PREPARATION

Our new finca was located about one-and-a-half miles to the south of Morón, just off the disaster called a road that we had driven over en route to the Peñón five years earlier. It was quite unlike all the other fincas we had seen in the area in that it had been partially remodeled in 1935, and was now considered a *finca de recrea* (pleasure ranch, or estate). Although such pleasure ranches are becoming fashionable today, what with the new-found wealth of the middle class and its mass escape from urban congestion, in days past all land in Andalusia was owned by a few rich families in each area (and still is, to a slightly lesser extent), of which no self-respecting member would have actually considered living in the country; all had sumptuous town houses as actual residences. Nearly all finca buildings, therefore, were strictly functional, with few, if any, amenities, consisting solely of storage space and rustic quarters for animals and farm laborers. (My grouping together of the animals and farm laborers in no oversight; except in the rare case of a truly humane señorito, animals and human workers and their families were treated similarly, which means to say they were maintained at a most basic level as long as they were productive, and afterwards discarded without benefits of any kind. But it is not fair unduly to condemn the Andalusian señorito for this attitude, for as we know this has been the human condition everywhere throughout the history of the world until a few exceptional individuals in certain regions came along and taught man, sometimes forcibly, to look beyond his blinding barrier of self-interests and be more considerate of his fellow man. Andalusia is just arriving at this revelation. Many parts of the world are still a long ways from it.

Our finca had a more unusual history than most. It was built at the base of the first mountain to break up the Sevilla plain, just to the south of Morón, in an area traditionally named *"Espartero"* because of the sizeable amount of esparto grass that grows wild in the environs (an *"espartero"* is, therefore, a gatherer of esparto grass). Thus the finca was named "Espartero," as were the adjoining mountain, the segment of river running at the foot of the property (the river as a whole is the Guadaira), and the country inn on the road on the other side of the river.

Finca Espartero was first deeded in 1865 as an olive farm complete with a large fruit orchard running along side the river. This site was chosen, no doubt, due to a spring that gushes clear drinking water from a hillock just above where the main building was built, and which was channeled partly into the building itself and partly into an adjoining fountain. This spring was the pride and joy of the finca, for water in the dry Morón area has always been at a premium. Even today Morón suffers from constant water shortage, always having to ration water in summer and oftentimes in winter as well. Thus the finca Espartero, with its fresh water spring, was a privileged plot of land indeed, and around the turn of the century took advantage of this when it was converted into a *venta* (country inn).

At first the Venta de Espartero catered to animal caravans, where by day the animals could freshen up at the fresh water trough by the fountain, the drivers likewise at the venta bar, while at night the venta offered beds for the drivers and shelter and feed for the animals. Before long, however, the owner was not content to cater only to such poor types, and soon the word got around that girls were available at Espartero, as well as some house flamencos. The finca surged to eminence, and soon señoritos were enjoying days-long juergas there with such renowned flamenco artists as Manuel Torre, la Niña de los Peines, Tomás Pavón, Antonio Chacón, and many other of the greats of the first twenty years of this century.

I have not been able to obtain corroborated data as to just why the venta discontinued its lucrative operation. Most say the owner died and his widow sold the finca, having had enough of such raucous and scandalous business. Others say that the owner started evading the periodic monetary gifts to the authorities that such a cabaret-type operation entailed, and he was closed down. Be that as it may, the finca passed through a series of hands and endeavors, including a period as a distillery of aguardiente (type of strong, dry anisette), before an eminent but ailing Morón doctor bought it in the hopes that the brisk mountain air would improve his health. This owner remodeled one wing of the large main house into his living quarters, including such touches of class as hand-painted floor tiling and a modern bathroom. After the doctor's death the finca reverted to farming and changed hands frequently. In 1964 it fell into the hands of its first foreign owner, and American painter who ran out of money after a year at the finca and reluctantly sold to us.

When I arrived in Morón that autumn of 1965, to begin the remodeling of the finca, I must admit I was completely unprepared for the snake pit that awaited me. Although thirty-six years old at the time, I was still a starry-eyed idealist, as innocent, in many ways, as a yearling. In my defense, how could I have known? My entire experience to date with Andalusia had been at the level of having fun and spending money. Under such circumstances the *Andaluces* are a most charming people, sociable and helpful like no one. But when self-interest rears its ugly head, watch out. Each man is out for himself in such an exaggerated fashion that I had trouble believing what I was experiencing. After all, I had been brought up in a society where these basic instincts certainly exist, but where we had been educated to be ashamed of them and constantly battle to subdue or at least hide them. Not in Andalusia. Here there existed a certain pride in being able to defraud your neighbor. Not just an enemy or an unknown, mind you, but on occasion a friend or even a relative as well. How many Andalusians have I listened to who boast about selling their neighbor a sick or dying animal at some exorbitant price, and similar low acts. The courts are full of members of families attempting to cheat each other, each standing firm on his own little island of selfishness. Deceit is everywhere, an intrinsic and accepted part of the Andalusian way of life.

If I had to find one word most representative of the way of being of the Andalusian male, it would be *guasa*. Guasa literally means "joke," "jest," "fun," "facetiousness," and this pretty accurately describes the scene in Andalusia. Very little is taken seriously, and joking and horseplay are constant. What a happy way of being! one thinks at first, until one discovers that most of the time the joking is at someone else's expense. And that is the usual meaning of guasa: making fun of others.

Guasa, in fact, is the principal source of diversion among the less educated in Andalusian towns, indulged in by all except those too intelligent, too dim-witted, or too nice to play such mean little games. The quick-witted and the aggressive stand at the head of the pecking order; on down the line we reach the weak and the retarded, who are constantly tormented. In all fairness, guasa *can* be extremely witty and relatively innocent, a good-natured pulling of someone's leg, but frequently it is sadistically inclined, and too often degenerates to merciless extremes, such as in the case of the crazy peanut vendor who used to have so many of his wares (laughingly) stolen or dumped on the floor that he had to give up this sole source of income, or the Mongolian idiot whom a group of jesters only slightly more intelligent than himself used to (laughingly) taunt and cuff about until he became enraged and lunged at them in his clumsy, inaccurate way. Only once did I see him connect with one of his tormentors *(guasones),* who, as

41

was to be expected, did not think this reversal a bit funny and somehow did not appreciate my clamorous approval.

Guasa obviously implies a complete lack of regard for the feelings of others, and is a natural prerequisite for the more sinister pastimes I have already described, when true self-interest enters the picture. However, practitioners of guasa that read or hear about this criticism will undoubtedly put me down as a crank. They have never analyzed their guasa, and believe it to be good, clean-cut fun. It is so entrenched in their way of life as to be nearly instinctive. There is no use attempting to fight it in Andalusia, to run around idealistically sticking up for the under-dogs. The guasones cross you off as a kill-joy, ignorant of their way of life. Even the victims are thrown into confusion by such unprecedented displays of concern. (3)

By 1965 I had become quite good friends with the regulars at Casa Pepe. We had juerga-ed together, laughed together, invited each other to numberless drinks, and I believed that true and lasting friendships had been established with many of them. Naturally, when it came time to select a work force for the finca, I turned to those of these friends who were masons, plumbers, and common laborers. In all, ten were selected, over half from Casa Pepe, and we went to work. These were my friends and I treated them as such, much to the amusement and outrage of whatever middle-class and señorito acquaintances I had in town. I made two trips each morning before eight and two more after work in our old Volkswagon to transport my friends to and from work. (Such a practice was unheard of at the time; workers were desperate for work, and transported themselves as best they could, usually by foot, a few by bicycle, even to jobs at a much greater distance from town than our finca.) I provided wine for lunch, and looked after their every care and complaint. Before long I had fame of being *"muy bueno"* (very good), which, I came to learn, is not a compliment in Andalusia. It means you are consi-dered weak and a little stupid, easy prey for the *listos* (the "smart ones"), for the typical Andalusian believes that the normal and intelligent way of being is grasping and unyielding. This he under-stands. Being "bueno," regardless of his religious education, is a concept that escapes him, for the vicious circle is complete. Very few are "good" if they can be otherwise, for who wants to be con-sidered a soft touch and a fool.

There are age-old reasons for this attitude, foremost among them the fact that life in underdeveloped regions everywhere has always been a survival of the fittest, in which the "buenos" normally do not fare too well. In other words, one cannot afford the luxury of being "bueno" until society has evolved beyond the stage of struggling for its most basic sustenance.

I must say I went through difficult times before I understood and assimilated all this both intellectually and emotionally, but once I had, I was able to accept it as part of Andalusian life and even admire the disarmingly charming fashion with which this creed was practiced. One almost forgot one was being had. I found that if the stakes were trivial, which was nearly always the case, it was more pleasant and practical to play along with the game than become embittered. Moreover, it was occasionally wise to put one over on one of the "listos." One's status in the community rose considerably upon so doing, as long as it was kept at an insignificant level.

When I hired my ten working friends, our relationship changed immediately. Suddenly I was their EMPLOYER, to be somewhat feared, for after all I could *also* fire them, as well as doubly fair game for whatever they could get away with in the way of slacking off, petty stealing, and such. I helplessly watched myself converted in their minds into a finca owner and therefore a member, however unusual and unwillingly, of the señorito side of the fence.

Still more confusing at first was the fact that after work, in Casa Pepe, their attitude would automatically switch back to comradeship, although not to the previous extent as long as they continued working at the finca. The same worker who might steal a section of lead pipe from the finca might turn around and spend the proceeds buying me drinks. Such incidents made it clear that there was nothing personal involved, but was just the old game of buenos-listos and also, in this case, employer-employee. One intelligent mason who is himself something of a bueno has become a very good friend and has long since refused to work for me in avoidance of just this paradox.

At any rate, I eventually became used to this strange relationship with the workers, and work on the finca progressed. A number of weeks were spent in remodeling the parts of the big house that had not been remodeled by the ailing doctor back in 1935: five bedrooms, a living room, and a bathroom were erected upstairs in what had been a large storage area (one of these bedrooms was later converted into an upstairs kitchen); new windows were hacked through the half-meter-thick stone and mortar walls; two new entrance doors were installed, one downstairs, another upstairs, both leading onto the back patio (the upstairs one with an outside staircase); a bathroom was installed by the downstairs main entrance; a large downstairs storage area just off the big old kitchen and pantry was converted into two bedrooms complete with Dutch doors leading onto the front terrace, and an adjoining bathroom; and so forth. In the patio behind the house a separate little building was constructed which became the bar-rumpus area, where most of our juergas were to be held, and on the hillock where the spring was born behind the big house an electricity *caseta* (little house) was built and equipped, and electricity was installed throughout the finca. Later on, in a separate building that had been used as a barn, we constructed a nice little apartment for myself and family (wife Luisa and nine-year-old daughter Tina), consisting of living room with fireplace, small kitchen, bathroom and entrance hallway, and two bedrooms looking onto what was to become a beautiful walled-in patio. My study was built in another part of this building, with a window overlooking the big house and the orchard and distant landscape. The rest of the building, which was considerable, was reserved for storage. Water was piped in to all the bathrooms and kitchens from the fountain, and a complex drainage and sewage system installed.

In short, an immense amount of work had to be accomplished to prepare this big old complex for a maximum of some fourteen guests, the three of us, and the help. The painting came last, of course, everything white-washed except the woodwork — German pine beams, doors, window frames —, all of which was painted mahogany, while the doors to the closets we had installed in every room were oak stained. We furnished the finca simply; chairs and tables of stained pine and wicker, curtains and matching bedspreads of country colors (olive, wheat, sky blue, etc.), hand-wrought iron lamps with parchment shades, esparto grass and hemp rugs, pictures of Spanish and flamenco scenes, and so forth. When the place was finished, about a month before the arrival of the first guests, it was quite fetching, truly unique in that part of the country.

Those six months of preparing the finca were divided roughly into two parts. During the three months of heavy construction my family stayed in Madrid and I lived in the big house accompanied only by Willie, our boxer dog, and a cat unimaginatively named Gatita (Little Cat). In the other building lived Paco the gardener with his wife, Dolores, and their several children.

They were exhausting months, full of work and play. Whenever I was not arranging for materials in town or on some other errand, I generally worked along with the workers, a most un-señorito-like activity that some workers admired but most scorned, for the true señorito never lowers himself to physical labor. I must admit I did not indulge myself in this type of work for the sheer pleasure of it, although it was somehow satisfying if taken in reasonable doses; it was rather that I quickly realized my working alongside them was the only way to keep them going at a steady pace. These people were truly professional in the art of prolonging a two-hour task into a full day's work. Work was very scarce then, and they wanted to stay on the job as long as possible. In fact, this mode of behavior was so prevalent that two wages could be demanded by workers, I came to learn in subsequent years; a normal one for the typical plodding worker, and a higher one for those rare workers who really pitched in and achieved a full day's work. The higher wage is well worth it, for one or two such workers, especially if they are in positions of authority, force the entire work force to work faster. The problem is, such workers prefer to work alone or with others of their same philosophy, for they are deeply resented by the goof-offs on the same job. I realized none of this at the time, of course, and my entire work force those first three months, with two halfway exceptions, was of the plodding variety. It was up to me to keep things moving.

At night, after driving the second load of workers into town, the play began. The flamencos invariably united in Casa Pepe, and the combination of the companionship and the drinks was delightful after the day's activities. During this period I got to know the flamencos better. Diego was unalterably charming and cordial, and his ideas, when loosened up with drink, made for fascinating listening. As previously mentioned, Diego was rather irreverent of the establishment, but not in the thoughtless black-and-white manner of most political objectors. Unless truly in his cups, when reason tended to escape him, Diego tried hard to understand both sides of the picture. He did not like the Franco regime, for instance, but at the same time shared to some extent a rather widespread belief that Mediterranean types need a heavier hand than usual to guide them. "Spaniards and similar hot-blooded people," he used to say, "tend to be undisciplined, and are likely to create chaos and anarchy if given the chance. Look at the Republic of the 30's. Liberty reigned and there were about as many political parties as there were voters, and crime and vice went on a rampage. At least at that time, Spain was not ready for democracy."

Although Diego considered nearly all the people surrounding Franco, including his immediate family, opportunists becoming wealthy at the expense of the people, he respected Franco himself as a man of integrity truly attempting to help Spain. "Look at his record," Diego would say, "he fired this man and that man and even his own brother from office because of corruption, but he simply cannot keep tabs on all the graft going on. True, in the beginning he used deplorable strong-arm tactics, but he mellowed considerably as soon as he was strongly enough entrenched in power that he could afford to mellow. He is a dedicated man who believes his mission is to save Spain from itself, not really a bad chap as dictators go." But above all, Diego considered Franco a political genius. He felt that Franco's keeping Spain out of war for such a long time (twenty-six years at that time) was commendable, and that his handling of Hitler in World War II was particularly brilliant (when Franco owed Hitler a favor and was fully expected by Hitler to join forces with him not only did Franco avoid doing so, he somehow even got away with forbidding Hitler to use Spain as a stepping stone to Gibraltar and Africa).

On a more immediate level, however, Diego felt that the local police in villages like Morón were overly tough throughout the forties and early fifties, and deserved to be feared and hated by the populace. Like everything else Spanish, this was revealed in joke. The local Guardia Civil cuartel (barracks) was referred to as the "Fábrica de Tortas." Literally, this means "Cake Factory," but *"torta"* is also slang for "slap; blow across the face." A sinister little play on words that invariably drew chuckles, if a few shivers.

The dictator previous to Franco, Miguel Primo de Rivera, was a great favorite of Diego's. Diego insisted that Primo de Rivera truly attempted to help the masses, initiating, among others, a program of public projects that gave everyone work who wanted to work, with the resultant contentment of the people and the best network of highways in Europe at that time (1920's). Equally as important in Diego's mind was the fact that Primo de Rivera was from Jerez de la Frontera and a renowned flamenco aficionado. At the drop of a hat he would contact twenty or thirty flamencos from Andalusia and hold two or three day blasts at his Madrid palace, treating those illiterate peasants with great dignity and rewarding them grandly at juerga's end. "That," Diego exclaimed, "is .truly unusual and democratic in the flamenco world. How many señoritos of far lesser category treat the flamencos like *mierdas,* humiliating them at every opportunity, knowing the flamencos have to tolerate the abuse because they desperately need the money. Fortunately, there do exist a few señoritos with truly noble spirits, such as Primo de Rivera possessed, just enough so that one cannot in all fairness cross off the entire señorito caste."

Diego was perhaps most revolutionary, from a Spanish old-establishment point of view, in his religious ideas. He felt that religion truly was used as an opiate for the people, and walked hand in hand with the powers that reigned. Not that during Diego's lifetime the Church directly oppressed, but it did do its best to resign the people to oppression while the powerful, including the Church, became wealthy. Diego often expounded that it was anti-

Christian for the Church to be so wealthy, an obvious instance of hypocrisy. There *was* a priest whom Diego rather admired, however, one who used to lift his skirts in juerga and swing into dance. If one's job was to deceive the people, Diego felt, at least be *gracioso* while at it. On the other hand, Diego was delighted with the modern movement of young Spanish priests, who actually go out on a limb to defend the rights of the poor. So much so that several have been defrocked, and some have even landed in jail. "Finally," Diego would exclaim, "the clergy is becoming Christian!"

Diego had quite definite ideas on an international level as well. He greatly admired Charles de Gaulle as the savior of France, felt Roosevelt had done a fine job pulling the USA out of the depression (using methods similar to those of Primo de Rivera in Spain), held Churchill's humor and indomitable spirit in much esteem, and thought Kruschev's new liberal policy excellent "if they let him get away with it" (they didn't).

Diego also enjoyed telling about his youth and, when in a certain soulful · mood, about his family, about his brother "who played the guitar better than I but who died young" (the only explanation of his death I ever heard), and about another brother who had been insane and had had to be kept chained up in his room so that they wouldn't take him away to one of those dreadful asylums. Occasionally the insane one got free and would go into his act, which was to strip bare and parade around town, stealing and munching on fruit as he proceeded, and sometimes singing romantic verses at the top of his voice to women he passed on the street. Then there was Diego's living brother, Mellizo, an alcoholic who was a constant thorn to Diego, for Mellizo knew no limits. He had a viperous tongue and was constantly sending people, including the authorities, to hell for no reason. He would beg, pass out in gutters, occasionally defecate at devastating moments or in original places, and whatever else one might imagine. But just occasionally — when sober enough to function — he would pick up his beat-up old shell of a guitar and play incredibly moving and delicate creations of his own. Then, as if embarrassed at his own display of emotion, he would often follow these beautiful moments with a barrage of profanity, accusing us in no uncertain terms of considering him a worthless old drunken reprobate when in reality he was the only guitarist, and gypsy, "of any worth in this whole goddamn province." His end, two or three years later, was as much a mistake as was most of his life. After one particularly obnoxious episode, when he went just too far, the authorities got together with Diego and the rest of the family and a course of corrective action was decided upon. For

Mellizo's own good, and that of Society in general, he had to be dried out. The question was, how? Mellizo would never agree to such nonsense. The solution was simple enough. One morning at dawn Mellizo was passed out in typical fashion in the gutter. The policemen winked at each other, awoke him and took him to jail amidst a barrage of abuse hurled at them by Mellizo. They told him he had really put his foot in it the night before, and had to be locked up for a whole month. Thus Mellizo began his drying out period, and everyone heaved a sigh of relief. This fine plan, however, had one small defect: no one knew of such refinements as taking him off gradually, and Mellizo's system could not handle this brusque change. Before anyone knew what was happening, he "died from lack of alcohol," as it was so aptly put.

Diego talked about his parents with love and respect. He considered his mother a saint, and when two or three days into juerga he would nostalgically sing the soleares from her Rondeñan mountain village she taught him when he was a child (in fact, I soon learned that these soleares were often preludes to some of Diego's more emotional guitar playing). Diego considered his father, a wealthy cattle dealer, the most generous man he had ever known. As long as his father was alive, no one in the village went without, providing his need was justified. Those merely too lazy to work were not tolerated, but Diego's parents gladly provided for those without any means of support until a more permanent solution could be found. "But woe to those who tried to deceive my father," Diego would say, "he could also be a very hard man if taken advantage of!"

Diego's parents spent a great deal of money supporting their immediate family of nine children, plus many of their relatives and the village needy, but there was still enough left, between cash and properties, to leave each of the children a sizable chunk when their father died. What did each and every one of them do with his/her inheritance? Blow it, of course, the men on booze, women and juerga, the women on their men and what have you, and by the time I met them they were all penniless and living in poverty, being supported to a great degree, as I have indicated, by Diego's earnings from the occasional paid juerga.

The finca operation, therefore, was truly to be an economic boom in the lives of the local flamencos, for of course the artists were paid for the organized juergas at the finca, and some of the artists, principally Diego, but also Juanito and Agustín, were paid for countless guitar lessons they gave at the finca. If the lessons were "countless," the juergas were nearly so, for I calculate that over the eight years of our finca operation we held in the neighborhood of four hundred paid juergas (the operation, and juergas, were limited to spring and summer, or there would have been far more).

But the economic was not the only boom the finca introduced into the lives of the flamencos. There were also the foreign girls who came to the finca and who provided the gypsies with abundant sex, as well as, in many cases, some of daddy's money to boot. I was quite surprised, as a matter of fact, at how eager many of the unattached girls were to bed down with, firstly, an "artistic" gypsy, and secondly, any gypsy they considered passably attractive. Up until this time, frivolity of this type was almost unknown to the flamencos other than with professionals – nice Spanish girls would not have dreamed of such pastimes – and at first the gypsies could not believe what was happening to them. They quickly recovered, however, and made the best of the situation. This phenomenon we review in more depth later in the book.

There was also the indirect activity caused by the finca's being in operation, as well as by my books, by now widely circulated. Many aficionados came to Morón in search of Diego and the flamenco way of life, and stayed in town. After a time, in fact, Morón became a "hippie" stopover point in their dope route; Marrakesh-Morón-Ibiza-Amsterdam-and/or India. Diego became a reluctant guru for these people, as well he should have been; he was no doubt more authentic and sincere than the others they would seek out. With a few notable exceptions, however, these types contributed little more than dope to the Morón scene, and their welcome wore off; the flamencos eventually saw they were out to take as much as they could, and give little or nothing in return.

Last but not least, by any means, there was the fun of the whole finca operation, the constant whirl of activity that the flamencos still talk about and badly miss even today, five years after ceasing operations.

But I am getting way ahead of myself. Back to the nights at Casa Pepe in the period of finca preparation. During this time I became good friends with Fernandillo, the wild, dark-skinned gypsy of superior intelligence, trigger-fast wit and incredible penchant for *"cachondeo."*

Fernandillo had been subjected to a much harder life than the rest of the Morón gypsies, which was reflected in his unusual wisdom and experience in a variety of fields. His father had been killed in one of the first battles of the Civil War (1936), shortly after implanting Fernandillo's seed. Besides having been a singer-dancer-fiestero of some repute, the father had been a wily cattle trader, as were nearly all the Morón gypsies of that epoch, and his family had never known poverty. With his death all this changed, and as soon as Fernandillo was old enough to walk he was out in the streets begging, borrowing and stealing the family daily bread. In those post civil war "years of hunger," as they are popularly and accurately referred to throughout Spain, this was no easy task, achieved only by the strongest and/or cleverest. After the civil war, throughout the forties and up until the USA came to the rescue with its mutually beneficial air base pact in the early fifties, no one offered aid to war-torn Spain, and its populace suffered accordingly. Fernandillo (and everyone else) often talked about the long bread lines, when just enough whole-grain bread was doled out to each family to keep it alive (Spaniards even today strongly prefer the nutritionless refined white bread as an unconscious reaction against the brown bread that was often their only food). Even after waiting in line for hours one could not be sure that the bread shop would not run out of bread before your turn came and you would go hungry for the day. He remembered what hunger does to people, how neighbors used to fight over a loaf of bread, and how the braver children used to snatch the recently distributed loaf from the hands of the aged and weak and run away like the wind, devouring huge chunks of the bread as they ran, stuffing in as much as they could before they were caught and beaten up.

Fernandillo and others described with disgust how many of the rich, with their storerooms brimming with hordes of food, got richer through black market activities, when they smuggled in normally unobtainable goods and sold them locally at exorbitant prices. If money was not available, the buyer had the option of working for hours or days to pay off the debt, until eventually he was owned heart and soul by the "company store."

During those years Fernandillo worked at everything and anything a growing boy would be accepted for, invariably receiving a pittance for long hours of labor, and often treated harshly to boot. He could never earn enough to support his family through work alone, and at night he would foray into the local orchards and gardens to steal whatever food he could, dangerous activity at that time, for sleepless caretakers might be behind any tree clutching shotguns they would not hesitate to use (usually, but apparently not always, loaded with rock salt).

During one extended period Fernandillo worked far out in the country on a brave bull ranch (a ranch we passed en route to the Peñón, where the old foreman still remembered Fernandillo and invited us to a bottle of wine once when we stopped to visit). Among Fernandillo's many jobs was tending the brave bulls, and he got to know their habits well. And he learned that cows occasionally can be just as dangerous as bulls, such as the time the cow he was milking turned on him in an effort to gore him (she had horns just as sharp as any bull's). Fernandillo took off like a shot and escaped the cow, only to trip over some obstacle and break his leg. As luck would have it, he was alone on the finca at the time, and had to lie with his broken leg, panic striken that the cow would find and attack him, for two days and one night, until the foreman and finca owner returned at sundown the second day. Many ten-year-olds might find this experience so traumatic as to never recover from it, but not Fernandillo. He took it in stride and learned from it. Life was tough then, and that's the way things were.

During his laborious childhood Fernandillo also learned about horses, becoming an excellent bareback rider in the process. He was one of the few brave and capable enough to break in wild horses, and was also trusted by established cattle dealers to take horses, mules or donkeys from one point to another and deliver them to their new owners. So between one thing and another Fernandillo made it through his childhood, turning over most of his earnings to his mother, who in turn supported the rest of the family.

When I first met Fernandillo he was about twenty-four, married to a *"castellana"* (gypsy term for a non-gypsy Spanish girl) and with two beautiful little girls, María, named after the mother, and Fernanda, after the father. By now the beasts of burden were rapidly losing ground to tractors, while beasts of transportation were being replaced by other noisy contraptions, and Fernandillo had had to turn to other back-breaking methods of earning a living. Being strongly built and very tough, he used to unload whole truckloads of grain, flour, canned goods, etc., by himself so as to receive the entire wage paid for the work. He often arrived at Casa Pepe so exhausted that he would not pep up until the third or fourth brandy. Even worse were his annual six to eight weeks of labor in the rice fields of "La Isla," a large, then mosquito-infested area adjacent to Las Marismas, south of Sevilla.

"There," Fernandillo commented wonderingly, "the work is so hard that I have had to quit early and come home. Can you imagine bending double all day long, wallowing in water and muck and being eaten alive by hordes of mosquitos? We start working at dawn, take an hour for lunch, and then work until sundown, some seventeen goddamn hours of hard labor seven days a week. There have been times I just collapsed right in the rice fields at sundown, to wake up at dawn and continue working, my body covered with mosquito welts. Jesus Christ! But such impossible labor doesn't even seem to slow down the workers who have been doing it all their lives. They just go and go, and at the end take home a poor man's fortune, while for outsiders like me it is torture. But there are also good times. Sometimes I say fuck it and go to one of those thatched-hut bars out in the field and get drunk and sing and dance and latch onto one of the girls who hang around out there waiting for their share of the loot. I get her drunk too, and then take her out in the middle of the rice paddies and lay her right smack in a pool of water, both of us giggling like we had just invented sex. And when I was in the mood, the more raunchy the girl, the better – one who really stank so that you had to hold your breath when she lifted her skirt."

During those nights I had ample opportunity to observe that Fernandillo did indeed prefer the raunchy types (with the exception of his wife, clean and decent as Spaniards insist the mothers of their children must be). One of his favorites was a local whore, a stubby, chubby little thing with a face that would stop a clock. But she was colorful, as full of hell as Fernandillo and given to even stronger language. They had a wonderful time together, exchanging obsenities, double-duty phrases, drinking up a storm, then disappearing for a little action. When Fernandillo was in money, he would give her twenty-five pesetas. When broke, she bought the drinks and would slip him a little money to boot, if she had any.

She wasn't the only one. Fernandillo never let up. One night he invited me to "make the rounds" with him. We walked through the dimly lit back streets until he sidled up to a barred window and tapped out some code on the pane. At the first house no one answered. "Not home," he said, "let's try another." At the second house there was a long silence, and then a hushed "Get out of here, Fernandillo, for the love of God. My husband is home!"

We got out of there. (4)

Other than perhaps Diego and Manolito, Fernandillo was the most loyal friend I have known in Andalusia. At that time there were "anti-outsider" feelings among some of the locals, and he used to stick up for me through thick and thin. Once out by the fountain he confronted four drunken rubes who were slandering *el americano* as fast as they could. Fernandillo told them they were all a bunch of *mierdas* and didn't they wish they could be half the man the americano was. When things looked like they might get out of hand, three of us who were listening from the veranda went down and joined Fernandillo. Now it was four against four. They quickly left. But the point is that Fernandillo did not know we were overhearing the argument. He was risking his skin.

52

He often verbally took on the younger gypsy flamencos as well. Once the finca was operating and they were being regularly hired for juergas, much to their initial delight, they started to out-macho each other, saying things like "We're being exploited and I'll be damned if I'll ever perform at the finca again."

Fernandillo would become incensed, and attack:

"You bloody assholes, worthless gypsy bloodsuckers, you've never made a peseta in your lives, performing or in any other way, living off of Diego and your parents, and you say you're being exploited! I know what work is, and I know what a soft touch the finca is. I've killed myself in the rice fields seventeen hours a day to earn less than you ingrates earn in a few hours of having a good time and doing what you do every night for nothing for whoever will listen to you. Go ahead, don't come. I'll tell Pohren to get his performers elsewhere!"

Oh, and how they would change their tune until the next inciter, usually one of the town foreigners who was envious of all the action at the finca, began rapping "exploitation." And the story would repeat itself. In reality, of course, none of them had any intention of abandoning the finca juergas. The important thing was to talk big. They were not expected to follow through.

Among the bonds that drew Fernandillo and me together was an unusual one: he admired hard workers, and he saw that I was then working on the level of a common laborer, and later continued to work hard to keep the operation running (far more than I had bargained for, I can assure you). In this he was unlike most gypsies, who scorn work and are amused by hard workers. Gypsies feel, as do most Andalusians, that work is for fools. They see no merit in it, nor do they derive any satisfaction from it. Up to a certain point, of course, they are right. When work takes over strictly for work's sake, at the expense of other good things in life, when executives work sixteen hour days and suffer a heart attack at age forty-six not because they need the money or the satisfaction but because it has become a sickness, then the gypsies are right. In the end, of course, one's point of view regarding work is basically environmental and educational, as is one's point of view about nearly everything. In this respect Fernandillo was truly exceptional; his superior intelligence enabled him to see through all the local prejudice and silliness by which he was surrounded, and draw his own concepts and conclusions. That, my friends, is extremely rare in any society, but above all in one that was as little educated and had as minimal contact with the rest of the world as did Fernandillo's.

The older flamencos never complained about being "ex-ploited" as did some of the younger ones. They knew a good deal when they saw one, and they prospered. There was one exception among the old-timers, however, who was so tightfisted that it became his trademark and, somehow, his major charm. This man was Luis Torre Cádiz "Joselero", Morón's finest and purest singer, with whom I also became close friends during those first months. Luis was illiterate like nearly all the rest, but one could look into his eyes in moments of economic calculation and see the money wheels spinning, somehow always in his favor.

Joselero had had TB (which crossed one's mind more than once when spooning out of the communal stew pot, I can tell you). It left him a bit withered, small in stature, with thin little legs that he delighted in showing when a bit tight and doing "his dance" at juergas. He was perhaps the most naive person I have ever known, and for this reason was a riot. His stories were always as straight, formal and innocent as can be, about his adventures in the flamenco world and above all his stay in Madrid, where he had been taken to perform some years back by a Morón señorito. When in the middle of one of his wide-eyed stories he could never understand why listeners would crack up and his sons exclaim "Oh, father!" and stomp out of the room. His naiveté was perfect and beautiful, but a dead giveaway when Luis had money on his mind.

"Pore", he said once before another finca season was about to get underway, "I've been thinking. *Ojú* has life ever gone up, and my wife is very sick of the kidneys, and three kids to feed, and life is hard, and..." triumphantly, the real kicker in his argument "my picture is in two books!!"

"Yes, Luis, but those two books are mine, and I put you in those books. Don't you understand, Luis, I am making you famous and charging you nothing for it?!"

"Well, you see, Pore, there is this intimate friend of mine in Barcelona who wants to hire me for the whole summer and pay me a lot of money, and another in Granada, so that if you can't pay me what I ask I just can't afford to stay in Morón, and YOU'LL BE WITHOUT A SINGER OF MY STATURE!"

"Well, gosh, Luis, good luck in Barcelona, and don't forget, if you decide to come back we'll always have a place for you."

At this Luis would look confused and saunter off down the street, wondering where he had gone wrong, and he would miss the first juerga or two that season before beginning to frequent Casa Pepe when he knew I would be there.

"Hola, amigo Pore, here you have me! What a surprise, eh, you thinking me in Barcelona all this time. How are things going at the finca?"

"Swell, Luis. What happened to Barcelona?"

"Well, you know, I decided to hell with Barcelona. I belong with my family, so why should I go trucking off at my age even if it means a lot of money. Besides, you being such a good friend, how could I leave you in the lurch? Now, would I ever do that, when you desperately need me?"

And we would settle for a middle price, up from the year before but something we could afford, for Luis was not the only one involved. All the other flamencos would be awaiting the outcome of our negotiating, but without, of course, missing any juergas. When Luis' fee was raised, so was that of all the others.

During those first months we had our little intrigues out at the finca as well. As I have indicated, Paco the gardener and his family were living in the adjacent smaller building. Paco had been nicknamed the "wolf" by the previous owner of the finca, who had hired him and then passed him on to us, due to his evil beady-eyed stare and wolf-like gait when loping after intruders attempting to relieve the orchard of some of its produce. Paco and Dolores worked the orchard for us on a fifty-fifty basis, meaning that they got free room, whatever they wanted to eat from the produce of the orchard and the rabbits they bred, plus fifty percent of the benefits from the sale of same. Dolores also earned extra money as our part-time maid.

Tending an orchard in Andalusia was (and is) no easy task. Other than the considerable work involved, Paco often sat up all night with his air rifle to protect the orchard from robbers, and we even had to keep our eyes open during the day. Although the "years of hunger" had ended long ago – hunger was very rare after the mid-fifties – orchard stealing had remained a tradition. Adolescents were the main offenders, motivated not by hunger, as Fernandillo had been back in the forties, but by the challenge and excitement involved.

Often during the day and above all at sundown Paco would visit the venta across the river to have a few, the result being that he was half sloshed nearly all the time, but rarely to the extent that he could not function well. Being an incurable gossip and feeder of fires, as are nearly all Andalusians, men and women alike, there was nothing he enjoyed more than telling Antonio, owner of the venta, and whoever else was around, that the workers were stealing me blind, but never in enough detail so that I could have done something about it were it true. As I too frequented the venta from time to time during the day I was sure to receive Paco's gossip, spiced up for double impact by Antonio. Then at lunch-break the workers would stop in, and Antonio would also tell them what Paco had said, no doubt adding that I was about to fire them all. And the workers in turn would deposit their venom, about Paco being a drunken wife-beater and the real thief at the finca, which would soon reach my ears via Antonio's grossly exaggerated version. Then I would drop my own bomb, telling Antonio that I didn't believe that anyone working at the finca was capable of stealing from me (ha!), but that they had all better start working harder or they would all be in the street. And so the game would go, the only winner being Antonio, who would serve wine as fast as he could while spreading the word and then somehow lose track of the number of glasses and always charge an extra five or ten pesetas, a significant amount in those days.

As it turned out, Pacos days at the finca were short-lived, but not because of the gossip game. One night after Christmas, when my family was living with me at the finca, we returned home from town to hear great shouting and screaming from inside the big house. We immediately assumed that Paco was drunk again and probably chasing Dolores around over some real or imagined remark. So one of us entered the front door and the other went around to the back, and trapped Paco, raging and ranting and looking for his wife. We sent Paco away to sober up, and finally found Dolores under a bed with the kids in one of the downstairs rooms. She had had enough this time, and the following day left Paco, and the finca, taking the kids with her (they eventually got together again). Not long after Paco followed suit, but not before bad fortune made Paco the laughing stock of his hated finca workers.

Early one morning it rained heavily in the hills upriver, and shortly after I got the workers across the river it started rising, not dangerously, but just enough so that I didn't want to take the Volks across to pick up two bags of cement a delivery vehicle had just left there. So I sent Paco, who always wore black rubber boots that reached well over his knees, with our little donkey, Platero. Paco did not like this turn of events one bit, but went, riding Platero across in a dignified manner, his black beret cocked to one side, an all-knowing smirk on his face. His instructions were to load the cement on the donkey and lead him walking back across, as the water was not as yet over the top of his boots. But Paco was not about to walk back across. He loaded the donkey, a sack of cement on either side, then perched himself high and dry on the donkey's rump and urged Platero back across. Little Platero did fine until about midstream, at which point his back legs gave way from the excess weight, pitching Paco straight back into the rushing water. With Paco off, Platero quickly regained his balance and resumed his trip, bats of cement intact and dry.

Paco stood up, sputtering, raging, sopping wet. Of course, the workers had observed all, as had a group of loiterers from the venta. All roared with laughter, holding their sides, rolling on the ground. Paco had no escape. He looked neither right nor left, did not answer the inquiries as to how the water was, and marched straight to his quarters, not to be seen again that day.

Antonio from the venta was delighted when Paco finally left, telling me I was much better off without such a drunken, shameless man at the finca. Antonio was a great one to talk, I was to find out.

The history of his venta is interrelated with that of the finca, for it was when the finca stopped functioning as a venta that the humble little inn across the river was inaugurated. At first the venta was merely a little thatched hut where the mule and donkey drivers stopped for refreshment, and it remained thus until Antonio came along and took over. As the venta is located on government land – an official resting spot along one of the old *caminos reales* (royal roads) – no one ever wanted to risk improving the venta for fear that one day the government would reclaim the land for some use or other. That did not stop Antonio, however, and little by little he made improvements that greatly enhanced his business.

On the positive side, it must be said that Antonio is a character worthy of admiration in many respects. He is an illiterate man who started out with zero and through sheer hard work and will-power had built up quite a decent business. And hard work a venta is. For years Antonio was up at dawn, milking the cow (later cows), then serving the early morning farm and quarry workers who would stop by on their way to work for a few aguardientes or brandies. The day would wear on, between one task or another, never to end until ten or eleven at night, when Antonio would fall wearily into bed, often to be aroused by some group pounding on the door who wanted to juerga. This usually meant staying up all night, preparing food, serving wine, and being amicable to a generally loud and drunken bunch of revelers, for Antonio could not afford to turn them away.

Although Antonio was constantly improving the venta, by Western standards it was still very poor when we moved into the finca, a little white-washed adobe building with neither water nor electricity. As is .true of most ventas in those parts, the bar and food business alone is not enough to make a go of it, and Antonio also kept pigs, chickens, and cows, and had two mules to help with his hauling tasks, which included carting water to the venta from our fountain across the river. He slaughtered his own chickens and pigs, and his homemade pork and blood sausage, and cured pork loin, were savored throughout the area. He also had a plot of olive trees, and prepared his own olives in the various delectable manners of the area.

Now we come to what might be considered the negative side of Antonio's character. He did not make it only through hard work and intelligent improvements. He was also blatantly cunning, and would stop at nothing to make that extra buck. Such as the old gypsy practice of perking up a sick or dying animal and selling it for a high price. Or the common practice of adding water to the milk from his cows which he sold around the neighborhood, sometimes to such an extent that protests would force him to decrease the dosage. But above all, his dexterity in presenting the bar bills to his customers.

As I have pointed out, Antonio was completely illiterate, but had learned the numbers corresponding to the price of each article and how to write them down. He did not know how to add them up, however, but this did not hinder him one bit. With a piece of chalk he would jot down the prices of the various items consumed, look them over rapidly, and come up with a lightening fast total that was invariably higher than it should have been. How he could consistently do this I do not know, but he was unfailing. As most of his clients could not add any better than he, they could not authoritatively contest his calculations and usually had to end up paying the exorbitant amounts, but not until very comical arguments had ensued.

"Antonio, this can't be right!"

"Why isn't it right?"

"Look at it, it just doesn't look right."

Antonio would then go into his act, pretending to add by columns as he had seen school-taught people do. His utterances were off the top of his head, but would come out to his original figure. Sometimes, of course, he would catch his fingers, when someone who knew how to add was there, such as myself. I did not like to see those poor country types cheated by such as Antonio, and would intervene and add up the column correctly. Antonio would swallow his venom and play it perfectly natural.

"Of course, what was I thinking about?" patting the client on the arm. "So sorry, hombre, must be this terrible headache I've got."

At times his little game proved dangerous. It is said that on one occasion (I did not witness this, I am sorry to say) he wrongly sized up a large table of country bumpkins who had consumed full meals, which at the venta included opening tapas, two main courses, accompanying wine, dessert, coffee and brandy. What an opportunity! Antonio had a long list of numbers chalked on the bar, and when it came time to pay effected his usual quick addition, arriving at some unbelievable sum. One of the biggest bumpkins marched right behind the bar without saying a word, grabbed the chalk out of Antonio's hand and quickly arrived at the correct amount, over four hundred pesetas less than Antonio's calculation. He grabbed Antonio by the shirt collar and said he ought to throttle him, but that this time he would let him off easy; they just wouldn't pay! And with that they stomped out, and the matter was ended.

Diego told a story about a juerga that was held at Antonio's venta. Included in the group were some señoritos whom Antonio did not know. The juerga lasted all night, and when paying time arrived Antonio had chalked up a line of numbers that took up half the bar. He was taking no chances this time. He knew that the señoritos would surely know how to add, so he made the list twice as long and intended to give the señoritos the satisfaction of adding it up themselves.

Diego quickly sized up the situation and called Antonio to one side, whispering to him in his most conspiratorial manner:

"Antonio, one of these gentlemen is a government inspector of bars and restaurants. *Ten cuidado, hombre.* Be careful, man!"

Nuff said. Antonio graciously invited his guests to a drink on the house, and when he thought they were distracted quickly rubbed away about half the column, leaving numbers corresponding at least roughly to what they had actually consumed.

The señoritos, none of whom were inspectors, of course, paid, and they laughed all the way down the road to the next venta, where they continued the juerga.

As nearly everyone in the area eventually learned about Antonio's habit, one would think they would stop frequenting his venta. But oh no, not in Andalusia. Instead, they admired his cunning, and as Antonio, apart from that, did have an ingratiating manner, they considered him *"muy simpático."* It seemed to develop into a kind of game of who could outwit whom, the customer feeling triumphant if he paid only what he should have.

These beginning months of preparation were somewhat hectic, due to the full-speed-ahead work and play schedule, but this was nonetheless countered by the general feeling of peace and lack of haste that still lingered on in inland Andalusia in 1965. The motorcycle invasion, triggered by the adoption of the pay-by-installment system, was still two or three years off, and automobiles and tractors five or six years, all noisy, evil contraptions that spelled eventual doom to horses, mules, donkeys and bicycles, and the way of life these represented. With what delight I remember sitting on the terrace of the finca watching the animals plod lazily along the road across the river, carrying riders who whiled away the time by singing flamenco melodies that sounded vague and haunting across the two hundred or so meters distance. At that time Andalusia was full of song. Most of the finca workers sang to themselves while they worked, their voices murmuring softly of amorous matters, perhaps reaching my ears from five or six different points of the property. Workers in the nearby fields also sang then while ploughing, planting, pruning, picking, harvesting, whatever the task, and their song made them forget they were insignificant cogs in an infinite universe. These were happy people forced by life's circumstances to move slowly and contentedly. How I was to mourn for them, and for myself, as I watched them change with mechanization. As the decade of the sixties died and that of the seventies was born, these people had faster and faster transportation and yet somehow less and less time to enjoy nature, each other, and life in general. In the beginning they used to bring their animals to freshen up at our fountain and perhaps fill earthenware jugs, lingering, joking, singing, rarely in a hurry. At the end they would drive up in their cars-on-credit in a swirl of dust, car radios blaring music of indescribably bad taste, fill their plastic water jugs, perhaps exchange a few complaints if anyone else was there, and drive hurriedly off to some other task.

Of course, the singing stopped. They no longer had time for it, and those few who did feel like singing were drowned out by the noise of mechanization. Singing was a pleasure when one's voice carried cleanly across silent space, perhaps echoing off distant hills, the rhythm measured by the beat of hooves, but a discouraging, even disgusting experience when in competition with a tractor's roar. In a matter of a few years noise replaced song and silence; screaming motors, transistors at full volume, and in bars and homes perhaps the most sinister mind-warping "progress" of all: television.

Animal labor and transportation encouraged not only singing, but multitudinous shouts of encouragement, compliments, or abuse at the animals. It seemed that most mules were named Carolina, and "Ca-ro-liii-naa" would often float through the air, followed by "guaaa-pa" (pretty girl) or perhaps something a little earthier, like "Doesn't my mother-in-law wish she had your behind!" The loudest shouts of all, of course, were those of abuse, when the owner would defecate on all the animal's ancestors or, more directly, in the milk it had nursed, or threaten to clobber the animal in a variety of colorful ways if it didn't shape up. One that struck me as particularly funny one day was: "I'm going to slug you so hard I'll turn your face inside out!"

60

Occasionally an animal would become so obstinate that the owner would flip and attempt to carry out his threats, beating the animal with a stick until the owner slumped, exhausted but relieved, to the ground. Such treatment used to shock me at first, but then I began to notice that the animal never seemed to get physically hurt and usually did become more manageable. The Andalusian male was convinced that their animals, like their women, needed an occasional beating to keep them in line, and I often suspected that both women and animals agreed with this deep-seated belief, as long as it wasn't overdone.

We had our share of animals at the finca during those years, lovable animals that somehow caused countless problems.

It was with Platero, our little white donkey, that we first learned that work animals need to work. As long as Paco or Dolores loaded him up with produce from the orchard and made the daily rounds to the less fortunate fincas without orchards around the area, Platero was fine. He seemed to sense he was a useful part of the team and was docile to the extreme, like a household pet. But after Paco and Dolores left, there was little for Platero to do, and he would hang around the orchard all day eating grass, bored out of his mind. As always, boredom bred mischief, such as the time he tried to mate with a female mule who was tied in front of the venta; she wanted no part of it and reared back and kicked, causing her six earthenware water jugs to crash to the ground. Or another time when he ate all the flowers that were tended with loving care by Antonia of the venta, Antonio's wife. We finally had to put Platero back to steady work, selling him to an *arriero*, a man who used his team of donkeys to carry sand from the river to construction sites.

We had a similar experience with Palomo (Dove), a white horse we bought for the purpose of pulling our newly acquired buggy. This horse-buggy episode is quite picturesque, and reveals some of the disappearing color of old Andalusia.

It all started very romantically in my head. A horse and buggy had always held deep meaning for me, symbolizing all that was most desirable in country living. Besides, in a more practical vein, I told myself, think of the savings on gas and motor repairs!

One day I mentioned this dream to Fernandillo, not believing it to be at all within my means. Fernandillo's eyes twinkled and he beamed broadly, signifying that the dream was soon to become a reality. First off, he set about finding a buggy, no easy task, since buggies had been out of fashion for a number of years already, and those rich folks who still had one for once-a-year usage at fair time would not even consider selling.

Nonetheless, one day Fernandillo told me he had located

a buggy. None had been available in Morón, but he had enjoyed better luck in the nearby village of El Arahal, and at the very reasonable price of fifteen hundred pesetas, payable directly to Fernandillo as he had already completed the deal with the seller. This was less than I had expected to pay and I was quite happy about it, but not so happy as Fernandillo; he later told me that in exhange for the buggy he had traded a pair of antique vases he had pruchased from an old lady for eighty pesetas while doing his house-to-house antique-buying routine (a common gypsy occupation that helped their economic situation considerably; Fernandillo, with his persuasiveness, had it down to a science).

We invested another fifteen hundred or so in fixing up and painting the buggy. Before long it was shiny and demanding to be used, and it was time to find a horse for it. Fernandillo, of course, knew where to go, and soon Luisa, Fernandillo and I were drinking *manzanilla* wine in the village of Montellano with two of Fernandillo's cousins, both gypsy horse traders.

"Have just the thing for you, yes sir, a beautiful white gelding in the prime of life (eleven years old), a former racehorse that has precisely spent the past two years pulling a milk wagon. And for only ten thousand pesetas!"

Fernandillo bargained with a great display of gesticulation and technique, and the price was lowered to seven thousand pesetas, still, no doubt, considerably higher than we should have paid, and certainly containing a nice percentage for Fernandillo (as a matter of fact, Fernandillo told me later that they gave him a stipulated twenty percent, I believe it was, normal in such transactions; he did not, however, demand any money from me, to which he was entitled under cattle dealing protocol). In reality, it is extremely hard to fix a fair price for a horse, for it is all based on the bargaining power of both parties and on the whim of the buyer. Ah yes, and on one other factor: the ability of all concerned to hold their booze. Many drinks, and hours, are consumed during a negotiation. No one is in a hurry. Everybody seems to enjoy such transactions so much he doesn't want them to end. The object of the drinking, of course, other than to have a good time, is to get the other fellow muddle-headed and carefree about the price. Although everyone knows the rules of the game, this does not seem to make them less effective. Often one hears boasting to the effect that "I got him so loaded he nearly gave it to me," or, less frequently, the loser ruefully saying, "How that fellow could drink; I don't even remember how much he paid me!"

That night the horse was delivered to us at the finca, the son of the seller having ridden him over from Montellano.

As it happened, we were heavy with *juerga* a the moment, and Fernandillo soon had his cousin singing some extraordinary gypsy *tangos* of the variety generally associated with the wandering gypsies of Extremadura. A most appropriate ending to our horse negotiations.

So now we had a horse and buggy. The next day Fernandillo hitched Palomo up for a trial run. Much to our surprise, Palomo was not a bit enthused about being hitched to the buggy. He reared, kicked, threw himself on the ground, and it dawned on us that we had been duped by the sellers, who claimed that Palomo was accustomed to pulling a milk wagon. Fernandillo, however, accepted the responsibility and, moreover, the challenge, and swore that in no time Palomo would be pulling the buggy like a champion. As Fernandillo had a way with animals, he did eventually dominate Palomo; but only Fernandillo could hitch him to the buggy thereafter, and then only with great cussing and difficulty. Before long the whole thing seemed so burdensome that we rarely went for buggy rides, eventually giving them up altogether.

On the other hand, Palomo was an excellent riding horse, but even of this we did not take adequate advantage. Having only one horse meant we had to go out one at a time, which was not so exciting as going out with company. So Palomo, like Platero, ended up spending most of his time in the orchard, and eventually also learned to unhobble himself and go wandering over to the neighbor's haystack or wheat field or, several times, back to the herd of horses and mules some twenty kilometers away he considered his true family. Ultimately, when it grew commonplace for irate neighbors to come to our door to complain about Palomo's latest escapade and sometimes demand damages, we decided to sell him. This was somewhat heartbreaking, for Palomo had finally come to consider himself a member of our family. When we called him from the top of the stairs leading down to the orchard he would come at a canter, climb the stairs, and nuzzle up with true affection. Nevertheless, we could not go on alienating the neighbors and shelling out, and besides, Palomo deserved to be worked and attended far more than we were doing. So I sold him to a man who took horses down to the Costa del Sol for tourists to ride, and Palomo left our lives.

Platero and Palomo were saints, however, compared to our boxer dog, Willie. Most animals come and go and are soon forgotten by the community, but Willie has become legendary around Morón de la Frontera.

Willie was firmly convinced that he was chosen to achieve two supreme goals in life: mate with all the bitches in the area, and whup all the males. With human beings, on the other hand. Willie was irresistible. Despite the more-than-boxer ruggedness of his demeanor, with a huge thick head and deep chest far more exaggerated than is customary in his breed, Willie turned on a most incredibly soulful pair of brown eyes, melting all resistance. Regardless of prohibitions to the contrary, Willie's habit was to sneak into bed with each new guest who left his door ajar, and the guest would wake up next morning nearly pushed out of bed by Willie's considerable weight curled up alongside. If he was not immediately scolded and thrown out, Willie would consider it his privilege and would scratch and thump against the guest's door every night until gaining entry. If ultimately rejected, however, it was no problem, he would simply move on to another door.

Willie was equally persistent gaining entry into juergas. He had been weaned on flamenco and his love for it was almost an addiction; he would not hear of being left out of any flamenco happening if he could help it. This presented difficulties, for at first many of the flamencos were afraid of Willie (as they are afraid of nearly everything new or beyond their understanding, like the ignorant and uneducated everywhere) and we would have to lock him away in some remote part of the finca where he would howl his heart out. Eventually someone would take pity and release him, and a short time afterward Willie would come creeping into the juerga and curl up unobtrusively in a corner of the room. As he gained confidence, Willie would single out one of the guests whom he knew to be an easy mark and sidle up to him/her and rest his head on the guest's lap, as if it were just too heavy to hold up any longer. If encouraging, the guest would eventually have Willie draped across his/her lap, with only his hind paws touching the floor. From this position Willie would closely follow the proceedings, enjoying every minute of it. La Fernanda summed up everyone's feelings once after Willie had been watching her with big liquid eyes the entire time she sang. Although she had been extremely fearful of Willie at the beginning of the evening, when she stopped singing she exclaimed wonderingly:

"Ojú, that dog is too much. He has the eyes of a human!"

If there is anything to the theory of the transmigration of the soul, there is no doubt that Willie's soul once inhabited the body of a flamenco. And judging by his excellent taste, a good one.

However, as previously indicated Willie was not quite so loving with other animals. This trait traced back to a definite incident that traumatized Willie for the rest of his life. One day, when still a clumsy puppy, Willie frolicked up to a full-grown

64

dog wanting to play, and was trounced in a most dastardly manner. He did not forget but bided his time for a few months, filling out, growing muscles. When he calculated he was ready, he laid in wait for that same enemy and gave him a most impressive beating. After such a signal victory Willie became King of the local canine population, reigning with such demoniac power and regality that the human beings in the area, who normally fear and hate dogs, began pridefully calling Willie "Clark Gable", or, in Andalusian, "Clar Gabley." His exploits were the talk of the area, both sexual and pugilistic. Actually, "pugilistic" is an understatement, for with animals Willie was a bit of a psychopath. He did not fight merely to defeat, as is usually the case; he fought to kill, a sickness that would usually have caused us much trouble expect for the fact that the Andalusian people admire a good fighter and tend to cross off the loser, even if their own dog, as worthless. If the Andalusians did not care much about dogs and cats, however, they did care about their mules, and mules were among Willie's most prized diversions. Although he merely chased them, nipping madly at their heels, sometimes the mules had riders, with whom we were not terribly popular.

As his fame spread, Willie became like the fastest gun in the West. Owners of other dogs wanted to try him out. One day a fellow came up to our gate with five *galgos* (of the greyhound family), and challenged me to let Willie out. We were working on the electricity caseta, and I wanted no nonsense. The fellow insisted. The workers urged me to comply, immediately setting odds. I saw no reason to hurt the galgos. The matter was unexpectedly resolved when the maid emerged from the gate and gave Willie his chance to escape. Such a whirl of snarls and dust ensued that we could not see what was happening until the pack broke and all five galgos took off at top speed through the orchard and into the river. Willie caught one of them in midstream and held him under water for what seemed an interminable time. When he figured the galgo was finished Willie let go and returned, amidst the cheers of the workers. And how they pulled the galgos' owner's leg! He had nothing more to say, and that was the last time we were challenged. Fortunately, Willie miscalculated, and the half-drowned galgo survived.

But even Clar Gablay got his occasionally. His favorite pastime of chasing mules backfired several times, and he came home with huge hoof prints on his head. His real comeuppance would come, though, when the neighborhood dogs would rove in a pack after some bitch in heat. Willie, being Clar Gablay, always had the honor of being first, never remembering that he would be hooked to the bitch for some minutes afterwards and virtually

65

defenseless. Then the pack would attack en masse, and Willie would come dragging home more dead than alive, gashes, rips and tears everywhere. But that Willie could handle; it was all part of the game, and I am sure he enjoyed even those wild, one-sided fights. What must have freaked him out were savage occurrences of an entirely different nature. Twice when he returned his head was beaten out of shape, which we calculate could only have been caused by clubs wielded by human enemies, perhaps owners of useful dogs, such as the hunting variety, that Willie had destroyed. With human beings Willie was incapable even of defending himself, and would have been a sitting duck when involved in the love act.

After the last of these head-deforming beatings Willie finally staggered away to die. The neighborhood animals heaved a huge sigh of relief (except the bitches, no doubt), and we at the finca a resigned sigh of mourning. It had to happen sooner or later. Willie had been asking for it. (5)

DIGGING IN

By the time the finishing touches were being completed on the finca, in March of 1966, the town of Morón was absolutely sure of one thing: the finca was slated to be a cabaret featuring prostitutes and flamenco. The town had searched its memory bank of experience, and that was the only use to which the finca, in its remodeled state, could be put. Downstairs for drink, food and juerga, upstairs, with its seven bedrooms, for "you know what" (winks, smirks, nudging). When we attempted to explain the true purpose of the finca people would look vague and disbelieving. As far as most of the townsfolk were concerned, what flamenco needed was a good stamping out, not a center to encourage it and the disgusting life style it engendered. Besides, who cared enough about flamenco to take it seriously? It was all right in its traditional context, as a background for revelers, but could by no means be considered an art, to be studied and learned as such. Flamenco was, after all, the primitive music and dance of Andalusia's lowest classes, obviously worthless if compared to the world's great arts. A flamenco center indeed! The town knew why we were there, only too well!

This firmly entrenched belief was to cause us many immediate problems. The finca is huge and we needed maids. The maids were willing enough, but as soon as their men – husbands, boyfriends, sons – found out where they were working, they made them leave. It was useless for the maids to tell them that we were not a cabaret, but rather a most innocent (comparatively speaking) flamenco center. Andalusian men are dead certain that all women will be promiscuous if given the opportunity, and must be protected from their own instincts. God only knows what their women would be up to out in that center of sin! In addition, even the rare man who had faith in his woman could not acquiesce; he might believe in her, but no one else in town would, and he was not about to face the disgrace this would bring about, no matter how badly they needed the money. And need the money they did. Not only were jobs extremely scarce, we paid far better than anyone else (another suspicious sign).

That we had a cabaret was such a certainty that carloads of

67

men from the area began visiting us, cautiously inquiring if we were open and if they might come in for a drink. None of them actually came right out and asked if we ran a cabaret, and they all retired in confused haste when we answered that they could get a drink at the venta across the river. But the cabaret rumor persisted even after several such rejections, although now in a more exotic light. My God, they thought, the finca must be truly exclusive, apparently solely for the decadent foreign elite. Everyone in town by now was dying to visit us. A few became friends and did attend the odd juerga. How disappointed they must have been when they finally saw for themselves that we were, after all, a flamenco center.

After some three years the cabaret belief began dying out, to be replaced by a somewhat more accurate description of our operation: a flamenco center, yes (of all things!), but replete with an abundant and everchanging crop of foreign girls rumored to be eager to please. Now the tables were turned. It became easier to keep maids, but our new reputation reaped a harvest of jealous wives who became a blight on our operation. Andalusian women could handle the flamenco cabaret idea: that was normal and traditional, and presented no real threat to them. Foreign girls, however, were unsettling, definitely not to be tolerated. Three of our local singers used to have to sneak to our juergas, and finally we had to drop two of them completely from our roster of artists. The problem also entangled several of our local friends, who were not artists but who were good flamencos and whom we used to invite out both for their friendship and for the animation they injected into a juerga, extremely important for the evening's maximum development. One night two wives of the latter group of friends appeared at the finca angrily demanding to see their husbands, absolutely certain they would be in bed with a dozen or so foreign girls. As it turned out, that night one of our larger and more formal fiestas was in progress, which included a group of Americans from nearby Morón Air Base. Everyone was nicely attired and on best behavior, including the husbands of the irate women. The jealous twosome, neither of whom liked flamenco in the least, sat glumly and in obvious confusion through part of the fiesta, leaving as soon as they thought it would be appropriate. I am sure they were actually disappointed at not having caught their husbands in the act.

Ironically, none of the men whose wives were so insanely jealous ever had anything going with girls at the finca, but the wives, feeling that their men must be terribly attractive to *all* women (a form of self compliment), could not accept this. One woman in particular, common-law wife of one of the singers, felt that *she* should know about the shameless eroticism of her species; she had been madame of Morón's most successful red-light house for years, until the lights were snuffed out by the authorities. The feeling that one's mate is the apple of everyone's eye also extends to the male species in Andalusia, to a most ridiculous extent. No one would touch with a ten foot pole many of the Andalusian women who are so jealously guarded: big, fat old mammas with dandy little mustaches and beards, and similar types long past their prime. Love and/or possession truly is blind at times.

If the cabaret/erotic foreign female beliefs made life more difficult for us, two occurrences around the beginning of the operation made up for them.

The first was a beautiful coincidence. Simultaneous with our opening for business, the highway department decided to repair and pave, for the first time, the horrible road that passed in front of the finca connecting Morón with Coripe (and the Peñón). The townsfolk, of course, credited the improvement to us, commenting with awe what impressive connections we must have in Madrid.

The second was even more desirable, but far more complicated. You will remember that the finca was once a venta and that cattle, mule and donkey teams and their drivers, and people in general, were encouraged to frequent the fountain and the venta (finca). In order to make leaving the main road, crossing the river and visiting the venta more desirable, the venta owners opened a path that led through the property and emerged again onto the main road, some hundreds of meters further along. Who could ask for more? The supplementary path was a great success, and the venta thrived. However, once the venta was closed and the property sold, who was to convince the passers-through that they were no longer welcome and the path was closed? The path was now tradition, and the locals convinced that the path had been public from "time immemorial." Furthermore, they were dead certain that they could not only pass through, they could linger and loiter and even picnic, if they so chose. And not content with that, they would ask the owners of the finca for water, or to use the toilet, and when no one was looking pick the finca flowers or dart into the orchard to steal a little fruit. Most irritating of all, however, was their throwing stones at the dogs, whom we were obligated to keep chained up as long as the path was considered public.

Such was the situation at the finca when we bought it. We knew about the problem but, being starry-eyed idealists, felt that if we treated people well they would naturally reciprocate. Actually, weekdays were fine, when country people passed through en route to some task or other. They were almost always genuinely friendly, extremely courteous, and prudent. These people were welcome, and we told them so. But weekends and holidays quickly established themselves as nightmares. Sundays and holidays, above all, the lower class town folk would congregate at the venta across the river to have a few. Upon arriving at the obnoxious stage of their drinking they would decide to take a walk, and where else than across the river and up to the fountain and finca? And obnoxious many of them were, to such an extent that I decided we somehow had to stop them from coming through before I lost control of myself and took more drastic measures.

Thus one fine day, after exhaustive research showed clearly that no legal public path crossed the finca, we fenced off the path on both ends. The dogs were let loose, and would-be loiterers warned that if they attempted to force entry it was at their own risk. This discouraged everyone except one old neighbor, who took the case to court, stating that "these here young foreign whippersnappers" are taking the law in their own hands. He was right, we were, and the law ordered us to take the fences down immediately. However, a ray of hope was added to the judicial order: it stated that the legality of the path was not being judged, only our methods of closing it off.

We immediately got a lawyer and began accumulating official documents that showed that the finca was one uninterrupted property, and opened a court case against the neighbor who had protested, as well as against "whosoever thought he had the right to use the finca path." In order to win we had to demonstrate to the judge that the path was not official, and that furthermore no one had a true need to use the finca path except us. When this had been accomplished, they no longer had a case and we won. This time we put up permanent walls and gates, and settled down at last to the full-time peace and quiet of country living.

That we won the case was a sensation in the area, for many of the most important *caciques* (town influentials) of Morón had opposed us. Not because they needed or used the path; the caciques were in the main rich folks who were opposed to only one thing – change of any type, unless initiated by, and benefitting, themselves. Besides, outsiders were always looked upon with suspicion, and found obstacles in their way at every turn of the road. My wife was an outsider from Madrid – that was bad enough – but far worse was an americano attempting to fight the traditions (and abuse) of the people. Who does he think he is? We'll show him!

Thus when I initiated my investigation and asked to see the official plans of the finca at the Morón town hall, I was courteously, if condescendingly, shown what any half educated person would immediately recognize as the wrong plans (they were so used to dealing with the illiterate they no longer even bothered to disguise their conniving). On subsequent efforts I was again given the run-around, leaving no doubt as to whose side town hall was on, or at least the employees I dealt with, who I assumed were following instructions from higher up. What a shock they were all to get when in the court case we presented the correct plans that we had finally gotten from a higher authority in Sevilla!

The master stroke, however, was provided by our lawyer, an outsider himself who was not related to any of the caciques and who would be, we correctly surmised, beyond their direct influence. He knew that the judge slated to decide our case had xenophobic feelings, being particularly prejudiced against Americans (who think they can run the world!) – the judge had given himself away by a couple of remarks when ruling against us in the first case – and felt that his xenophobia might affect his decision, if only unconsciously. Our lawyer, therefore, dragged the preparations of the case out until vacation time arrived for the judge in question, and then vigorously pushed the case into court. In the absence of the judge, a substitute judge was appointed to handle the preliminary hearings and investigations, and his findings, unbiased and therefore favorable to us, were irrevocably entered in the records. In view of which, the xenophobic judge, upon his return, had no choice but to decide in our favor.

First the road being improved and paved simultaneously with our entry into the finca, and then winning the court case against the caciques, including town hall! We must indeed have powerful connections, Morón thought, and we were thereafter treated with growing respect.

As a last move before opening the finca – about the time the electricity was being installed, a welcome addition, I can tell you – we decided we needed a Land Rover in order to conduct the finca operation properly. This was a major decision, because we were nearly broke by now, after the construction, remodeling, furnishing, law cases, etc. However, the Land Rover company agreed to let us buy on installments, and we soon had the long model that seats nine persons. That is to say, nine people can be seated comfortably in the Land Rover, the number that is also the maximum permitted by the law for this particular vehicle. However, the Rover is built like a small tank, and as on the back Andalusian roads traffic police were extremely scarce it was not unusual to see our Rover rolling along bursting at the seams with perhaps sixteen or eighteen passengers, one or another flamenco singing por bulerías, the rest of us beating out a staccato rhythm on the aluminum roof and sides. Some pedestrians were quite startled to observe this mobile machine-gun thunder by, while others would light up and wave delightedly, wishing they were aboard.

The Land Rover took us places inaccessible to normal transport, permitting a most diversified schedule of activities intended to squeeze the maximum enjoyment from life in Andalusia. In addition to four-wheel drive, the car also possessed a lever that cut the Rover's speed in half while doubling its power factor. When both the double power and the four wheel drive were in use, the car could do almost anything; go over any terrain, through rivers, up mountains, all of which were on its nearly daily itinerary. Many were the after-juerga jaunts to town when we would shun the road and roar through the olive groves, dodging the trees that showed eerily in the headlights, and the just-for-the-hell-of-it climbs up steep mountain slopes when the wine had done its job. Countless were the flamenco picnics, when we would pack all the non-human ingredients on the roof rack – a sixteen liter carafe of red wine, another full of water, a cooler full of beer and a bottle or two of white wine, another full of soft drinks and extra ice, plates, glasses, silverware, the huge stew pot, and the assorted meat, vegetables, fruits, condiments and spices – and the human element inside; four or five flamencos, plus nine or ten of us. These excursions always sparked much excitement, and before long Diego, Fernandillo, Juanito, Gitanito, Joselero, Agustín, Andorrano, Dieguito, whoever happened to be along, would be singing happily, then piling out at the odd venta for refreshments and stretching of legs, then back in again and merrily on our way. The Peñón was a favorite destination, as was the Charco Charcal, an ideally-formed water hole far in the country, surrounded by rolling hills and made unique by high rocks at one end of the pool from which one could dive from various levels into the deep water.

We had several formulas for these picnic excursions. Sometimes we went in the morning and spent the entire day there, eating our meal at two or three in the afternoon. Although we took flamencos along on most of the day excursions, they were mainly merry social affairs involving little serious artistry. By the time we returned to the finca, at eight or nine in the late afternoon, we would be ravenous again and ready for the light meal of salad or gazpacho, and cold cuts the cook had prepared. The flamencos would nibble with us — they rarely ate much before performing — and the all night juerga would follow. This, however, did not prove to be the best formula for good flamenco. After a full day of drinking, eating and sun, many of the guests quite understandably did not have the stamina for a late juerga and often deserted in midstream.

For artistic purposes the best formula was to leave for the picnic after a light lunch, say at three or four in the afternoon (although in July, August and September it could be unbearably hot at that hour). We would arrive at the picnic spot by five, still in time for a couple or three hours of swimming and hot sun, then have the meal at sundown. We would all eat somewhat lightly and consume a goodly amount of wine, and be ready for the juerga after dark, seated around the fire, a clearing being left for the dancing.

Occasionally, on warm nights, we stayed all night, and the awesome setting, especially at the Peñón, invariably touched off the profound in the artists. After the first two or three hours of opening gaiety the fire would be allowed to flicker low, causing the millions of stars to move into more intense proximity. I often scheduled these outings to coincide with the full moon, under which conditions the setting would become even more ethereal. Nearby, water tumbled over rocks, splashing softly and hypnotically. The setting was bewitching, and a spell never failed to be cast. The notes of Diego's guitar then seemed to spin a web of wonder, hanging suspended in pure silvery design in the moonlit silence. It was not sadness on such nights, but the most profound musical philosophy. As if overwhelmed by the miracle of nature, Diego was asking what it is all about. The rest of us sensed this, and we awaited the answer, feeling that it would be revealed to us in the magic of the night.

One night after Diego had set the mood Joselero got to his feet and looked up at the awesome Peñón cliffs towering high above us. He stood quietly for a few moments, and then started singing *martinetes,* one of flamenco's most ancient and profound forms that traditionally admits no instrumental accompaniment. His voice rang with emotion as it echoed off the cliffs and soared high in the night air. The effect was such that Joselero felt a surge of power, and sang on and on in a way that he has probably never equalled, before or since. He, too, was questioning, almost demanding an answer, for a Presence was in the air. We all felt it. This mood of awe carried far into the night, and somewhere along the line the question "What is it all about?" seemed to be

73

answered. It was all about right then and there. The answer was perfection, and perfection was that night at the Peñón.

INSIDE THE OPERATION

We were ready for the first guests at the appointed time, just before Holy Week in April of 1966. Guests were sparse during that entire first season, but not bad considering that our publicity was even more sparse. We simply did not have the money for an adequate publicity campaign, and besides, we felt publicity would attract too many dude ranch types in no way committed to flamenco, but just out for a good time; we preferred to limit our clientele to aficionados, which we knew would be the only way to maintain the purity of the idea. Thus we relied initially on my mailing list, built up over the previous four years from readers of my books who had written in. Later, we calculated that word-of-mouth publicity would complete the job. The news did spread, and we did attract enough guests throughout the years to support the operation.

Just barely, for the operation contained one built-in snag that we had not envisioned. All aficionados do not share the same beliefs. We were dedicated to offering the pure, as opposed to the commercially sophisticated. I had tried both, and compared to the highly emotional flamenco found in towns like Morón, Utrera, Alcalá, Jerez, and so forth, commercial flamenco as performed throughout the world is banal and insincere, good business but no longer authentic folk art.

What is inconceivable to me is that many flamenco aficionados prefer the commercial. Perhaps "prefer" is the wrong word, for most such aficionados are ignorant of the authentic and thus cannot compare. But when they do get themselves into a comparing position, the results are often disconcerting. I know of several cases in which aficionados immersed in the teachings of some slick or unknowing instructor have found themselves quite distressed after experiencing the real thing, but have had the character to attempt to discard their mistaken education and start all over again. Others in the same boat take the easier road; they condemn the pure as "too primitive" or "outmoded," and slide along with the commercial. Still others simply do prefer the commercial. They are used to it, and they find it easier to identify with, a revved up musical form that does commingle nicely with our industrial age. ("Flamenco must keep up with the times," they say, when in reality the phrase should go, "Flamenco is being destroyed by the times.") Also, one's built-in defense mechanism is partly responsible. Unless the aficionado resides in a town like Morón, he necessarily has to live with the commercial variety elsewhere and might as well make the best of it, since it is probably better than nothing. In fact, several aficionados have written to me stating that we spoiled flamenco for them. Where they live they do not have access to the pure, and can no longer tolerate the commercial. This, indeed, is a dilemma without solution. So was the limited appeal our operation was to have. But back in that first year we did not know all this, and it would have made no difference if we had. We were irrevocably committed.

With the arrival of the first guests the operation quickly fell into a sort of loose routine, necessarily flexible and open to frequent innovation. For a set price $60 a week, I believe it was, during the first year — the guests were fully provided for: room, three meals a day, maid service, laundry, transportation, and three organized juergas during the week. Needless to say, the profit margin was exceedingly small, by no means compensating for the immense amount of work the operation provided. Regardless of this monumental truth, however, the word quickly spread, both among the local Andalusians and the foreign element in town, that we were charging exorbitant prices and, in addition, were shamelessly exploiting the flamenco artists and getting rich fast in the process. This stigma was upon us until the end, played upon with delight by the groups in question and only too often believed by guests and gypsies alike.

I keep referring to the work load. Could it really have been that bad? Had we considered it work, it would have been ridiculous. For my part, I had to make the early morning (7:30 a.m.) run into Morón to pick up the maids, for during this first year none would live at the finca. When this worked out well and the maids came, we heaved a sigh of relief, for when they decided to take the day off Luisa, Tina and I got stuck with the maids' work as well. After delivering the maids to the finca I had breakfast, then again headed to town to do the day's shopping. Often some of the guests would come along to do their errands, help with the shopping, or simply to sip something or other at one of the market bars (the Morón market is quite delightful, sporting two busy bars where the men congregate in the morning to gossip and discuss business while the women gossip and do the shopping). Sometimes a guest would stay on in town for a guitar or singing lesson, to be picked up on the

76

next town run. Upon completing the shopping I would take the groceries, cases of wine, beer, siphon water, butane bottles, and so forth, back to the finca so that Luisa could begin preparing the midday meal (when we had no cook), our biggest of the day. Often I would take advantage of the shopping run to bring Diego or one of the nephews out to the finca for lessons. This was not so easy as it sounds, for Diego did not enjoy giving lessons when he was drinking. During these not infrequent occasions he would often be in half hiding, hoping we would forget about his promise (he was incapable of saying no to anything and always graciously agreed to teach). Thus I often had to search him out, except when he was sober or on the mend. At those times he enjoyed teaching, as a relief from boredom.

Around noon I would round up whichever of the guests were interested and make the pleasure run into town. This involved the first wines and beers of the day at Casa Pepe, where the noontime crowd was always spirited. So much so, in fact, that many were the days we would get caught up in the scene and arrive back at the finca late for lunch, much to Luisa's very understandable irritation.

The midday meals were always exciting affairs, involving two courses, dessert, and all the wine we wanted. Our carpenter, a true artisan, had made us a long wooden table to Luisa's design and specifications that comfortably seated up to fourteen (but not infrequently hosted as many as twenty), and when the house was full of guests from diverse backgrounds and the wine began taking effect, conversation became quite animated and interesting. What with one thing and another these meals lasted between two and three hours, until drowsiness set in and we all retired for a *siesta*. Any number of errands usually cut my siesta short, and before long it was 8:00 p.m. and time to take the maids home, while Luisa prepared or supervised, the evening meal. Generally the guests would come along, and after dropping off the maids we would spend another hour to two chatting it up in town before returning home to a less copious meal that often lasted until midnight or after. Two or three nights a week, however (depending on our organizational format at the time), I excused myself at about 11:30 p.m. and went to town for the artists for the night.

This, again, was no easy task. Although the artists benefitted from the juergas and decidedly wanted to come, they had no sense of time or organization. They were just as likely to be waiting for me at Casa Pepe, prepared to go, as to be dispersed all over town, drinking with friends, involved in amorous matters, whatever. Even under the best of conditions Diego never remembered to bring his guitar, or a capo, or a replacement for a broken string, to our rendevous spot, and always had to send for it (them). Sometimes I had to spend an hour or two tracking the artists down, and the condition in which I found them determined just how quickly the juerga would get off the ground. If they were waiting for me as arranged, it indicated they were relatively sober and would need half-a-dozen mood-setting drinks before a juerga culd even be thought of. If they had been drinking all afternoon and evening, however, they would already be in the mood, to say the least, and the juerga would start in the Land Rover on the way to the finca and carry straight on through the night.

Still other complications arose on the frequent occasions we hired artists from out of town, such as Manolito de María, El Poeta or Manolo Heredia, from Alcalá de Guadaira, La Fernanda, La Bernarda, Perrate, etc., from Utrera, Juan Talega from Dos Hermanas, Francisco Mairena or others from Mairena del Alcor, El Farruco or a number of others from Sevilla, or still others from Jerez de la Frontera, La Puebla de Cazalla, Osuna, and so forth. The problem was that the only way to get these artists to come for sure was to pick them up before the juerga and take them home afterwards. I quickly learned that no matter how badly they wanted to come or needed the money, they would rarely take any reasonably priced transportation, such as the bus. A favorite trick was to agree to take the bus, but somehow always miss it and have to take a taxi, sticking us, of course, with the fare, always high between towns. So unless the artist in question could convince a friend with a car to accompany him to the fiesta, the job of fetching and delivering was mine except on the rare occasions when someone reliable was around who was willing to do the job. This meant an extra two or three hours round-trip roving the highways of Andalusia if one was reasonably efficient about it, and often a lot longer if one gave in to the whims of the flamencos to have a quickie in this bar and that venta along the way.

Between one thing and another, I rarely slept at all on juerga nights, and as the morning routine was always waiting, I had to catch catnaps at odd hours and try to extend the siesta as long as possible. But then there were the organized activities that did away with many siestas, such as the picnic excursions (about once a week) and out-of-town juergas. Pinpoint scheduling was essential in order to work it all in and stay reasonably healthy.

Another factor that could cause one to lose sleep was the very difficulties inherent in organizing juergas. In a town like

Morón there are at any one moment hundreds of intrigues. Half the town is not talking to the other half, making it likely that a temperamental artist will walk off in a huff if any number of people show up, or refuse to go if another goes who just the day before was his best friend. (6) Before each juerga it was actually necessary to talk to each of the chosen artists in order to calculate just whom one could and could not invite. On the other hand, at times it was clever to pit one foe against another, and let them fight it out artistically, just so you didn't let them know about it ahead of time, and providing they weren't enemies to the point of physical violence. It was truly a job for a computer.

One might say to hell with them, he who pays gives the orders. Yes and no. I have been through too many disagreeable experiences to follow that tempting but impractical line of thought, such as artists sulking in a corner refusing to perform because of such and such, or simply walking away from the juerga. A little pampering, it turned out, went a long way.

Luisa also had her burdensome share of work to accomplish, especially the first year or two, when much of the time she had to cook two major meals a day for all of us, in addition to her roles of mother, hostess, keeper-of-the-keys, flamenco dance instructor (often giving three or four hours of classes daily), featured female dancer in many of the juergas, sometime gardener, and substitute maid during the not infrequent occasions the maids failed us. All of this, combined with the fact that she was not nearly so enthralled as myself with the whole scene – in truth, she was living in Morón and caring for the finca more or less against her better judgement – caused her to have a much more difficult time than I. For me it was an extremely desirable, if exhausting, life. For her there were few compensations. On the one hand, she did enjoy many of the guests and activities. On the other, she did not enjoy the overabundance of work and, like most women everywhere, she longed for the peace and quiet of a normal home, and the security of a job with an assured future. Obviously the finca operation offered none of these.

Actually, we had foreseen that there might well be an excess of work, and I had attempted to prepare for this by making an arrangement with a friend, an American flamenco guitarist who had lived in Morón, to come live at the finca and help out in exchange for his room, board, and flamenco activity. In the interim he married, and we agreed that he could bring his bride, an American girl whose main enthusiasm in life was to learn flamenco singing and guitar. This sounded even better than the original plan; Luisa would have a helper, too.

Let's call the couple George and Mary. They arrived by

taxi, and were left on the other side of the river because the driver did not want to wet his tires in the two or three inches of water (when a cab was acquired in a village it was usually for life, and the cabbies took no chances). Several of us walked down to meet them and help them carry their luggage up to the finca. We crossed the river stepping on the stones placed for that purpose, greeted them, picked up some luggage, and recrossed. Nary a foot even got damp. It was a crossing accomplished with ease by men, women, and children. But not by Mary. She whimpered and clung to George, who looked helpless and gave me a pleading look. Mary, a girl in her early twenties, I would estimate, was afraid she would fall and hurt herself. Wasn't there some way we could get her across? I was damned if I was going to bring the car down just for Mary, who looked spoiled enough as it was, and compromised by sending the donkey. George got Mary mounted with some difficulty, but once mounted, Mary rode triumphantly all the way to the finca without falling off once!

All right, we thought, perhaps she has a thing about rivers. So let's get their luggage into their quarters. All of us pitched in, including a couple of guests who had already arrived, except … guess who? After watching Mary completely ignore the moving of their considerable luggage for some time, I finally suggested that she might help. After all, it was her luggage. She immediately went into what we learned was her helpless act, stammering and whining like a little girl.

"Ah, he he he, George is showing me how to play the guitar, he he heh, and I really have to take care of my hands, they're so small and delicate, he he he".

Our hearts sank. God, what had we gotten into. I smiled at George; he looked most embarrassed and tried to hide the fact that he was wondering the same thing. Although I am optimistic by nature, I had to admit that the situation did not look very promising. What an understatement! As it turned out, the only things Mary accomplished around the finca were to create a great amount of tension and to play the protagonist in colorful anecdotes, such as those that follow.

Shortly after the river and luggage incidents came that of the water. One day our pipes were being repaired and the finca had no running water, making it necessary to carry water in from the fountain in buckets, which we all set about doing. At least, almost all. At one point Luisa noticed that Mary was nearly dragging a bucket that contained about two fingers of water. Luisa naturally asked her what she was doing. Mary reverted to instant childhood and stammered that she couldn't carry any more. Upon which

Luisa picked up the bucket with one finger in a most effortless manner. Mary knew she had been had and had no recourse but to throw a tantrum, stomping her feet and rushing off to her room, not to be seen again that morning until, of course, mealtime.

Mary had by then proven entirely useless to us. She could not cook, or wash dishes (her hands), or mop, or sweep, or carry, or lift, but oh how she could eat. But even that she muddled up, invariably arriving late to the midday meal, just out of bed, all sleepy-eyed in her robe, with her hair a complete tangle. Luisa and I had been bustling about for several hours by then, and on such occasions Luisa would comment dryly:

"We'll wait for you to dress and comb your hair, Mary."

Mary would answer: "Oh, I don't mind, I'll just eat this way."

Whereas Luisa would have to give her an unmistakeably hard stare and say "We'll wait!"

Mary would stumble away, grumbling and whining about being picked on, but quickly be back to eat the hugest helping of all, serving herself and George before the guests, gobbling that serving down in record time, the heaping their plates high again, "just in case." They usually left most of the second serving, which had to be fed to the dogs. We had to put a stop to that practice when several of the guests confessed they would enjoy seconds occasionally "if Mary ever left any."

Then came a truly humorous incident. We had finally thought up an activity that we thought Mary could handle and might even enjoy. She could put her guitar playing to use by accompanying some of Luisa's dance classes.

Long face, disapproving look. "Oh, I don't know how to accompany the dance."

"You'll learn. Come along."

This was a warm May morning, when all of us were in shirt sleeves, enjoying this most delicious time in Andalusia. Mary, on the other hand, always wore thick wool sweaters, stocking and skirts, but none of us were prepared for her performance in this first lesson. Luisa was busy teaching and the student learning, but somehow the music was not coming through.

Muffle. Thuph. Plaufgh.

"Mary, for goodness sake, please play a little clearer," the student pleaded.

"Ah he he heh, I can't. I'm doing the best I can, he he."

With this both instructor and student looked at Mary for the first time, and both burst out laughing. Mary had on thick fur-lined mittens, protecting her little handsies from the bitter eighty degree cold.

That was when Mary divulged she suffered from low thyroid and was always cold and tired, summer and winter, day and night. Luisa asked her why in the world she didn't take medication for it, and Mary answered that she couldn't take both thyroid medication and the pill, and that she would rather be cold than pregnant. Both instructor and pupil launched into an explanation of various methods of birth control other than the pill, sincerely trying to help Mary. Then Luisa left the room to see how the food was coming along. Mary had only one comment to make to the dance student:

"Boy, if I get pregnant Luisa will have to take care of the baby!"

It had been obvious that Mary was suffering from some condition or other, and the reason she got away with as much as she did was that we all felt sorry for her. Before long, however, we observed that she always had plenty of energy to accomplish whatever she liked, but was invariably much too tired or sick to tackle unpleasant tasks. Such as when we all went to the Holy Week processions in Sevilla. We advised Mary to stay home, as we would be up all night and it would definitely be cold in the early morning hours. But oh no, she insisted on coming along. Now it happened that our maids took the last four days of Holy Week off, so upon arriving home from the processions the women would have to clean up all the dinner dishes that had been left the night before, as well as get everything in readiness for the next meal. Only then could everyone sleep for awhile. Mary agreed to all this, and still insisted on coming.

We returned to the finca late afternoon the following day. Mary had held up beautifully, bubbling, gay. Upon arriving back at the finca, however, we noticed that both Mary and George quickly disappeared. I knocked on their door. No answer. I tried to open. Locked from the inside. I pounded on the door. No answer. Mary and George had copped out.

The temptation was to get them up and throw them out of the finca right then and there. But I still considered George a friend, and decided to count to ten. Which, as always, was wise, for not long afterwards George and I agreed amicably that it would be better if they left. That day they moved into Morón.

I was soon to find out that George's friendship was questionable. At the finca we had strict rules against any and all types of drugs, including pot. Nothing moral was involved. All drugs are against the law, and if word got around that there was dope at the finca the owners, not the lodgers, would be held responsible. (7) As it turns out, both George and Mary were potted a good deal of the time, one valid reason for their ineffectiveness. In addition,

I found out later that George attempted to grow marijuana on the finca grounds, which fortunately did not take. Who would have taken the rap if it were discovered? Not friend George, to be sure.

In subsequent years we came to realize that the formula of exchanging room, board and flamenco for work around the finca, so seemingly beneficial to all concerned, was not practical. The people that filled these roles invariably harbored unrealistic and romantic views of finca life – constant juergas and hell-raising – with little idea of the work involved. They would see the paying guests having the time of their lives, and the temptation was strong to identify with them and follow their examples. This line of reasoning makes no sense, but such is human nature. We did not fully realize this, however, until a second and then a third experience with hired hands.

Unwisely, I decided to try again our second season, and when two young American aficionados wrote requesting employment, I wrote back stating the work conditions and the benefits, and made a point of emphasizing that absolutely no dope of any type could be brought onto the finca. As an added precaution, I requested photos of them both. They answered quickly, enthusiastically agreeing to everything, and sent recent photos. They looked fine, and I agreed to take them on.

To make a long story short, they turned out to be dedicated potheads, California hippies who had washed their faces and gotten haircuts for the photo taking. One was a nice fellow made ineffectual by the dope he was secretly taking all along. The other, a Haight-Ashbury graduate, was a more serious drugs case, so spaced out it appeared that drugs had permanently damaged his mind. Before long it was agreed they should move to town.

The following year a final try was made for an ingratiating young fellow who drove up to the finca one day in his own van, which he offered to utilize in accomplishing his duties. He came well recommended by mutual friends, and I figured I could lose nothing by trying him out. He was informed of the rules, including the dope bit, and agreed to everything in a most sincere manner.

For awhile he worked out well, helping considerably in the gathering of maids, groceries, flamencos, and other miscellanea, but gradually seemed to fall into a confused, energy-less state. The symptoms looked all too familiar. He confessed he had an entire kilo of high-grade hash he had brought back with him from Morocco, and swore he would stash it outside the finca and smoke it only when off duty. It was made clear that if he brought it inside the finca grounds, he was out. Of course, he did exactly that, and he *was* out, the very same night. Another hashhead for the Morón foreign population.

With those experiences under our belts we thought we would never again consider taking on more non-Spanish help. We did, however, in our sixth and seventh years of operation which, I am happy to report, turned out very well.

The first of the new series was Arnie, a fellow who had been a finca guest par excellence for several years running, by now more part of the family than guest, whose main enthusiasm, other than flamenco, women and booze, was cooking. So much so that he wanted to open his own restaurant but felt he needed experience cooking in quantity before jumping into such an ¡endeavour. It occurred to us that the finca would be an ideal proving ground, and we had ourselves a cook.

The changeover from finca guest to finca cook was at times frustrating for Arnie. He was extremely flamenco by nature, having the same quality of surrounding himself by excitement and good times as was possessed by many of the flamencos. As a guest Arnie had been most active, never missing a thing. As finca cook he suddenly had responsibilities, and big ones, for hungry people are not to be toyed with, and as Arnie had to turn out two sizeable meals, midday and evening (guests were now preparing their own breakfasts in the upstairs kitchen), he found he could not partake as fully of flamenco life as before. This he made up for in part, however, by creating his own very colorful scene in the kitchen. By eleven in the morning Arnie was back from shopping and beginning the midday meal preparations. The kitchen door was opened wide, a bottle of wine plopped on the table, and guests encouraged to share in Arnie's wit, wine, cutting, chopping, mincing, preparing. It was a hard scene to resist, and by noon there was often quite a jolly little gathering chuckling along in the kitchen, at times complete with rumbas and bulerías played by the nimble fingers of the chef himself when not by Diego, Juanito, and/or Agustín, at the finca for guitar classes, irrepressibly attracted to Arnie's morning merriment. Not infrequently the gypsies would also burst into song (Diego sang rarely but well, Agustín excellently por bulerías, while Juanito's bubbling good humor was constantly overflowing into wild, happy song), and then it would be the dancers who could not resist. High noon in Arnie's kitchen was often a highlight of the day.

Despite, or because, of all this, Arnie consistently managed to turn out complex, well-prepared meals with a minimum of temperament — when he did have a chef-like seizure, watch out; pots and pans were likely to fly in the finest culinary tradition — and Arnie passed his first cook-in-quantity period with flying colors, while in the process adding still another dimension to the picturesque life of the finca.

By our next season (1972) Arnie was down on the southern coast investigating opening his restaurant, and could not repeat his successful effort of the year before. (8) In lieu of which, an arrangement was made with a young couple, friends and aficionados, to take over, she as cook, he the logistical side of the operation.

Different natures, different scene. This temperamental cook insisted on working in solitude, and the kitchen became her inner sanctum. Although a good cook, she had trouble coping with quantity (for those who are not cooks I can testify that it is a thousand times more difficult cooking for sixteen than for six). She did make it through but was out of her element and not happy with the situation, even though she was cooking only one major meal a day instead of the two prepared by Arnie the year before (the other meal that year the guests ate in a local restaurant, or prepared themselves in the upstairs kitchen). He worked out well, and the desired effect, that of taking some of the workload off our shoulders, was successfully achieved.

In 1973, our last year, the kitchen again became everyone's ideal: a center of good cheer and visible culinary delights in the making. That season daughter Tina, then seventeen, was chef, displaying an even temperament, organizational ability, and talent for cooking possessed by few. Her efforts were applauded by one and all.

Then there were the maids, well deserving of mention in that they played an enormous role in the finca operation. So much so that our very existence largely depended upon them; had we run out of maids we would certainly have had to close shop.

Our initial maids, back in the first year of operation, were two sisters, both extremely pleasant and good workers. They lasted only a few weeks, however, before their father made them leave when our reputation reached his ears. In some ways their replacements were better, for one of them, an aging widow named Adela, had worked as a cook and knew how to prepare many savory Andalusian dishes: stews of various types, *gazpacho,* and fried foods, mainly. The most surprising thing about her was that she was also willing to learn new dishes from Luisa. Although Luisa had to supervise most of her preparations so that they would be suitable for the guests – above all her usage of olive oil – Adela took a great load of work off Luisa's shoulders and made life more pleasant for her during the three or four months she was with us. Adela finally fell and injured herself out at the fountain. She stayed home in bed recuperating for some days, and her sons talked her out of coming back.

The other replacement was Ani, a lame, quite lovely girl with a pleasing personality, who stayed with us for about a year, as her family had moved to Barcelona and there were no men folk around to pull her away. Ani lived with her grandmother, who chose to ignore our reputation and believe Ani's account of us. When she finally did leave, it was to join her family in Barcelona.

Like Luisa and Tina, Ani loved gardening, and I remember with what delight the three of them would go down to the garden they had planted in the orchard and pick the vegetables for the day's meal, and how the guests, who came mostly from industrial countries of beautiful but insipid fruits and vegetables, enjoyed this freshly picked produce that was bursting with flavor.

As the seasons passed we did manage to make our lives at the finca easier and more pleasant by experimenting with and adopting everchanging organizational formats, but above all by finally encountering maids who agreed to live in, at first part-time, and finally full-time. Foremost among the part-time live-ins were two: Pepi, whom we see in the chapter on Fernandillo; and Isabel, a small woman in her sixties with thin brown hair pulled back in a little bun that was forever in disarray. Isabel kept us going for awhile after Pepi left, but cannot be said to have been very clean or efficient. She did, however, have some endearing habits, such as singing in a most startling high-pitched voice while she worked, coquettishly raising one foot off the floor while washing dishes, sewing the hems of her uniforms up so at least an inch of her slip always showed (she never divulged her reason for doing this; perhaps she was proud of her slip?), and daily making herself a corsage from petals of the jazmine bush that grew on the terrace to put in her unwashed hair (she only bathed when we insisted). She also gave us emphatic daily lessons in her version of the Spanish language. The Spanish of the lowest class around Morón is astoundingly dissimilar to correct Castilian Spanish, and even varies considerably from the Spanish of the educated locals, in itself quite unlike Castilian. Before eventually settling down to enjoy Isabel's esoteric language, Luisa used to attempt to correct her in proper Castilian, much to Isabel's annoyance.

"Isabel, its *petróleo,* not *pretóleo,* and *película,* not *pinícula.*"

"Ha," Isabel would answer indignantly, "that may be so in your country, but in *'españolito'* (her word for *'español,'* or 'Spanish') it's like I say it and always has been!" For Isabel considered anyone from outside her direct theater of operations native of another country, including such distantly vague places as Madrid.

Isabel finally decided to take a prolonged vacation just when

Luisa was in bed with hepatitis and we needed her the most. We looked for a substitute and came up with our first full-time live in maid, a woman in her early thirties so full of boundless energy and bubbling good spirits that she earned the title ROCIO THE WONDER MAID. (As human nature will have it, as soon as Isabel heard that Rocio was firmly established at the finca she was filled with desire to return to work. We gave her a gentle but firm "no.")

Ladies, sit back and read what Rocio used to do, and then start counting your blessings. First off, every other day about six in the morning she would wash by hand and hang up to dry the laundry for as many as twenty people (our washing machine and dryer both burned out somewhere along the line, and in any case Rocio insisted she preferred washing by hand due to the increased cleanliness), which she would iron, fold and distribute in her "spare time" during non-wash days. After that came the daily sweeping and washing down of our huge front terrace (some eighty square yards of it), as well as our nearly as large back patio. If it was a morning after a juerga she would then clean up the juerga sector, which meant washing a multitude of glasses, ashtrays and sometimes dishes if food had been involved, sweeping and mopping the floor, moving a dozen or eighteen chairs back to their normal locations in scattered parts of the finca, and so forth. If there had not been a juerga the night before, she would often entertain herself by washing a car or two, usually at no one's request. Afterwards into the kitchen to feed herself and her son before packing him off to school. She would then attack the downstairs, both big and little houses, followed by beginning preparations for the midday meal. By that time most of the guests would be up and she could start on the sleeping areas, which involved cleaning eleven bedrooms, the making of nineteen or twenty beds, cleaning of five bathrooms, and so on and so forth. She would then help serve the midday meal, and clean up afterwards, including all the dishes, after which she would get in some ironing, weed and water the plants, and begin preparations for the evening meal (Luisa or one of our string of cooks did the actual cooking, although Rocio's stews were in great demand and she would oblige by whipping one up once or twice a week). After helping serve the table and cleaning up after dinner, Rocio allowed herself some entertainment. If a juerga was scheduled, she would get a little dolled up and dance a *sevillanas* or two with Luisa or Tina, and flirt with the flamencos. Otherwise, there would be horseplay with us or the guests. Or a look at the TV. A "look" is an accurate statement, for as soon as she was seated and her guard was down, she would be fast asleep.

Not only did Rocio do all the above plus lots of other odds and ends in the ·endless work of the finca (as well as off-season whitewashing, painting, oiling and waxing of furniture, woodwork, floors, etc.), she did it happily, singing and joking her way along. We insisted we should hire another maid to help her, and did so a couple of times. However, the new maids would only get in her way as she flashed about, and did not last long; Rocio correctly insisted she could do the job better without them. And besides, working alone she garnered all the abundant tips from the guests, which often equalled her salary, already sizable by Morón standards.

Aside from her gargantuan appetite for work, Rocio was a delight, personally clean, extremely loyal, forever defending us and the finca against town gossips and slanderers. She stayed with us until the end, and was crushed when we closed up and moved to Madrid, as we were when we had to part company. I can even say that if it hadn't been for her, the finca operation may well have ended sooner. Her incredible output of work and good will made the last finca years feasible. So *Viva* Rocio, Wonder Maid!

We of course look up Rocío every time we return to Morón. She remembers the "easy" finca days with nostalgia, for she is at present the SOLE worker, other than the bartender, in a Spanish air base canteen and is in charge of preparing the midday food for two hundred or more men, plus cleaning up the whole mess afterwards. And there is no modern equipment involved. She personally peels a sack of potatoes daily for the enormous stew, makes hundreds of sandwiches, does all the dishes by hand, and on and on. Compared to this, she says, the finca was a breeze Her salary: less than $5 a day at last report. However, on the positive side she has been included in a social security retirement plan, a newly innovated luxury for Andalusian workers, and at least feels secure about her old age.

(Since writing the above we returned to Morón and looked up Rocio. She is quite happy. Not only have her salary and work conditions greatly improved, she was granted an apartment in a new group of buildings constructed for families whose previous living quarters were condemned to demolition. If it is correct that Morón is in the throes of an economic crisis at present, with factories closing and a very high unemployment rate, it is certainly going down swinging. Demolition of old tenements, and new construction, are in evidence everywhere, serving, of course, the double purposes of improving the living conditions of the poor and providing work for the unemployed. How is it all financed? From what I gather, the new buildings are sold at cost, payable in comfortable installments within nearly everyone's means over a long period of time. A down payment, however, is necessary, and this is where a modern miracle enters the picture. If the story is true — Rocio and others swear it is — an old priest returned to Morón after having been absent since the Civil War, and commenced digging in a remote catacomb of one of Morón's churches. Sure enough, it was still there, a fortune in church silver and other valuables that had been hidden at the beginning of the war. This is all normal enough. The miracle is that a large share, if not all, of the resultant money was channeled directly to the needy! Although Rocio herself was able to get an advance from her employer for the down payment, many of her neighbors, including her sister, were not so fortunate. In such cases the 40,000 peseta down payments on the new apartments were provided by the old priest.)

PART III

PORTRAITS AND SKETCHES

ANZONINI AND PACO

Our guests that first year were as heterogeneous a group as can be imagined. In such a flamenco atmosphere, in which a great deal of wine drinking took place as a natural part of the activities, differences were likely to be magnified, generating numerous personality clashes. I, of course, being male in all of his innocence, did not pick up on many of these innuendos at first. I was friendly with each guest, taking him or her at face value, and found it difficult to realize that all others did not do the same. To the contrary, petty nit-picking seems to be a major diversion of much of humanity, and in an ambiance as homey as the finca, in which we all shared the same table three times a day, as well as the same terrace, bathrooms, juergas, picnics, and outings in town, it flourished. Pretty soon I was hearing that two of our initial five guests could not stand each other, the society woman labeling the middle class house wife as "petite bourgeoise," and the house-wife scorning the beautiful grand dame as "disgustingly *sexy,* always touching herself and attracting attention." On the other hand, these two enemies got together and branded another of the female guests as "terribly boyish," and still another, who kept to herself a great deal, as "dull." I was to find out that they were *all* agreed on one thing: they were instinctively agraid of our sole male guest at the time, whom they named "Jack the Ripper." As I was on quite friendly terms with Jack and was, besides, too busy to indulge in such gossipy pastimes I paid no attention until hearing that after one particularly long binge Jack had gotten a bit out of control, becoming somewhat offensive with the women and culminating the scene by roughly pinching my ten-year-old daughter. With this Jack had gone too far, and he and I decided the next day that he should leave, one of the rare times such a situation arose with guests during our entire operation. This was all taking place during the reign of George and Mary, so one can imagine the chaos had it not been for the all-important binding factor: flamenco. We all had that common interest, and it was a strong one.

Oddly enough, our first five guests were all students of the dance, which meant that Luisa had her work cut out. There were days when she gave all five classes, in addition to her other multitudinous duties, days at the end of which she would fall into bed exhausted. Fortunately, this was not the norm, for during most of the finca operation guitar students were in the majority. It was not unusual to sit on the terrace and hear the simultaneous practicing of five or six such students issue through the open windows of separate rooms, much to the confusion of the ears and alarm of the neighborhood birds.

Shortly after Holy Week, which I mentioned briefly in the last chapter, Sevilla celebrates its famed spring fair. We made a point of visiting that fair two or three times that first spring at different hours of the day or night: the all-night juerga scene, that carried through until ten or eleven in the morning in the gypsy *casetas de los buñuelos,* where all the artists gathered after their performances in the señoritos' casetas to continue juerga-ing together while consuming the traditional early morning *churros con chocolate* (fritters deep-fried in oil, eaten after dipping them in thick hot chocolate); the afternoon bullfight, and afterwards talking it over and drinking at La Marina before perhaps dining at El Mesón (bull's tail stew during bullfight days) and then on to the fair; or the scene from about eleven in the morning to bull-fight time, when a good part of Sevilla donned traditional costumes and watched the señoritos and their women, also costume clad, ride around splendidly from caseta to caseta on equally as splendid horses, the horses heads high and tails stiff and the humans' backs straight with ramrod pride.

This particular year we reaped an added reward at the fair in the form of two fine flamenco artists of the old school: Anzonini del Puerto and Paco de Valdepeñas. I had frequently hired them for juergas in our Madrid club two years earlier, and we were by now good friends. They were fair-hopping this year – going from fair to fair in Andalusia, being available for paid juergas when the opportunity arose – and had a few days with nothing much to do between the Sevilla and Jerez de la Frontera spring fairs. This seemed a fine opportunity, and I invited them to stay with us at the finca during that period, promising them two or three juergas during their stay. They were delighted, as were the guests to have such close contact with gypsy artists of their stature.

Both Anzonini and Paco are excellent unschooled singers and dancers, as well as expert juerga animators (fiesteros). Any juerga in which they are involved is likely to be a memorable one. Both are over six feet tall and cut fine, slim, masculine figures, so unlike the minute effeminate types of which the flamenco dance is largely comprised. Paco was in his late forties, Anzonini in his late fifties at that time.

Paco de Valdepeñas is perhaps the better dancer of the two, with fine arms of unusual elegance for his type of dance, while Anzonini, with his thin, foggy voice, suitable for small juerga rooms only, sings with a *duende* that can be truly moving. Anzonini's completely unique dance is so bizarre that there are those who do not realize that it is dancing. But, as I pointed out to two of our guests in the first finca juerga in which he performed, if we accept the dictionary definition of dance as being "to move rhythmically to music" and add to the definition "in a flamenco manner," his dance not only fits the category but is highly praiseworthy, never failing to please his viewers. Paco's dance, on the other hand, is excellent in a far more conventional way but still falls under the unschooled classification. (Unschooled gypsy dancers are completely unlike their far slicker theatrical counterparts, whom we are used to seeing in tablaos, nightclubs and theaters. The unschooled rely far more on personality and magnetism, rarely using complicated footwork, oftentimes singing and dancing simultaneously or at least in the same number, perhaps acting out the verse story in their dance. Theatrical flamenco dancers, on the other hand, rely almost completely on footwork and other schooled techniques. The unschooled dance is spontaneous and creative, the theatrical choreographed. There are a few performers who successfully dance a middle road between these two extremes, El Farruco, whom we shall meet later in this book, being the most notable.) Paco's singing is not on a par with his dancing. His voice, a bit bullfroggish, can be downright disagreeable in the higher reaches. However, the combination of the singing and dancing of each is superb, and both enjoy fine reputations among knowledgeable aficionados.

Anzonini's background is nearly as unusual as his dance. Born in Puerto de Santa María (near Cádiz) of gypsy parents, his direct lineage includes both Italian and English gypsy blood, from whence stems the name Anzonini, as well as another of his names, Leighton (which has given rise to a nickname, appropriate when he is in one of his grandiose moods, of "Lord Leighton"). By trade Anzonini is a butcher, as are others of his family. He had a pleasant and prosperous existence in El Puerto until one day the lure of the artistic life led him throughout Spain and to various parts of the world, mostly with the troupe of Lola Flores. When I met him in 1964 he was performing in a Madrid tablao that was dedicated to presenting the truly authentic in flamenco (as a consequence of which it went bankrupt; knowledgeable flamenco artists and aficionados loved it, but the tourists preferred the slick).

Paco de Valdepeñas was born of gypsy parents in Valdepeñas,

capital of Spain's largest wine producing region. He early developed his dance and accompanying song, and began frequenting the *colmados* and other establishments that catered to flamenco, mainly in and around Madrid, where he could hope to be hired for juergas. His marriage to a gypsy girl from Barcelona was quite fortunate, for she turned out to have a talent for another time-honored gypsy trade: peddling goods from house to house. Previous to Spain's recent entry into the international merchandise market, when foreign goods were nearly non-existent or outrageously high-priced in Spain, there was an excellent market for goods smuggled in from such ports as Gibraltar and Tangier. Paco's wife specialized in fabrics, and the combination of her good looks and gypsy persuasiveness brought her great success. She found South America a better market than Spain, however, for in South America gypsies are scarce and hold a certain fascination for the people, rather than the blatant dislike and fear of them that so often exists in Spain. So she began making yearly trips to South America, taking with her bolts of unusual Spanish cloth as well as English and Indian fabrics from Gibraltar and Moorish and Middle Eastern from Tangier, all of which she would sell at an excellent profit before returning to Spain. Running out of goods before she was ready to return to Spain was not much of a deterrent. In such a case she would seek out the specialty shops in the big South American cities and buy bolts of uncommon fabric, which she would take out to the nearby provinces and sell as merchandise from such and such an exotic land. On each of these trips of two or three months she made a killing, enough so that they could live in relative style the rest of the year. Paco often accompanied her on these journeys, helping her during the day, and sometimes bringing in extra money through his flamenco at night.

Both Paco and Anzonini fitted well into finca life, although the rest of us had a hard time keeping up with them. Both are live wires who never seemed to run out of energy. They got along extremely well with the Morón flamencos, and their entire stay with us blended into one long juerga. For instance, we threw a grand juerga to celebrate their first night at the finca, with Diego, Luisa, Fernandillo and Joselero in addition to Paco and Anzonini. With artists of such quality and high spirits the juerga was incredibly animated, and coasted through to morning without one moment of letdown. Everything was going full blast when I went to pick up the maids, and still was when I returned. Then I had to go shopping. Great! We'll all go!

Soon we were at the marketplace, boisterous, crazy, but still artistic, Anzonini, Paco and Fernandillo competing in the large space between the two market bars, singing, dancing, amusing all the early morning shoppers and the bar crowd, drinking constantly but wisely, never passing over the line. If you have never lived in Andalusia you cannot really imagine this scene; the authorities of industrial countries would never tolerate such carryings-on. But here, in the Morón marketplace, everyone, including the local cops, was delighted. Before long, Manolo de las Alhajas took a break from attempting to collect jewelry money owed him (convincing the women to pay the latest installment before they spent the money on food for their families) and was in the middle of the circle, singing and dancing and challenging each of the fiesteros to try equal *that*. Then Juan Cala, the mason of the perennial hat who happened to be working near the marketplace that day, burst loudly into the circle and did his caricature of the dances of Anzonini and Andorrano. Peals of laughter, and he was declared the greatest, which again spurred Manuel de las Alhajas into action, and in turn Anzonini, then Paco, and so forth. Someone had the not-so-bright idea of pushing one of Diego's gypsy nieces, reputedly an excellent dancer, into the circle. She resisted, refusing to dance more than a step or two, then escaped, blushing and self-conscious, fully realizing that if she danced her parents and the whole gypsy community would be furious with her. This was a man's world, and only men could expose them-selves publicly in this manner; decent gypsy women have to reserve their dancing for family gatherings.

A small, slim gypsy cattle dealer replaced her in the circle, carrying the short staff of his profession. He silenced the crowd with a manner of authority and quietly proceeded to explain that all the dancing we had been witnessing, with its hustle and bustle and moving around, was not true gypsy dancing. In true gypsy dancing, he went on to say, one barely moves one's feet (many old-time purists shared this belief). He then proceeded to draw a small symbolic square on the floor with his sraff, from which, he said, he would not stray during his dance. He placed his staff on the floor carefully, stepped into the space, perhaps a half yard square, and proceeded to dance. The *palmas* recom-menced the *compás* of the bulerías, and the serious little man began to move his arms and body in a most dignified and fluid manner while, as promised, moving his feet only enough to mark the rhythm. His facial expression was absolutely deadpan through-out, but it did not take long to discern a well-developed sense of humor when he comically accentuated the climaxes of the bulerías in perfect harmony with the staccato hand-clapping. Here we had the Buster Keaton of flamenco, and his performance was received with great enthusiasm. When the little man stopped dancing he picked up his staff and symbolically erased the square, thus ending the ritual. Only then did he grin broadly, while bowing low to the crowd. The approval, clamorous, was soon ended by another spectacle.

A pretty young thing stepped into the opening with a shawl draped daintily over her head and shoulders, and with a broom in hand. The palmas started up as if on cue, and this little miss began sweeping in a most feminine manner in perfect rhythm, her face largely hidden by the shawl. Only when she started singing, with a voice like a bull in heat, did everyone realize who it was: who else but Fernandillo? As he danced around with his broom Fernandillo parodied a popular ditty of the period:

> *If I had a broom (repeated three times)*
> *How many things I would sweep...*
> *First,*
> *What would I sweep first,*
> *I'd sweep all the ugly things*
> *That there are in this world...*

At that moment a large object leapt into the circle, entirely covered by a piece of white material and, arms outstretched under the covering and making loud ghost-like woooooooing noises, proceeded to pursue Fernandillo around the circle. Fernandillo opened his eyes wide and pursed his lips in a most delicately shocked manner, and danced away from this terrible ghost. The ghost, peeking out from time to time to get its bearings, was in hot pursuit. When it started gaining, Fernandillo had no alternative but to wheel around and clobber the ghost a good one with the soft end of the broom.

Thunk.

"Woooooooooooooooo-eee, *hijo de puta,* I'll get you for that!"

Finally the ghost caught Fernandillo and enveloped him in whiteness. Fernandillo stopped struggling and cooed:

"All right, you caught me. I'm your's."

Only then did the ghost expose himself. It was Bernabé the Butcher, who had his business in this market and who could not resist, as always, the temptation of cachondeo. Like a true showman, Bernabé kept the best surprise for the end: he had a string of five or six link sausages dangling from his fly that reached nearly to the floor. The crowd roared with laughter that must have shook the marketplace to its foundations. Fernandillo let loose a delighted "ayyyyyyyyyy" and threw his broom away, and he and Bernabé danced arm-in-arm out of the circle.

That broke up the gathering. Nothing could follow that act,

and besides, I had to get the shopping back to the finca or no one would eat. Great! We'll all go back and cook the meal! I invited Bernabé, and he said he would be out as soon as he closed shop. Meantime he donated his sausages to the meal.

And back we rocketed, the Land Rover virtually alive with beating and stomping out the rhythm, singing, shouting... Upon arrival, all the gypsies made a rush for the kitchen, each declaring that he was going to cook today's meal a la gitano. Anzonini and Fernandillo won and took over the kitchen. Luisa gladly acquiesced and came out to the terrace with the rest of us.

There we sat, basking in the late morning sun while munching on tapas and sipping red wine. The moods alternated between the deep and philosophical and the wild and rambunctious. Those who wished took refreshing dips in the pool and then returned to the group on the terrace. The surroundings were exquisite that spring morning. The orchard was a series of vivid greens, set off by pink and white blossoms of the fruit trees. Platero munched on the thick green grass and occasionally let off a questioning hee-haw, to be answered promptly by one of the donkeys tied up in front of the venta. Both edges of the river were thick with high trees and cane, and beyond, the as yet dust-free olive trees sparkled gaily across the rolling hills to the horizon. Nearby, the swallows were still at their morning congress, perched in dignified and orderly fashion along the two wires that ran between our electricity caseta and the venta. They were deep into their business of the day and argued most heatedly, unruffled by our presence and activities. The venta shone whitely across the river, the sounds of its morning bustle of customers and animals carrying to us softly. One by one the guests, all of whom had open second story windows facing onto the terrace, were awakened by our somewhat noisy vivacity and peered sleepily down at us, each to be greeted by some king of clowning, perhaps a bit of raucous poetry by Diego or, if female, an innocuous proposition from one of the flamencos.

The guests would take in the scene at a glance, get ready quickly and join us, kicking themselves for missing the action when told of the marketplace scene. That was one problem with finca life that could never be solved. The guests usually were there for a short period and did not want to miss anything. But coming from a sedate life with set hours and lets of sleep, they couldn't even attempt to keep up with the flamencos and their round-the-clock activities, and they would have to settle for those times when they calculated that the highlights would take place. This, however, no one could calculate, and the guests invariably missed out on some of the best moments.

Not long after all the guest were assembled with us on the terrace our chefs for the day announced that the meal was ready and would we kindly be seated in the dining room. The table was nicely set, and placed in the middle of it was a huge stew pot containing enough *paella andaluza* to feed a regiment. Which was just as well, for there were about twenty of us for that meal. While the paella settled and gained flavor we were served Bernabé's sausages, just fried and delicious, with *pan cateto* (hick's bread). Then came the paella, very soupy and eaten with a spoon, as is customary in Andalusia, unlike the dry paella from Valencia. (It must be said that the Valencian paella is far more of an art, but the Andalusian variety is also very tasty, consisting of rice and a variety of vegetables highlighted by tomato, garlic and bay leaf in this case, as well as a goodly amount of pork). For dessert they had made an enormous salad, which contained about everything they could find in the kitchen and pantry: lettuce, raw spinach, garlic, onion, bay leaves, pepper corns, radishes, tomatoes, green peppers, cucumbers, olives, tuna fish, asparagus, thyme, rosemary, shallots....

Anzonini was turned on and entertained us with stories of his adventures during the meal. One never knew what to believe of his stories. He possesses a vivid and famous imagination, and much of what he recounts is pure fantasy. However, at the most unexpected moments, when one is sure he is telling blatant lies, along comes someone who verifies his story. Such as the time he was telling about Haiti. It just happened that one of the guest knew Haiti well, and at our insistence began questioning Anzonini in detail. Much to our surprise, Anzonini rattled off names of local characters, places and events in Haiti that were absolutely accurate.

Regardless of having only one tooth left in his mouth, right at the front, Azonini was popular with the ladies (or perhaps because of it – a few years later one of his ladies had him fitted with dentures which, besides being uncomfortable, were so unpopular with his fans he stopped wearing them after a time; with them, he was simply not the Anzonini we all knew and loved). He is tough, upright, and extremely gracioso. And, like Fernandillo, not afraid of work. In fact, he is an excellent worker if the conditions are right, as he has demonstrated by his long-term affairs with foreign, ladies who have successfully put him to work.

One was with a girl who was apparently doing research on the sexual habits of gypsies, for she went through nearly all of them I knew. Anzonini became the favorite at one point, and she decided to buy a finca and have him run it for her. All went well for a spell until Anzonini made the mistake of falling in love with the girl, who in the meantime continued in her diversified research, although in a slightly more clandestine fashion. Love, and above all jealousy, had no place in this relationship, and they eventually parted company. But he remained in love with the promiscuous miss, and the subsequent juergas in which he sang of her charms with tears in his eyes were extremely moving, or hilarious, depending on one's bent. It never struck me as funny to see a friend suffer, and he suffered intensely during those moments, but the local Andalusians almost without exception laughed at what they considered an absurd display of love for such a woman.

Another serious affair was with just the opposite type of foreign lady, which carried him to the opposite extreme. She attempted the impossible – reform. She set Anzonini up in a butcher shop and began discouraging him from participating in his flamenco life. For a time it worked. Anzo worked long hours and was a good partner. He disappeared from flamenco almost entirely and toed the line. Oh, there were times when he would break away for a weekend of hell-raising and flamenco, but it wasn't that much fun, knowing he had his woman, and business, waiting impatiently. Finally, after a number of years, the regular hours and bourgeois life got to him, and the overwhelming lure of flamenco seduced him back. He left this secure life to return to the nomadic, usually penniless existence of the disappearing and today largely unsolicited old-time gypsy flamenco.

Have no doubt that Anzo misses many of the benefits of the secure life. His foreign women had money in abundance which they had shared with him generously, and nothing makes Anzonini expand like a pocketful of money. Under such conditions the ever-flamboyant Lord Leighton would exceed himself, inviting grandly, throwing money around almost insanely, as if to make up for his many periods of poverty. He would show the world who the true Anzonini was!

Both Anzonini and Paco de Valdepeñas had a defect which greatly hindered their ever accumulating much cash in their preferred flamenco world, a defect shared, usually to a somewhat lesser extent, by most of the old-style flamencos. They were incapable of holding to the law most basic to those who desire to make their living as performing artists that of doling out their art in amounts calculated to excite but not satiate the appetites of those in a position to hire them. To the contrary, with Anzonini and Paco all that was needed was a flamenco ambiance, a little wine, and the sound of a guitar, voice or palmas for them to burst immediately into the scene and take it over, singing and dancing for minutes, hours or days, whatever it took to demonstrate definitively where the real flamenco lay and who possessed the true gracia and duende. Then when the session ended and everyone went his way, their artistic airs would dissipate like the crowds and they would usually be as penniless as before, if not more so (for at the height of their splendor they, above all Lord Leighton, were likely to pick up part of the tab, if not all of it, depending on their finances of the moment). No señorito doubted their artistic merits, but why hire them if they performed constantly just for the sheer pleasure of it? Anzonini and Paco's attitude, of course, is traditional to the core. In the old days, when no one considred making a living at flamenco, all flamencos were that way. Flamenco was simply part of a pleasureable life style. But today, when flamenco artists are trying to sell their art, this attitude is decidedly impractical.

We held a farewell juerga for Anzonini and Paco the night before they left, and then took them down to Jerez and dropped them off at the fair the following night. After they departed the finca operation carried on in its usual energetic fashion, but it now seemed calm after the almost frantic activities of the previous days. Today, eleven years later, both of these fine old-school artists have calmed down a bit, but are still guaranteed to outlast in juerga all but the most formidable and determined of young people. They are among the last of their breed. The spirit that drove them on (and on) has nearly disappeared in this more "reasonable" age of materialism and regular hours.

DIEGO

Only after knowing Diego for several years did I come to fully realize just what a singular person he was. Behind his affable exterior there raged a fierce pride, both in himself and in the gypsy race in general, that was never extinguished. This pride cost Diego many thousands of pesetas during those hard years and occasionally could have put him in personal danger. Fortunately, the latter never came to pass. The señoritos and authorities tolerated Diego's idiosyncrasies because he possessed genius. They took from him what no ordinary man would have gotten away with in those totalitarian times. The following two anecdotes show Diego at his most typical and/or daring.

Diego and his immediate group of Morón gypsies were once hired for a juerga by a flamenco club from a nearby town. On arriving, they were greeted effusively by the club officials, all friends of Diego's, and drinks were placed in their hands. Everything was most pleasant until one of the señoritos pulled a pack of expensive American cigarettes from his pocket and offered them around to the other señoritos, pointedly ignoring the gypsies in his offering. This was, of course, a slight that Diego did not let slip by. Instead, he spoke up.

"How about us?"

The señorito looked at Diego condescendingly and replied: "Since when do gypsies smoke blond tobacco?"

Diego reacted as if he had been struck, jumping up and declaring:

"*¡Ya está!* This 'gentleman' can find a guitar and play for the fiesta. I'm leaving!"

Everyone protested and tried to stop him, including the other artists; they saw their money for an entire week slipping through their fingers, for they knew that without Diego there would be no fiesta.

"Diego, *por Dios,* think of my children!"

"You think of your children. I'm leaving!"

And leave he did, the rest of the gypsies having no choice but to trail along behind, telling the señoritos they would try to talk him into returning.

103

All their persuasion was to no avail. Diego had other ideas. He bought them all several rounds in the local bar, and when the wine began having the desired effect of causing the lost fiesta to seem far less urgent, the twinkle came to Diego's eyes and he proposed:

"Let's go over and see El Cojo and play for the prisioners. They're our people, not those bloody señoritos."

Quirky ideas appeal to gypsies, and they all rallied around and thought it a fine plan. The flamenco club was completely forgotten as they carried a case of wine over to the local jailhouse and barged in on El Cojo, the lame jailer and quite good flamenco singer himself.

"Cojo, we are here with offerings of good cheer for you and your friends."

"Diego, *hombre,* welcome! It is probably against the rules, but what isn't these days? Cell No. 3 is free. Go right in."

And dawn found them still in and around cell No. 3, the prisoners, the gypsies and El Cojo all happily in their cups, singing, dancing, playing, telling tall stories, brothers forever.

Another occasion could have been more ominous if Diego had not been Diego. The same group of Morón gypsies was hired for a juerga in a mountain village in the Serranía de Ronda, not far from where Diego had been reared. It was quite an occasion to have Diego, and the turnout was large and enthusiastic. Everything was going fine until the opening bulerías died down and a man conversing in a loud voice became noticeable. No one seemed to hush him up, so Diego amicably put his finger to his lips and politely tried to get the message through. The man kept right on talking, paying no attention to Diego. Diego started up another bulerías, trying to see if this talkative chap would tire of his own babble. But no, he was still going strong at the end, causing Diego to call out a pointed comment about how impolite people who don't know when to stop talking ruin juergas. The man paid no attention, so Diego tried one more time by announcing that he would play a solo and would appreciate complete silence. To no avail. Blabbermouth carried on.

By now Diego was furious. (I have seen him in this state once under similar circumstances, when he was about to smash *my* Santos Hernández guitar over the head of the culprit had I not restrained him.) He stood up and shouted:

"Hey you!"

Everyone looked shocked and turned timidly to look at the talker. The mounting pressure finally seeped through to him, and he gave Diego a hard stare and replied:

"Are you referring to me?"

Diego got the message. Here was a man of power, not to be trifled with. But that did not stop Diego.

"Are you either going to shut up or get out, or do you want to be responsible for this fiesta breaking up right now!"

The man's eyes turned to ice. He smiled sardonically and replied:

"You apparently don't know who I am. I am Don Fulano de Tal, *Cabo* (Chief) *de la Guardia Civil!*"

The chill of fear hung heavily over the room. Everyone else present knew only too well who he was, of his complete power in the area and of his dangerous nature. Their hearts pounded while they awaited Diego's answer. It came immediately.

"And I am Don Diego del Gastor, and you can start looking for another guitarist!"

And Diego packed up his guitar and left, again followed by the other reluctant artists bemoaning the fate of their children. The Civil Guard Chief did nothing, no doubt knowing that Diego, although a lowly gypsy, included among his friends and admirers many influential people, including the governor of the province. That is a bit much to cope with, even for a Cabo de la Guardia Civil.

All Diego ever wanted was basic respect for the gypsies and their art. If received, he was the most affable of fellows who would do anything for a friend. However, that was asking a lot from most of the señoritos of that (or any) era, educated by society to consider the gypsies far inferior to themselves. By the same token, the existence of this attitude explains why the flamencos of Morón and other areas so readily and even eagerly accepted the foreign aficionados who came to them. Here were people who truly appreciated their art and considered the gypsies as equals. The flamencos opened their arms to them far more than they ever have to the usual Spaniard.

The combination of Diego's bizarre way of being and his extraordinary guitar playing made him a legendary figure while still relatively young. Nevertheless, as he stuck close to Morón and its immediate environs and played almost exclusively for private juergas, few other professional guitarists had ever heard him play. This, naturally, aroused their curiosity to the bursting point, and many of them contrived to get Diego to play for them. Two such guitarists were Niño Ricardo and Sabicas. However, the prospect of playing for guitarists of such renown terrified Diego, and he rarely let it happen. Diego reasoned that such guitarists had been immersed in commercial flamenco so long that they no doubt would have forgotten what true flamenco is all about, and would probably laugh at him and his unsophisticated playing. Technically, these guitarists were superior to Diego, and he knew it. Furthermore, although Diego did not much like their playing, he did greatly respect the immense creative ability of both, founders of their own playing styles, each with hundreds of followers. In short, he was not about to play in front of either of them for love or money.

He did, though, and the results are now part of flamenco lore. Niño Ricardo himself told the story of his first meeting with Diego.

"I decided to see just what all the hubbub was about, this Diego del Gastor fellow, so I got some señorito friends of mine to hire him for a juerga. When he showed up they explained to him that they had hired another guitarist as well, so that he wouldn't have to tire himself out.

"Diego recognized me right away – I was well-known, and my photo was splattered about here and there – and it was obvious the poor guy was dying to get out of there. But he was stuck and he knew it; he couldn't have just left without losing face. I watched him while I played. He seemed to shrink, and refused to touch the guitar throughout the night. All he did was drink, and I was feeling quite contemptuous after some hours. I was warmed up and playing well – really well – and it was painfully obvious that Diego had been had.

"Then around five or six in the morning, when Diego's hair began springing away from the back of his head, he began looking more animated, started talking it up and encouraging me with olés', and I must admit I felt a tinge of worry deep in my stomach. But he continued refusing to touch the guitar until about eight in the morning.

"He then actually asked for the guitar. I handed it to him, and he started playing a slow-motion soleá like I didn't know existed. He played about a tenth of the notes I had, and each note rang clear and true, emotional like no playing I had ever heard. When he made tears spring to my eyes I knew the one who had been had was I. The very essence of this man emerged through his playing. He arrived directly at the soul of flamenco without frills or bullshit. You might say that Diego *is* flamenco. The rest of us are something else, professionals only too often lost in the technicalities of the instrument."

Anzonini tells the story of the time Sabicas was staying on the Costa del sol with his brother. One day Anzo was telling them about Diego, and Sabicas decided on the spot that he wanted to pay homage to *ese gitano* that he had heard so much about. So they grabbed a cab and traveled the four hours ride to Morón, taking with them three excellent guitars – a Santos Hernández, a Domingo Esteso, and a José Ramírez – one of which Sabicas intended to give Diego as a gift.

Upon arriving in Morón Diego was located in the Nuevo Pasaje bar. Anzonini got out of the cab and entered the bar.

"Diego, I've brought two friends who want to meet you, and make you a gift of a guitar."

"Who are they?"

The crucial moment had arrived. If Anzonini said Sabicas, he knew Diego would bolt. On the other hand, if he deceived him, Diego would never forgive him. And besides, Anzo knew where Diego would hide.

"Sabicas and his brother."

Diego took off out the far door without even saying good-bye. Anzo went back to the cab and reported that the expected had happened, and that after a time he knew where Diego would be.

Diego, of course, went directly to the house of his friend, Chimenea, the hard-drinking shoemaker whose house was Diego's principal refuge since his other shoemaker friend, Lechuza, had left town. Both Chimenea Lechuza (9) were illiterate, hearty bohemians in whose presence Diego felt completely at ease. They both loved to drink and listen to Diego play, and he in turn loved to drink and play for them. The perfect union, it was said about town.

Sure enough, they found Diego at Chimenea's humble little house on the outskirts of Morón, where roads were not paved and the bars charged thirty percent less than elsewhere. They were drinking cheap *fino,* and Diego was playing for Chimenea and his wife.

When Anzo and company entered the house unannounced, Diego knew there was no way out and directed a cordial, if furtive, greeting to Sabicas and his brother, and a killing glare at Anzonini. Sabicas immediately set about putting Diego at ease.

"Diego, I am only here to present you with one of these three guitars. Take your choice. I've heard so much about you that I feel it is the least I can do."

"Hombre, this cannot be. I cannot accept a guitar just like that."

"Of course you can. You deserve it, and I want to do it. I don't want you to play if you don't feel like it, mind you, just accept one of these guitars."

"Have a drink and we'll talk about it. But we don't have any whiskey or anything. Just this local fino."

"My favorite drink," Sabicas replied.

With that the ice had been broken and Sabicas and Diego

became friends. Diego could see for himself that Sabicas was still a regular guy at heart, despite the oversized rock on his finger and his reputation of being the world's greatest flamenco guitarist. Diego felt at ease with him, and felt that he probably would, after all, understand and appreciate. Thus, when Sabicas suggested that Diego try out the guitars to see which he preferred, Diego did so without reticence, strumming all three until he determined which he preferred (the Santos, apparently). Then he settled down to play.

Diego was feeling good, somewhere in his second day of drinking, and he launched into his unique bulerías, at moderate speed, laying only his own creations, all gypsy to the core. He was at ease, confident, playing very well, and before long Sabicas' perennial smile widened into an ear to ear beam. This was more like it, after all those years of big cities and razzle dazzle! This was gutsy, downhome flamenco, and Sabicas loved it. Later on Diego played por soleá, then siguiriyas, also all his own creations, with the incredible sensitivity and depth of expression that characterized Diego's playing when he was turned on. Anzonini recounts that Sabicas was deeply moved, as they all were.

As it turned out, Diego accepted the least of the three guitars, the Ramírez. He felt he would be abusing his friendship with Sabicas if he selected one of the better ones. Sabicas saw through this, and insisted that Diego selected the guitar he really liked best. Diego insisted on the Ramírez, and Sabicas finally had to give in. After the pact was made, Sabicas and party climbed back into the waiting taxi and headed back to the coast. Diego now had another follower. So did Sabicas.

Actually, someone was always giving Diego a guitar. The late Juan Talega once told me the story of how Diego came by his first good guitar. I have already printed this account in my book "Lives and Legends of Flamenco," but feel it would be appropriate to reprint it here. In Juan's words:

"Like now, Diego used to be our favorite accompanist, except for one thing; the guitar that he played was so inferior and beat up that it could not even be tuned properly. So we decided to organize a juerga and present Diego with a fine guitar. If I remember correctly, it was a Santos Hernández. Everyone chipped in, and what a juerga that was. Diego was like a child with a new toy, and played and played and accompanied us all like never before. Finally, late at night, he grew tired of playing and wanted to rest, but couldn't find a safe place to put his guitar, as none of us had thought of buying a case for it. Diego solved the problem by locking it in the cab outside. He rejoined the gathering jubilantly, and amidst the ensuing drinks and merrymaking completely forgot the existence of the guitar. At juerga's end, still unusually exuberant for some reason he could not quite recall, Diego danced out to the car, hurled himself drunkenly into the back seat, lit atop his beloved Santos and smashed it into pieces. The guitar never could be properly repaired, and was the last good guitar, to my knowledge, that Diego has owned."

The refusal of the best guitar offered by Sabicas and the smashing of that given at the juerga may not have been purely through politeness in the first instance and drunkenness in the second. Strangely enough, Diego had a certain disregard, even disdain, for guitars. He thought that far too much veneration was afforded them, and made his point frequently by making beautiful music on any beat-up, tough-as-nails guitar that happened to be around. In fact, he seemed to prefer such guitars, and as a result usually ended up giving the good ones to whichever of his multitude of nephews was guitar-less at the moment. Nonetheless, he did seem to enjoy playing good guitars, even if he resisted owning them. Among his favorite habits was to borrow one of the guests' guitars when he played at the finca, often to the subsequent dismay of the owner, for Diego was all over a guitar with his hands (and nails) and managed to mark it up considerably regardless of the size of the protective tapping plates. However, such treatment of a guitar had a happy ending once. One of our female guests was so delighted with Diego's nail markings that she preserved them visibly intact by covering them with transparent plastic.

Which just gives an inkling of Diego's power over women. I would say, without exaggeration, that nearly every woman who came to the finca fell in love with Diego to some extent. Diego did not plan or even particularly want it that way – he was certainly no Don Juan – but his shy charm and manner were so ingratiating that it just happened. Diego did not chase women. They chased him.

It might be said that in amorous matters when the finca opened Diego struck gold, followed more or less closely by his nephews. Until the influx of foreign girls hit Morón, the love life of the town's respectable had been limited to normal sexless courtships that generally dragged on for years. Men had the outlet of an occasional tumble with a prostitute. Nice girls in the towns and villages, however, had only each other or no one until marriage.

Thus, being a bachelor, Diego's sex life had been limited to prostitutes – and apparently few of them – before the foreign element arrived in Morón (various old cronies claim that his pre-finca existence had been *completely* devoid of sex).

109

Prostitutes all loved Diego. He treated them like human beings, just as he would treat any respectable woman, and they adored him for it. Diego well understood that most prostitutes were in the business because they had no other choice. Many were girls from poverty-stricken families who spent most of their earnings supporting their parents and younger sisters and brothers. Many others were girls who had gotten pregnant and had been promptly deserted by their male friends. In this case they not only had to support themselves and child, but had to bear for life the humiliation of being an unwed mother. And this, in the hypocritical Spain of a few years ago, was truly disgraceful. Among these unmarried-mother prostitutes a surprising number were maids who had been wooed by the masters of the house and then rapidly dismissed when they became pregnant. None of these women had legal recourse in macho Spain.

Diego felt deeply for such prostitutes, and in fact admired them far more than the lucratively married "decent" women whose lives were so very easy by comparison, and who on top of it had the gall to scorn the prostitutes. Because of such out-spoken beliefs he was known as the friend of whores, drunks and derelicts. Like his father before him, Diego was a soft touch for the needy, whatever the cause. He always managed to give them something, no matter how poor he was himself at the moment. This deep humanitarianism, free of such considerations as tax deduction, is so unusual that it was another of Diego's attractions for women, causing them to flock to him like Mary Magdalene to Christ. (Most of Morón, predictably enough, considered Diego's generosity just another of his crazy eccentricities; when speaking of it they would twist a finger in a temple and call him "very good," meaning, as we have seen in another section, "very foolish.")

Diego often berated me for not popularizing Morón when he was younger, so that he could have enjoyed his new-found amorous relationships more fully. He would say mournfully that when in his prime he had been womanless, and now that he couldn't do much about it he was besieged by women. I could only advise him to keep trying, and we would laugh and drink to it.

I cannot say that Diego's loves made him happy. To the contrary, he seemed bewildered and frustrated by the passions that were awakened in him at this late stage; jealousy, possessiveness, desire he claimed he could not fulfill. Besides, his loves cramped his style considerably. Diego's life was juergas and bars. Both made him blossom, and he could handle all the drinking with case. The same, however, could not be said for his women. If they tried to coax him away from his preferred life, he would feel trapped and rebel; and if they tried to keep up with him, it was even worse, for chances were they would end up terribly drunk and more than likely put their foot in it in ways greatly embarrassing to Diego, for in Spain there is only one rule about drinking: drink as much as you wish, but always maintain your dignity. The refrain goes, *"Hay que saber estar,"* "Proper comportment is essential." Once dignity is lost, one is dismissed. For this reason one rarely sees a falling down or overly boisterous drunk in Spain. The drinkers' creed has been so strongly ingrained in them that it overcomes the effects of great quantities of alcohol, amounts that would have men in other countries brawling or staggering around blindly. The creed is even stronger for women. I have never seen a Spanish woman drunk. Such a condition is unthinkable. In view of which, you can well imagine Diego's perplexity and embarrassment when his loves, above all the last, would get drunk and unruly. In such cases, Diego would have to swallow his own feelings of overwhelming disgust and attempt to justify the offending woman in the eyes of his friends and fellow townspeople. It was not easy for him.

To add to his amorous problems, two out of three of Diego's principal loves were extremely neurotic women to start with. Take Love No. 1, for instance. She was a good-looking young girl who came to the finca one of our first years of operation. We noticed right away that she had a kind of distant look in her eyes and that we were never quite sure we were reaching her. She also had a thing about her hair, almost an obsession, that set us to wondering. She was always impeccably coiffed – never a hair out of place – and revealed to us that she had brought along a year's supply of a certain hair dye because none of the dyes in Spain were exactly the same platinum-beige color that she used at home. Her meticulousness carried over to her dress, and she looked every inch the Vogue model while sitting quietly in a gathering, lost in her thoughts, occasionally participating in the conversation when her mood permitted, but just as likely to come out with some startling comment, such as the time she asked us to stop talking because our voices disturbed her.

We were soon to find out just how disturbed this young lady was. During her stay that first season she became involved with one of the finca bachelors (who else but Bachelor Jim, whom you will meet again later in the book), who made a truly alarming discovery one night while trying to persuade her that it was too hot for clothing: she carried a small pistol in a pocket of her skirt! Her explanation to him of this phenomenon was that she had been raped as a child and had ever since harbored a horrible fear of men that many years of visiting psychiatrists had not dispelled.

If the story was contrived to dampen the fellow's amorous instincts, it worked! However, in lieu of future incidents, I am inclined to think she was telling the truth.

At any rate, this young miss fell in love with Diego during this stay at the finca, no doubt because of his gentle, fatherly manner that could scare no one, and determined to return the following year in an attempt to pursue a relationship with him. Meantime, during the intervening months she spent her time wisely, studying Spanish language and literature, with an emphasis on poetry. She also carried on a correspondence with Diego — rather one-sided, for writing was not Diego's forte; one of his friends wrote his letters for him — enticing him with many poetic allusions in her improving Spanish. When she returned the following year, he was eager to bite the bait. She stayed at the finca until she was sure, then took an apartment in town.

They soon became very close. This was Diego's first important relationship of such intimacy, and the delicate, platinum beauty of this young creature combined with her poetic nature to send him spinning. A first problem, of course, was Diego's life style. He could not afford to leave it even if he had wanted to, so the alternative came to pass: Love No. 1, a non-drinker by nature, adapted herself to his life, frequenting the bars and juergas with Diego, learning to drink and to tolerate the long, sleepless hours standing in bars or sitting in smoky juerga rooms. Her love for Diego put strength in her frail body, and in time she was keeping up with him far more than could have been hoped for. More important than endurance, however, was the prudence she displayed in her drinking. She quickly learned to pace herself, and very rarely became a problem or an embarrassment to Diego. Thus he was delighted with his new companion, and they carried on around town like love birds, Diego in his late fifties, she in her early twenties.

This happy courtship eventually was marred by only one thing: jealousy. They were terribly jealous of each other, each without reason, but that didn't help. Diego, in his fatherly manner, had a habit of caressing young girls' faces with both hands, while exclaiming "How pretty this little thing is!" The gesture was completely innocent (at first; later it became a technique), but Love No. 1 would bristle and boil while pretty young thing nearly swooned in ecstasy. On the other hand, Love No. 1's ethereal beauty attracted many men to her in the bars, with whom she would politely converse in order to improve her Spanish. She thought this perfectly natural, as *she* knew she wanted only Diego, and could not understand his growing rage over this practice and the increasingly frequent scenes that ensued. Finally the inevitable came to pass. Diego forbade her to enter even the Casa Pepe unless she was on his arm, prohibited her to talk with all men except Diego's most trusted companions, and so on. Like all the girls that became involved with the flamencos, Love No. 1 thought such treatment extremely romantic, a sure sign of true love, and happily sat by herself for long hours practicing her guitar and writing romantic poetry, waiting for Diego to make his appearances.

This romance had its culmination in a most unusual manner. Diego and Love No. 1 were attending a fiesta in someone's town apartment when something happened to spark another flame of jealousy. Everyone had been drinking heavily, and what could have been a few angry words ended up in a wild scene in which Diego told Love No. 1 that he had had enough, he could not go on with her, he was fed up and unhappy and wanted to split. Upon which she pulled her famous little pistol and told him that if he left her she would kill them both.

"You'll what?" Diego shouted, his cool fast escaping him (a hero type he was not).

"I'll kill us both!" she sobbed, waving the gun wildly.

"Jesus Christ, she's nuts!" Diego exclaimed, darting out the door and down the street as fast as he could (quick on his feet he was). When he heard the shot, he says he did the next fifty meters in one leap, rounded a corner on the fly, and kept right on going.

Did she really shoot? Everyone says she did. She claimed the pistol was never even loaded. Be that as it may, she had Diego scared stiff. For days afterwards he sent friends ahead into bars in case she was there waiting to pump him full of holes. One day he sent for me, to meet him at an out-of-the-way bar where he calculated we'd be safe.

"We've got to get that gun away from her," he said. "Got any ideas?"

"How about waiting until she goes out, then ransacking the house?" I suggested.

"No, she always carries it with her."

"How about telling your municipal police friends. They can take it away from her on the pretext that it's illegal, without having to press charges?"

Diego thought this over.

"Not too bad. Might just do it."

But nothing was ever done, and in another two or three weeks the matter was largely forgotten. Diego was still petrified of her, however, and they never did get back together. After a time she packed up and sadly went away, and Diego emerged from

113

his half-hiding heaving a huge sigh of relief.

I never had the pleasure of meeting Serious Love No. 2, having been away from Morón that part of the winter and spring. She was, apparently, a beautiful South American girl with a penchant for poetry whose connection with the finca was only indirect: she was introduced to Diego by a finca alumnus who found her in Sevilla and who, in his campaign to impress her, made the mistake of taking her to Morón. They caught Diego in the advanced stages of a binge, when poetry flowed from him as fast as the wine entered, and the young miss was swept off her feet. When she reciprocated with some poetry of her own, including sensitive recitations of one of Diego's favorites, Pablo Neruda, Diego in turn was captivated. In the process, my friend, as he says, "lost a potential girl but gained some great times; she had Diego bubbling along at top form during their entire affair, and I was guest of honor.

This relationship, my friend reports, ended with one of Diego's attacks of possessive jealousy. It was at the spring fair in Sevilla. Diego was playing at one of the casetas, and his love entered with three males, friends of her family from the home country whom she was showing around the fair and whom she particularly wanted to meet Diego. The proceedings were gracious enough until Diego insisted that she leave her friends and sit alongside him at the artists' table. She told him she couldn't be so rude to her friends and steadfastly refused under pressure. This infuriated Diego and he split with her then and there, disavowing, gypsy-style, not only her but *all* foreigners including, my friend says, himself. Diego would not speak to him for a number of weeks thereafter. After all, it had been my friend's fault for introducing them!

By the time we opened the finca that year, later than usual for some forgotten reason. Diego was calmed down and again himself and ready to be caught up on the rebound in another affair that was to prove to be the most violent, the most colorful, and the longest lasting.

Love No. 3, whom we shall call Lisa, was a married but childless woman, in her early thirties at the time, I would guess, who loved flamenco so much that she had spent periods of two or three summer months at the finca during three consecutive years. She seemingly had everything: money, a good husband, liberty to do what she pleased, charm when she wished; yet she was not happy. Except, that is, when drinking, and then only when it caught her right.

Lisa had a unique schedule at the finca. The days following juergas, usually thrice weekly, she would not emerge from her room until dinner, at eight or nine in the evening. The other days she would come to lunch, eat silently, and quickly disappear again after lunch. When sober, in fact, above all the last year, it might be said that she was not really there, a sort of zombie who did not come alive until the corks popped. As during the first years she pretty well limited her drinking to the dark hours, we learned to live with her habits: cold, disapproving, distant in the daytime, charming, effervescent, sociable during the first hours of her drinking, and impossibly obnoxious when she passed the line. How many times would Rocio, Wonder Maid, come to use in the morning and exclaim happily (she loved any and all intrigue, even if it cost her more work) that Lisa had been preparing herself food last night or rearranging the furniture! Which was her way of saying that Lisa had come home plowed and had had a seizure, during which all hell broke loose. She would storm into the upstairs kitchen and hurl everything she could get her hands on against the clean, white walls: eggs, ripe tomatoes and other sundry fruit and vegetables, glasses, silverware, pots and pans, and lots of highly stainable red wine, after which she might roar into the living room and tumble the furniture around a bit. Sure enough, we would go over to the big house and up to the area of chaos, and it would be a shambles. In the kitchen the floor would be littered with broken glass and egg shells, a gazpacho of cracked-open vegetables and a *sangria* of fruit and wine, while the walls would shame many modern painters, who seem to use similar techniques but do not have the inspiration of Morón booze: long steaks of egg yellow had passed through clusters of tomato red set against a background of deeper wine red, while the whole contained scattered pummelings of other vegetables in a variety of colors, mostly greens. In the living room the furniture would be upside down in never-repeated patterns. Lisa was indeed quite the artist, we consistently agreed before the cleanup crew spoiled her work.

It sounds worse than it really was, I must say. The furniture was tough, built for abuse, and rarely got damaged. The walls were whitewashed and a few coats would cover the stains after the walls had been washed down, while the floor would be cleaned and then mopped with water containing red powder and floor wax that brought it back to normal. Lisa would be nowhere to be seen, invariably plunged deep into depressed sleep. We would merely chalk up the cost of the damage and present her with the bill when again she reappeared, which she would pay glumly and usually without comment, her head still throbbing with hangover.

Each year Lisa became more difficult, until she began offending other guests, spoiling juergas, and in general overly complicating finca life. Thus, when she wrote wishing to take up residence in her favorite room the fourth year, I wrote back warning her that this year she had to promise to behave, and would have to leave the first time she caused a scene. From that moment on, Lisa was my devout enemy. She did not answer my letter, instead renting an apartment in Morón for the summer season. Thank God, for that year she was really over the hill, drinking at all hours of the day and night, causing scene after scene. If the town bars refused to serve her more wine upon seeing that she was too far gone, she was apt to attempt to smash up the bar if not quickly restrained and taken home. Another favorite little trick was to misplace her car keys, or her car, and then rant and rave at whoever she thought had stolen them/it. On one infamous occasion in the market bar she was close to violence with some innocent bystanders, abusing them with vile language and accusing them of stealing her car. The police were called, and upon their appearance she threw herself upon them, pounding them ineffectually with her fists. That time only Diego's influence saved her from permanently being thrown out of town.

And now reenters Diego's humanitarianism. Diego observed this poor unhappy woman, churning with uncontrallable demons, felt she badly needed his help, and took her under his wing. Oh, how he was to regret it when his instinct of self-preservation was dominant, and how he enjoyed it when self-destruction ruled, for she quickly commenced to drag Diego down with her. He repeatedly attempted to break away, especially after she would throw some terrible scene, usually embarrassing him in public (the worst of tortures for a Spaniard). But Diego somehow was bewitched, incapable of breaking off. His health was failing due to too much drink, and the doctor told him he must lay off. He would for a time, if he became frightened enough, during which periods Lisa would also attempt to dry out a bit, but as soon as Diego felt better they would go right back to it.

All of this did the finca operation no good during our last two years. Besides spreading a ceaseless barrage of anti-finca propaganda around Morón to anybody who would listen to her, Lisa made it difficult for Diego to attend juergas and teach at the finca as revenge for my "abusive" letter. She never did achieve enough control simply to prohibit him from coming to the finca, but when juerga time came occasionally she did manage to deter him with one contrivance or another: an attack of sobbing loneliness, violent sickness, desperate flirting with someone, some fetching scheme that sounded more fun than another juerga... Much to her wrath, however, Diego's sense of friendship and loyalty to me usually caused him to ignore her and come anyway, during which times he would visibly unwind and again become himself, often swearing to me and his other friends that he was going to break with her immediately, right now, as soon as he arrived back in Morón. But she would be waiting for him when we returned to town the next morning, often dead drunk, and he would feel compelled to go take care of her.

By the second and last year of their romance Lisa had left her husband and was living full-time in Morón. This was believed by some to be a determining factor in Diego's death, for in his weakened condition and at his age he could not keep up with a woman like Lisa, some thirty years younger. With Lisa he had an ever-eager drinking companion. When she was on good behavior they would drink together; when she was on bad behavior, he often escaped and drank with his friends, attempting to purge her from his mind. On the other hand, it also was argued that Diego was an old hand at drinking and needed no one to spur him on. If it hadn't been with Lisa, it would have been with his drinking buddies, or whomever.

Be that as it may, during the last months of Diego's life he became a different person. Lisa was getting to him, bringing out in him a certain baseness that before had been non-existent, or lying dormant. Violence began creeping into his conversation when he was well in his cups; he would carry on about how he had finally discovered that what Lisa really wanted and needed was physical punishment. Although he was too close to her to see things in complete perspective, what in effect Diego came to realize was that Lisa threw many of her tantrums much as a child does who desperately is hoping to be put in his or her place. Lisa's husband apparently had been too civilized for this, and she left him in hopes of finding a stronger father figure who could more or less control her.

Diego first began realizing this one night at a juerga in Antonio's venta. (Antonio's recounting of the incident, his eyes agleam, was soon verified for me by several others of those present, all of whom were delighted that Diego finally took a firm stand.) On this occasion Lisa got even more out of hand than usual and began insulting some of Diego's oldest and dearest friends, calling them the most offensive names she sould conjure up and in general shoveling out her most effective brand of abuse. They all took it for a time, trying to calm her down through use of reason (the worst approach to use on Lisa, I knew through experience). Ultimately, Diego's friends decided to leave. This was going too far for Diego. Lisa's driving his longtime buddies away so incensed him that he finally exploded and lashed out with an open-handed right that caught Lisa on the side of the face while she was seated at the table, causing her and her chair to spin around completely before toppling over backwards.

If Diego's action surprised the little group clustered about, Lisa's reaction did so even more. She instantly became subdued, and hero worship shone from her eyes. This is just what she had been after during those years of obnoxiousness. Here was a *real* man!

So Diego's course was clear during the remainder of their relationship. Although violence conflicted strongly with his pacifistic nature, he had no choice but to play the stern authoritarian. Lisa needed and demanded it, and she would make his life impossible if he held back. When drinking late at night he used to tell me about it, at first in bemusement, wondering how the hell the relationship had reached this point, and later on in a more assertive fashion that was completely out of character.

Lisa, indeed, was getting to Diego.

At long last Lisa had to return home in order to take care of some business or other. She urged Diego to accompany her, to which he reluctantly agreed under pressure. All the preparations had been made when Diego, predictably, backed out, getting a doctor friend to testify to Lisa that his health wouldn't be able to take the long trip and the change of climate. As a consequence, Lisa left alone, vowing to return as soon as she possibly could.

Diego had mixed feelings about Lisa's absence. Predominent was an enormous feeling of relief. His nerves began to untangle and a calm goodness again began taking possession of his eyes. But there is no question that he did miss Lisa; they had been too close for an immediate dismissal. He swore he hoped she would not return to Morón but knew she would, and also knew he would probably not have the strength to break with her when she did return.

As it worked out, Diego never had to face the problem of Lisa's return. Diego's doctor's ominous prediction – that Diego would not pull out of one of his binges if he did not slow down considerably – finally came true. On this occasion Diego had invited a group of his oldest friends out to his little country house for an all-night juerga, after which those who did not have to go to work went up to Casa Pepe for a few morningcaps. I was not at the juerga but did drop into Casa Pepe around noon the following morning, after doing the shopping for the finca operation.

"Hoo-la," Diego called out, bounding up and giving me a big, bearish hug, full of life, feeling on top of the world. "Hombre," he continued, "come have a drink, por Dios! Where

118

were you last night? We had a great time!"

At this point one of diego's nephews informed Diego that he would run him out to his country cottage so they could clean the place up. Diego told me he'd be right back and we'd have those drinks, and bounced out to the waiting car. I turned to the bar and ordered a tinto, but before receiving it was interrupted by "POHREN! POHREN! COME QUICKLY!"

I ran out to the car to find Diego slumped over in the front seat, his eyes glazed over, spittle escaping from his open mouth. We quickly carried him into Pepe's house and called his doctor. By the time the doctor arrived Diego had recovered miraculously and, apart from being frightened, was quite himself again. We had all insisted he go to bed, but not Diego. He remained standing most of the time, quite impatient to get back to the rhythm of the day.

The doctor told Diego that he had had a stroke and that he was lucky to be alive, and that furthermore he had better lay low from now on; his customary wild life must be avoided like the plague. Booze, women and juerga, above all, were strictly prohibited. Diego was too shook up this time to give the doctor any back talk, but I did notice a defiant arching of an eyebrow. The doctor finally gave Diego some medication and left, promising to return soon.

Diego was in a quandary, for precisely that day he was to be honored by the town of Morón. It was July 7, 1973, and that evening Morón was to celebrate its annual flamenco festival, in this case dedicated to Diego and in which Diego was to be presented with Morón's top tribute, a small golden rooster. (10) Diego did not want to let everyone down, and he determined to attend the festival, doctor or no doctor.

When Diego seemed completely back to normal I left, having to get the groceries back to the finca. That was the last time I saw Diego alive. After another hour or two, which Diego reportedly spent sitting outside Casa Pepe, he began feeling strange and started up towards his sister's house where he could lie down without disturbing Pepe's household. There he suffered the fatal stroke, and died quietly at age sixty-five.

Diego had done it again! He died in exactly the manner he had wanted to; quickly, without suffering, his strength still intact, with no sign of weariness with life, or senility in either his art or his person. Furthermore, that very day he had reached the pinnacle of his life. Artistically he was by now of international fame and, perhaps more important to Diego, his adopted town had chosen to honor him "exemplary citizen and artist" while he was still alive. After this he could only have gone downhill.

For the sake of mere survival he would have had to give up his life of drink and juerga, and Diego already knew from former periods of convalescence that books, dominoes and checkers are no substitutes. However, such a life could have been tolerated. What truly terrified Diego was the probability of more strokes — he had already had several — one of which would likely leave him paralyzed and/or damage his mind. He could not bear the idea of spending his last years a rotting vegetable, a burden on his family, having to be cared for in every detail as he had done with his beloved mother the last years of her life. I can almost feel Diego's mind musing over these possibilities while seated in front of Casa Pepe and deciding to give it up while he was on top.

All Morón went into mourning. The flamenco festival was called off. Artists and friends poured into his sister's house to attend the all-night wake. Telegrams arrived from everywhere. The funeral, village-style, with the casket carried through the streets followed and surrounded by pedestrian mourners, was massive.(11) Diego was loved and respected by everyone in town, for he had always had time for everyone, from the vagabond to the richest señorito. But above all for the humble: the prostitute, the illiterate shoemaker, children, forgotten old-timers. Diego stories were exchanged. It seems that everyone in town had had at least one grand experience with Diego during his active lifetime, experiences that now were remembered and revered. The gypsy women carried on during the proceedings in a most remarkable fashion, wailing and screaming over his body throughout the night of the wake, and during the funeral procession rushing out from doorways screaming "DIEGO," tearing at themselves, sobbing wildly, eventually to be restrained and led away by their menfolk.

Diego was carried from the church down the calle San Miguel to the city hall, where the golden rooster was placed on his casket, and then to the cemetery for burial.

The proceedings to divvy up Diego's possessions must have provoked many a gleeful chuckle from Diego if he happened to be looking on from some new dimension. Although he was not even on speaking terms with some of his five sisters when he died, and had not been for years. that did not deter them from participating in the material tug-of-war. Although Diego left no will, everyone knew that he wanted his little country house to go to the young schoolteacher friend who had once won a soccer pool and had given Diego a goodly share of the winnings, nearly enough to cover the house's construction and installation costs. Obviously, the cottage should revert to this good fellow, but oh no, the Family would not hear of it. They were Diego's rightful heirs, and they should get it!.

Then there was the guitar. In typical fashion, Diego was playing a borrowed guitar at the end of his life, a mediocre instrument that a young American friend had left in his care during the American's extended absence from Morón. The small detail that the guitar did not even belong to Diego was overlooked by the entire Family. What they did know was that the guitar, being the last that Diego had played, had gained a certain value, and it was therefore much coveted. One family removed it from Diego's last living quarters (a room at the local fonda) and took it home for "safe keeping." Another of the families quickly took the matter to court, and the amused judge instructed the family presently in possession of the guitar to keep it until the Family itself could work the matter out in a civilized fashion.

And so forth.

A few weeks after Diego's death a benefit was held in his honor, the proceeds of which went for the erection of a bust of Diego in the little park to the right of the Sevilla entrance into Morón. The bust is simply done in a classic style, making Diego appear every inch the Roman ruler forever watching the loiterers and children at play with blank, irisless eyes. Further honor was paid him by the naming of the pedestrian walk leading from Capa Pepe up to the Peña, where the statue of Morón's featherless rooster is located as well as one of Morón's flamenco clubs, the calle Diego del Gastor.

Thus, Morón did indeed paid homage to its adopted gypsy son, who brought Morón de la Frontera fame, as well as a degree of fortune.

FERNANDILLO

Fernandillo, like Diego, Manolito de María, Anzonini and Paco de Valdepeñas, was another gypsy who epitomized the disappearing flamenco life style. He was unlike those mentioned in only two basic respects; he was younger – his uncle Diego was some thirty years his elder – and had extremely dark skin, as opposed to the others mentioned, who were all considered "white gypsies" to a greater or lesser degree. He could probably, therefore, have boasted of purer blood, but never did to my knowledge.

Within the world of flamenco, so teeming with picturesque individuals, Fernandillo was undoubtedly the most colorful character I have known. He was so chock-full of the joy of living that it was constantly spilling over in a never-ending variety of schemes, dominated as it were by those of a hedonistic, financial and/or artistic nature. He had a mind like a whip: flexible, cracking with energy and ideas, in no way hampered by his nearly complete illiteracy. His memory was as all-retaining as his mind was active, which once led us into a unique situation that causes me to chuckle even as I write this.

Prelude: while having a few in Casa Pepe, Fernandillo requested that I and a couple of other english-speaking finca-ites who were present teach him some off-color words and phrases in English. He repeated them several times, we all laughed, and it was forgotten.

Incident: one night of juerga, some two weeks after Fernandillo's English lesson, a Rover full of guests who had arrived that very day accompanied me into town to pick up the artists. These guests, none of whom I had known previously and who as yet hardly knew each other, were composed mainly of very respectable-appearing professional people from the United States. They were thrilled at meeting the artists, and were of course instantly charmed by Diego. Fernandillo, however, was not there as scheduled, and the search began. A tip from a mutual friend placed him at a little bar in the lower part of town, to which we quickly arrived. I ran in and found him, heavy with booze, disheveled, one shirttail in, one out, eyes red and veiny, a three-day growth of beard, but still coherent in a fuzzy sort of way.

"Porrr-en!" he exclaimed wonderingly.

"Juerga time, Fernandillo."

"*Coño*, been working so hard here in the office lost track of time."

I led him out to the car and he climbed into the front seat. Diego had the group enthralled with some story or other, during which time fernandillo sat silently, apparently nodding off. When Diego finished his story, I turned back and said something like

"Folks, meet Fernandillo, King of the Gypsies."

They all looked at Fernandillo and smiled pleasantly. He turned around in his seat to face them, grinned most graciously, and stated in very understandable English:

"Cock-suck Cunt. Shit. Hi baby, wanna fuck?" (12)

Oh no, there was never a dull moment around Fernandillo. His methods of insuring this, however, were rarely so direct. To the contrary, most of his schemes were quite elaborate, obviously products of a fertile mind. Many involved intrigue, for the sheer joy of it, and others deception, for the sheer money of it. But make no mistake, he was not just another conniving gypsy out to con everyone and anyone. He was too much the artist for that. He far preferred deceiving presumptuous, boastful types who were often deceitful in their own right. For one thing, they deserved it. For another, that's where the challenge lay. Fernandillo was an acute observer, and he would study such types until he was sure he could bet them at their own game. Then he would strike, well realizing that if he were successful these victims would keep quiet about it for the sake of their reputations.

There was, for instance, the Case of the Watch Boaster. This took place perhaps twenty years ago, before the influx of imported watches into Spain, when a good watch was an object of extreme envy among the well-to-do. At this time a gentleman in Morón possessed a fine Swiss watch reputed to be the best in Morón, if not in all of Andalusia. And he never let anyone forget it. It was said that he paid people to ask him the time so he could pull his cuff way back and say something like "It's twenty to twelve on my fine Swiss watch and if any other watch says differently it's wrong because mine is the best in all of Andalusia!"

You get the idea.

One day Fernandillo heard the Boaster once too often, and decided to try him out. He went by his watch supply contact and asked if he had any exotic looking watches. The man did, a luxurious-looking German model that in reality was not worth even the one hundred pesetas Fernandillo paid for it. Fernandillo then sought out an accomplice, instructing him to maintain that the watch was an heirloom which he loved so dearly he would not part with it for love or money. Then the two of them strolled down to the bar where the Boaster hung out.

Sure enough, he was there, talking watches and matter-of-factly stating the immense merits of his own. Although neither Fernandillo nor Rafael, his accomplice for the day, had peseta one in their pockets, that did not stop Fernandillo from entering grandly and ordering a bottle of expensive sherry and glasses for themselves and their friends, including, of course, the Boaster. Rafael was stunned. How the hell were they going to pay for *that?* When the bottle was half-way down and the Boaster was really warming up to his topic — he now had the watch off his arm and was showing it around to his friends — Fernandillo leaned over and looked it over carefully before pronouncing:

"This watch is a turd compared to Rafael's!"

Rafael, quick on the uptake:

"Hombre, don't be so brash. His watch is really fine. Just cause it can't compare to mine doesn't mean it's not a terrific watch."

"Ha!" the Boaster exclaimed, faltering slightly. He had never before been challenged. "I would like to see your wonder watch, if you will."

Rafael handed the man the watch, explaining humbly that it was given him by his father, whose father in turn had been presented it by a wealthy German nobleman for whom he had been working at the time in Germany. He finished by stating in his most goody-good voice that it was very dear to him and he'd never sell it. The Boaster appraised the watch in a most professional manner, then said:

"How much do you want for it?"

Fernandillo cut in angrily:

"Didn't he just say he would never sell it? I merely brought it up so you'd stop bragging about that *mierda* you say is the best watch in Andalusia. If you must boast, at least have something to boast about. Now Rafael here can boast, if anyone can."

The poor Boaster could see his exclusive little domain crumbling about his feet, and he leaned over and ingratiatingly said to Rafael:

"Rafael, hombre, you really shouldn't wear such a good watch around at any rate. After all, being in construction (Rafael was a mason's apprentice at the time) you'll only break it one day, and then what? Actually, for the sake of your father, you should sell it to me, if nothing else for safekeeping. How about one thousand pesetas?"

Fernandillo laughed sarcastically:

"*Venga ya,* hombre, even if he wanted to sell, he wouldn't let it go for that ridiculous sum. Vamos, Rafael, let's get out of here before this one steals your watch!"

Upon which Fernandillo reached for his billfold, as if to pay the bill, loudly instructing the barman to include what the other gentlemen had consumed previously as well.

"Now wait a minute, Fernandillo." The Boaster could not stand the thought of being second best in Morón. He couldn't let them walk out. There were too many witnesses. "Let's have another bottle and talk this over."

Another bottle of Tío Pepe was ordered, with tapas, and the Boaster asked Rafael if he might inspect the watch once again. With each sip of wine his desire increased, as if the watch were a provocative woman.

"I'll have to grant, Rafael, that this is a fine watch, propably nearly as good as mine. I'll give you three thousand pesetas."

"HA," roared Fernandillo, "you still have the gall to compare your watch with Rafael's? Besides, Rafael doesn't want to sell at any price. Do you, Rafael?"

"Well, man, I wouldn't say at any price." Rafael simulated a slight stagger and slurred his words. "But certainly not for a paltry three thousand pesetas." (Fifteen hundred of which would be for Rafael, more than his earnings for a full week, or sixty hours, of construction work at that time.) "Why don't we just forget about it and part friends. I've got to run now. Bartender, the bill please."

The Boaster, truly excited now, downed another glass of wine and pulled out his wallet. He counted the contents carefully, then exclaimed:

"All right. I have seven thousand pesetas here. That's my last offer!"

Fernandillo's heart took a leap, but he turned to Rafael and shook his head:

"It wouldn't be right to give up such a valuable heirloom, Rafael. Let your conscience be your guide."

Rafael looked perplexed and sad, muttering how the circumstances of life cause one constantly to compromise oneself, but that times were tough and his family could certainly use the money, and...

"All right, it's yours!"

The Boaster looked triumphant. Now there could be no

125

question that he was the watch king of Morón (if not all of Andalusia). The exchange took place, and they all shook hands. Rafael asked for the bill, but the Boaster insisted it was on him. He wanted there to be no doubt as to just who was the señorito around there.

Fernandillo and Rafael hit it up the hill to Casa Pepe, split the money, and celebrated for three days. If the Boaster found out his new watch was worthless, which he no doubt did, he never let on. As long as no one else knew, what difference did it make? The story of his triumphant purchase spread around town like wildfire, and the Boaster basked in more prestige than ever. A happy ending for all concerned.

Fernandillo truly scorned arrogance and feelings of superiority, and went out of his way to punish carriers of same. Like the time he and I were knocking down a couple in Casa Pepe. He was deep in thought, obviously scheming. After a time he muttered that he had to raise some cash to leave with his family so he could run off for a couple of days with some new chick he had come across.

That was one thing about Fernandillo, he always did leave his family provided for before running off. He could have just asked me for a loan against juerga earnings, as he often did, but this time he conceived a better plan.

"Come on," he said, "I've got a little business to attend to."

Down to the watch supplier, where he purchased a dandy looking model, running temporarily, for seventy-five pesetas. We then walked up far beyond Casa Pepe to a neighborhood rarely frequented by Fernandillo and the other gypsies, where the art and *gracia* of the gypsies was little appreciated. We went from bar to bar, sipping *tintos* while he looked the possibilities over. Finally, standing outside of bar number six, he pointed out a stern-appearing country fellow and whispered:

"That one is a real son-of-a-bitch. He's wealthy through screwing his workers and whomever he can. Let's give him a try."

As this was my first (and last) experience of this nature, I said "Give what a try?"

"You just look impressed with the watch when I hand it to you. He'll be impressed by a foreigner's opinion."

In we went, and Fernandillo was suddenly feigning drunkenness, making boisterous pronouncements, slurring his words badly, all in a most convincing manner.

He held onto the bar, swaying, giggling, then exclaimed loudly:

"Shay, Jesus Christ, Goddamn it, am I ever an unlucky bastard. My children ill and hungry, my wife so furious with me I can't even go home. And me with no work, and too drunk even to look for any. God am I a worthless son-of-a-bitch!"

By now everyone in the bar was looking and grinning in a most superior manner. There is nothing they enjoy more than someone down and out, above all a gypsy.

"Goddamn it, all I have is my saintly father's watch..." His attention riveted on it. "Lookedit" – he put it directly under my nose, where I couldn't possibly even see it – "isn't it beautiful, absolutely beautiful? Worth a lot of money, too, but I promised I'd never part with it at my father's deathbed. Isn't it beautiful, *me cago en la mar?* Oh my poor father..." And he broke down and cried on my shoulder.

Obviously I hadn't known what I was getting into.

"I unload on all my ancestors, I can't even drink my sorrows under." Sob. Sob. "Bartender, you'll give us credit for a few rounds, no?"

"No."

"Then I have no choice but to go down and pawn my watch, and that bloodsucker won't give me anywhere near what it's worth. The very best watch in Morón, and he'll try to steal it from me." He turned to me and handed me the watch for close inspection. "Look at it. Don Fulano de Tal gave it to my father. Terribly expensive, and I have to go down and pawn it and probably won't get more than a miserable fifteen hundred pesetas for it."

I examined the watch and tried to work up the proper enthusiasm.

"Exquisite! My God, it's a ———————— (whatever the brand name was)! I'd give you three thousand pesetas right now if my check had come through."

Sr. Stern had been taking the whole scene in, and now walked up to Fernandillo and demanded:

"Let me see it."

Fernandillo looked surprised and held it out of his reach. "Why?"

Stern looked cunning and answered:

"Maybe I'll buy it and help you out of your dilemma."

"Oh no you won't. I'll never sell my father's watch. Besides" – he looked Stern up and down – "you certainly don't have what the watch is worth!"

That stung Stern. The whole bar was attending the negotiation closely, and it was Stern's move. He reached into his wallet, pulled out a bill without even inspecting the watch and slapped it on the bar. He was moving in for the kill.

"I'll give you five hundred pesetas for it right now." (13)

127

Fernandillo reeled drunkenly and exclaimed:

"That's a bloody insult to my saintly father, may he rest in peace. This watch is worth ten times more, at least. Here, see for yourself."

At this, Fernandillo handed Stern the watch, and befuddledly pointed out its marvelous features. He then turned to the bartender:

"How about another round, for chrissake."

"Set them up," Stern ordered. "All right, how much do you want?"

"I absolutely won't sell, but if I did I wouldn't let it go for less than two thousand pesetas. And that is a special price just for you cause you set up another round."

"I'll give you seven hundred."

And on and on, Stern buying round after round in an attempt to wear Fernandillo down. In the process, Stern himself got a bit loosened up and began bargaining more freely. Finally they agreed on eleven hundred pesetas, Fernandillo protesting that it was robbery but what could he do, Stern had him up against the wall.

On the way down the hill Fernandillo wiped his brow and had only one comment to make about Mr. Stern:

"Coño, he *is* a tough customer. No wonder he's rich."

Second only to such business dealings, Fernandillo loved intrigue and dissension. Not long-term, malicious intrigues, but rather little harmless ones which everyone involved could eventually chuckle over. His philosophy was that small towns can be crushingly boring and that in reality there is no need for them to be. All that is needed is a little imagination.

For instance, the trick he pulled on Pepe, the cabbie generally utilized by the flamencos whenever they had out-of-town juergas. On one occasion Fernandillo had to hire a cab to take them all to a nearby town, and he knew that Pepe the Cabbie was already on another trip and wouldn't be back in time to take them. This was enough to plant the seed of mischief in his mind. Upon entering the bar where the cabbies hang out, he said pointedly:

"Who wants to take us to a juerga, other than Pepe?"

"Why not Pepe? He's the one you always hire," one of the group replied.

"You mean you don't know?"

All the cabbies immediately clustered around Fernandillo, urging him to reveal his secret.

"Hombre," he said, "it's none of my business, but human decency demands that I disclose the ultimate shame. You know

Fulano de Tal?"
    They all did.
    "You know his twelve-year-old daughter?"
    They did.
    "Pepe has gotten her pregnant!"
    Exclamations of anger and disgust. Although Pepe was an excellent fellow and a favorite among his fellow cabbies, no one thought to doubt Fernandillo's story. They turned on Pepe with gusto. One of them always knew Pepe was shameless but didn't think he'd go that far. Others said of course he would, you can see it in his eyes. And so forth.
    Fernandillo finally hired one of the cabbies and went to the all night juerga, leaving the rest of the cabbies to work themselves up. In a couple of hours Pepe returned from Sevilla and entered the bar, looking forward to a beer and a little comradeship.
    "Hi gang. How they hanging?"
    Complete silence.
    "I said, greetings and salutations."
    Continued silence. Pepe confused.
    "What the fuck's wrong with you guys? Is this the mute society or something?"
    At this they all broke the silence simultaneously.
    "You bastard, how dare you show your face around this town? After what you did, how can you even live with yourself?"
    "Now wait a minute! What did I do, if I may know?"
    "Oh sure, act innocent. Fernandillo told us all about how you knocked up Fulano de Tal's twelve-year-old daughter!"
    "I'll be damned!" Pepe exclaimed, visualizing the intense gleam of mischief that must be glowing in Fernandillo's eyes. "That dirty bastard. And you simple assholes believed him. You'd believe him if he told you I raped the Virgin, too, wouldn't you?"
    Now the group looked confused.
    "You mean it isn't true?" one of them blurted.
    "Go ask her. She won't even know what you're talking about."
    Anger mounting against Fernandillo.
    "Let's go get him!"
    "Can't. He's out of town for the night."
    And by the time Fernandillo returned the following day, everyone had mellowed and thought it a fine practical joke, just as Fernandillo knew they would. Colorful guy, that Fernandillo. Yes sir!
    Other of Fernandillo's intrigues were of more constructive intent, such as those involving artists, the ultimate objective being to anger an artist to the point where his reserve would disintegrate

and he would perform to the fullest of his capabilities. On some occasions he would use himself as target, telling another dancer or singer that he was spiritless and without creativity compared to himself. After a time, however, the artists caught on and did not take such bantering seriously; they all knew what Fernandillo was up to. It was more effective, if a little sinister, when he would pit two artists against each other by use of the old trick of telling first one, then the other, that each thought the other artistically mediocre, or slipping, or getting old. I have seen this method work wonders, when the artists in question outdid themselves, their professional pride at stake, in an exciting contest to put the other fellow down. One such juerga ended most humorously when one of the artists, after delivering the best performance of his life, confronted the supposedly offending artist and said:

"I don't suppose you'll go around saying I'm too old to dance anymore after tonight, right?"

"But I never ... now wait a minute ... YOU were the one who said I was ... "

As awareness seeped in they both looked at Fernandillo, feeling duped but satisfied, for they knew the desired effect had been worth it. Fernandillo was standing behind the juerga-room bar, pouring himself a tinto. He grinned, winked, and lifted his glass in salute.

During our second year of operation Fernandillo set up quite a nice deal for himself at the finca. The plan, mutually beneficial to himself and to us, consisted of two parts: one, Fernandillo would take over the juerga-room bar full-time, sell drinks to the guests and visitors at Casa Pepe prices, and pocket the profits: two, in return ꞌ for this privilege, he would scour the town in an attempt to supply us with maids who would be willing to live at the finca at least part-time, thus saving us the immense bother of picking them up in the morning and taking them home at night.

Part two of the plan was solved immediately. It had been solved, in fact, before we made the deal, he later confessed. The maid in question turned out, of course, to be Fernandillo's newest girl friend, and what better place to stash her away than at the finca, well out of sight of his wife and the town gossips? Above all considering that he would have the bar excuse to be at the finca much of the time.

Pepa, it turns out, had nothing to lose by living part-time at the finca, for she was one of those maids-gotten-pregnant-by-the-boss-turned-prostitute we discussed in Diego's chapter. Now, with the whorehouses closed in Morón, she had no choice but to revert to maiding as a means of support.

It immediately became evident that Pepa was a fortunate addition to finca life. As a maid she was energetic, clean and proud, as a cook quite adequate, and as a person intelligent, bubblingly gay, and good. Her only problem was incurable hot pants, which Fernandillo took upon himself to alleviate. As he had time on his hands — other than at the pre-lunch and pre-dinner cocktail hours, and after dinner drinks and juergas, the bar did not give him much to do — touring the less frequented recesses of the finca was touch and go for a time, for one might stumble upon the love birds in most awkward situations and positions. I had to warn them a couple of times to be more prudent. Not everyone would be so understanding, and there was our young daughter to consider.

They seemed to take my advice to heart, for everything went along smoothly for a time until, I suppose, desire overwhelmed reason. But now, instead of climbing into the nearest closet, they would disappear for any number of hours. One occasion must have been particularly pressing, for we returned to the finca from town to find a roast and potatoes in a hot oven, the table set and the salad half made, but no Pepa or Fernandillo. Nor did they show up during the rest of the day, finally straggling in sheepishly the following morning looking thoroughly hung over and worn out.

Actually, Fernandillo was not in the finca bar business for the sake of mere money, nor solely to be near Pepa. Very prominent ulterior motives were provided by potentially available female finca guests. He patiently spent hours in the bar singing and dancing for the female guitarists so they could practice accompaniment, or showing the female dancers gypsy dance movements. But all in vain. Even those girls who were spreading their charms around quite democratically would not go with Fernandillo, much to his frustration and shattering of self-image. He, after all, was Fernandillo, charming, impish, irresistible to the more racy type of low-class Spanish girl. He finally came to me to ask just where he was going wrong. I did not know, being as surprised as himself at his lack of sucess, so I asked one of the more liberal girls. Her answer was that he was just too much of an animal; the girls weren't sure they could cope with him. He, in short, frightened them. I repeated this verbatim to Fernandillo. He remained somewhat perplexed and extremely sorrowful at all the potential action escaping him, but was also flattered. Fernandillo, King of the Animals, Ravishes Another Lovely!!! The reputation was almost worth the loss.

Even more than as a womanizer, however, Fernandillo excelled as a juerga artist. But not merely in the "normal" sense of being a fine and imaginative singer, dancer and *jaleador*. All these he was, but such accomplishments took a back seat to his true forte: dreaming up unusual situations and themes that invariably led to good times and memorable juergas.

Examples.

One Sunday afternoon an up-and-coming young non-gypsy singer from a nearby town came to the finca to juerga, bringing with him for moral support a few of his good friends, also flamenco enthusiasts. Fernandillo, Juanito, Agustín, and others of the locals rounded out the artistic roster. In all, there were some twenty-five of us packed into the little juerga house by about six in the afternoon.

The juerga got underway in quite normal fashion, the young singer dominating the scene with his very pleasant and occasionally moving *malagueñas* and related song forms. The trouble was, the singer didn't know when to stop. Had he been more experienced he would have realized that the numerous gypsies in the room would soon tire of such lyrical and poetic song forms and would insist on inserting at least a fair share of raucousness and hell-raising. Sure enough, before long Fernandillo was on his feet, looking his usual zany self, announcing to the group that he intended to honor them with his famous rendition of the typical middle and upper class Andalusian girl, "*hija de mamá*", or mamma's daughter, at her Sevillanas dance class (no one had ever seen Fernandillo do this, nor could we ever get him to do it again). The scene is a large room with chairs lining the walls upon which are seated many mamma's and their daughters. The girls alternate dancing in twosomes for their professor, and are occasionally corrected or encouraged. As each girl dances, her respective mamma goes into near ecstasy. I have attended several such classes, as has nearly everyone else in Andalusia, and can vouch that Fernandillo's interpretation was accomplished to perfection. He had the girls performing the movements in the usual *cursi* (corny), stilted manner, their hands revolving non-stop from busy little wrists, then quickly switched over to the delighted mamma squealing excitedly that her little precious was simply a *natural*, so fluid and graceful, just as her mamma had been. While playing the mamma Fernandillo had been seated in a most feminine, coquettish manner on the edge of a chair. When she became so excited she simply could not sit still another second, Fernandillo jumped up and became the over-ripe mamma attempting to pick up the dance where she had left off ten, twenty or thirty years ago, moving around ponderously, panting heavily after a few seconds, soon plopping back in her chair smiling

132

triumphantly at her show of grace, fanning herself full blast.

Fernandillo was hilarious. I venture to say that his was the funniest performance of any type I have ever seen. I was not alone. The small room literally shook with roaring laughter, all had tears streaming down their faces, we were holding onto each other for strength. In the uproar no one noticed, except myself and probably Fernandillo, that our guest artist and his friends did not so much as crack a smile throughout the entire performance. When it was over and we were drying our tears and attempting to compose ourselves, they got up, stiffly excused themselves, and left. Fernandillo had hit too close to home.

With them gone and the mood set so beautifully, the fiesta roared along at full tilt until well after midnight, when we repaired for final nightcaps to Casa Pepe.

Fernandillo also masterminded the craziest *juerga* anyone can remember taking place. But before recounting it, there is essential background to establish.

One summer day we were sitting on the front terrace chatting, enjoying the midday quiet, watching the distant olive trees simmer and shimmer in the heat, when up floated a powerful baritone voice issuing from a little man wheeling slowly down the road on a bicycle. The man was singing a *fandango,* Pepe Marchena style, but doesn't Marchena wish he had had such a voice. I became excited and asked Fernandillo who the devil that was. His eyes lit up, and he jumped to his feet and yelled:

"PEPE! BOLERO! OYE, PEPE!"

The bicycle stopped and the voice answered:

"*Qué quieres?* What do you want?"

"Come here, hombre, I want to introduce you to friends who might want to hire you for some juergas."

"*Voy,*" shouted Bolero joyfully. "I'm coming!"

Soon Pepe el Bolero had pedalled up to the finca and was with us on the terrace. It was hard to believe that such a beautiful, almost operatic voice had emerged from this scrubby little man, his pants all patches, his beatup old cap slightly awry on his big round head. Pepe's enormous black eyes, however, were his principal characteristic, terribly expressive eyes that instantly registered all moods and emotions, invariably giving Pepe away. They also helped him project himself, a most effective asset when Pepe felt comical, for Pepe was to prove over and over again that he could be one of the funniest men alive.

That Bolero, probably in his early forties, ever felt like being funny was a miracle, for his existence was most precarious. He had been born in poverty, raised in poverty, and still lived in poverty. In reality, as a seasonal farm worker Bolero could have done better than he did. A basic problem was his laziness (which I found out about when I felt sorry for him and hired him to do some work around the finca. Each time I checked on him he would be stretched out, jumping to his feet when I approached with the excuse that he had worked so hard he was plumb tuckered out; however, somehow there was almost no sign of his having worked at all). Independent gathering was his favorite type of work, when he could bicycle far into the country, singing all the way, and search for snails or wild asparagus or capers, depending on the season, and bring back a sackful to sell to the bars for tapas. Being poor and a flamenco type, Bolero had lived in the caves up by the Morón castle side by side with most of the rest of the flamencos of Morón, including all the gypsies, until the caves began falling in during a particularly rainy number of years. The government then built them housing in the lower part of Morón and made them all vacate the cave area. It was then that Bolero, as well as Joselero and his family, moved down to the Pantano neighborhood into the new housing, while other gypsy flamencos, with Diego as their leader, moved into the courtyard tenement near Casa Pepe. The new housing that Bolero and Joselero acquired was actually quite nice and financially almost a gift. They paid for their two-story apartments over a period of twenty years in monthly installments of something like 150 pesetas per month during the first five years, 225 pesetas per month for the next five years, and 300 pesetas a month for the last ten years. At the end of the twenty years they would be sole owners of their apartments.

To visit the apartments of Bolero and Joselero, of exactly the same year of construction, design and specifications, is like visiting two completely distinct worlds. Joselero is married to one of Diego's sisters, who keeps her apartment spotlessly clean, as is generally the Spanish custom. It is airy, furnished cheaply but tastefully, filled with sunshine and light. Bolero, on the other hand, married a "castellana" who was one of the beauties of her day — vestiges of a former beauty can still be discerned — but whose mind seems to have ceded to the strain of their hard life. She keeps all the windows of her apartment shut tight, blinds drawn against the light, and uses neither the bathroom nor the kitchen facilities; they do their "necessities" in the nearby fields, and she washes the dishes and clothes in the street with a bucket of water. The place is rank, airless, dark, without furnishings that I have been able to see in the blackness. In other words, she still seems to think they are living in a cave and proceeds with her daily activities exactly as if they were. But I have been in many caves throughout Andalusia and none have been so depressing as this. Yet Bolero drifts through life singing, telling extremely funny jokes and stories, happily working just enough to get by. His home life must be hell, but he seems to take it in stride and survives better than most of us. I came to respect this man more and more as I learned of his circumstances.

Bolero shook hands with me upon climbing the steps of the terrace, shy, seemingly a little frightened. Fernandillo knew the quick remedy for this, thrusting a tall glass of red wine in Bolero's hand. Bolero downed it in one long gulp, as the peasant class in Spain does. It knows nothing about savoring wine, only that bolting it down is the manly way to drink and achieves the effect sooner. Then another. And another. When Bolero's eyes were alive with dance, Fernandillo suggested that he might sing for us a little so I could judge if I might use him in juergas. And out came that incredible voice, singing por *malagueñas, fandangos, guajiras* in the most commercial style of Andalusian-type singing, made passable in this case because of verses that were poetry and because of Bolero's emotion (wine)-charged delivery and beautiful voice with the perfect pitch.

After a time Fernandillo eased Bolero into storytelling. He had some beauts, told in such a colorful manner that those among us who could understand his thick Andaluz accent and local jargon were cracking up. There was the story of his mother-in-law, for instance, who took her sow out to the local garbage dump in the country for a special feast one day. When the pig had eaten its fill, the mother-in-law tied it to her leg, to avoid its wandering off, and both lay down for a siesta. Meantime, back home the fresh litter of piglets the sow had recently produced were getting mighty hungry, which desire must have been transmiteed to mother pig by telepathy or instinct, for she suddenly woke up, snorted loudly, and took off across garbage dump and countryside in a straight line to her brood, dragging "poor" mother-in-law behind her "like an old broken-down umbrella." Bolero's eyes were wild with joy as he told this part and finished by saying that the "old bag" was in bed for a week after that nursing her "well-deserved bruises."

As this tale demonstrates, the content is the least of a story. What matters is how it is told, and Bolero was a master at that. Like all good comedians, he saw comedy in almost any situation (a most enviable talent) and had no reserves about going all out for an effect. Needless to say, Bolero was to become a regular at finca juergas, which never ceased to delight him. He loved the juergas and captive audiences, and even more so the money, for in one juerga he often received more than he made in a week at his type of "hard labor." Nonetheless, this did not stop Bolero

135

from succumbing to normal human greed. Once he saw that he was a popular figure at the finca, he began comparing himself with some of the true artists and began demanding more money. To his credit, this was not entirely his fault. A favorite game in little towns is baiting the simple-minded, and soon all were filling Bolero's ears with grossly exaggerated tales of his artistic merits and his indispensability to us at the finca, comparing him with such as Diego, Joselero, Fernandillo, etc. All this he would swallow whole, forcing me into deflationary action by leaving him out of a few juergas. The mischievous gossips would think this terribly funny, I would have to resign myself to it, for village life is that way, and Bolero would suffer. However, in a few days he would again be bicycling by down on the main road, singing at top volume to be sure we did not miss him, we would again call him, and he would again join the roster at the fee we all knew he was worth.

But back to the first time Bolero joined us on the finca terrace. As soon as Fernandillo heard Bolero sing down on the road that day he was already planting the seed for the craziest juerga ever, in which Bolero was going to play a principal role. In fact, the idea of the juerga was to dupe the guests, and Bolero. Above all Bolero, for by the time the juerga rolled around most of the guests had already deciphered the secret in the bustle of activity. The theme was the following: Fernandillo was to dress in drag and masquerade as the harem favorite of a rich Arab potentate visiting the finca. Juanito, another of Diego's nephews who plays a very nice guitar and had by then developed into a fiestero nearly on a par with Fernandillo, was chosen to act the potentate; and Juan Cala the exhilarant mason, his country's ambassador to Spain. Both Juans located Arabic-looking clothing for the occasion, including flowing burnooses and turbans, and for further disguise painted on false whiskers and the like (Juanito's dress looked suspiciously like Holy Week garb, it was noticed by some). Luisa dressed up like a little girl, supposedly the Harem favorite's dancing daughter, decked out in pigtails, freckles, a little girl's dress, boby sox and tennis shoes, and sucking a lollypop; while Tina, then twelve or thirteen, played the sophisticated wife of the ambassador. Although the latter four were cleverly costumed and played their roles well, creating an evening of very comical situations, Fernandillo's guise and performance fell into the masterpiece category.

I brought Fernandillo out to the finca at least four hours before the juerga was to begin and secreted him in the separate little house where my family and I lived. Then Luisa, Tina and Rocio, Wonder Maid, went to work on him. First they convinced him to shave his legs, for he was to wear one of Luisa's looser black skirts. They made him wash under arms, for an unwashed Fernandillo possessed an odor so strong and peculiar to him that he could have been picked out in a mob. He then shaved his face carefully, after which he was appropriately foundationed, eye-shadowed and lined, rouged and lipsticked. A bra was found that made it around his ample back (with the help of a length of cord) and stuffed with cotton until he had a fetching bust, full but not exaggerated. A red blouse set off his dark gypsy face, followed by a matching red neckerchief which made him even more alluring. A pair of brief leather sandals with slight heels were found for his feet, and then came the master touch: a brown wig, perfect for the occasion. Adornments were elegantly few: an unassuming necklace and small, very feminine earrings. When the job was finished not even his own mother would have known him. He looked exactly like a scrubbed version of the beat-up whores he loved so much, except that he was decked out in a far more refined manner for this important diplomatic occasion.

Shortly before I went to pick up the non-masquerading artists and friends, Juanito and Juan Cala arrived with Manuel de las Alhajas in Manuel's car replete with Arab costumes and already practicing their version of the Arabic language. Luisa and Tina were ready by the time I arrived back, and all five of the masqueraders kept out of sight until the other flamencos and all the guests were in the juerga room with drinks in hand. I then explained to everyone that we were honored with special guests that night, the emir of an oil-rich Arabian country and his retinue, consisting of his Harem favorite, her daughter, the Ambassador to Spain from this distant land, and his young wife. The emir's favorite, I was careful to explain, was suffering from a bad case of laryngitis and was unable to utter a word at present.

They made their grand entrance amid much a-wa-ha a-wa-hu and similar babbling. At first, only those in the know recognized them. Shortsighted Joselero squinted at them in awe and gravely shooked each one's hand. Bolero was equally grave. Luisa looked every bit a pampered young child. Tina played the sophisticate well, with her floppy blue hat and long cigarette holder. The two Juans hammed it up in their most Moorish fashion. Eventually, of course, they were recognized even by Bolero and Joselero, but no one except those in on the secret recognized Fernandillo. Everyone figured we had hired some cheap whore for the occasion, causing the proceedings to unravel as planned.

As the juerga got under way Luisa performed a couple of knock-kneed little girl flamenco dances while sucking her lollypop, much to everyone's delight, while Fernandillo sat next to Bolero and started eyeing him in a most provocative manner. Bolero flushed and didn't know what to do. Soon Fernandillo's hand caressed Bolero's leg. Bolero jumped up and called me aside.

"*Oiga Usté,* Pori, for the love of god, that woman is provoking me, and I respect your house, and besides, what will her husband think?"

(This was before bolero recognized the rest of the masqueraders.)

"Don't worry, Pepe, this is normal in their country. If you reject her she'll become terribly offended, and so will he. It's a matter of courtesy. So go to it, Pepe." A wink. " "She's not bad, eh?"

"But Pori, hombre, this cannot be! Her husband will kill me!"

"He'll kill you even more if you reject her, Pepe. She is his favorite and all men should desire her. Be discreet, but receptive."

Meantime, Fernandillo sat there mutely, hamming it up to the limit, gently snapping his fingers or clapping his hands, always completely out of rhythm (which must have been difficult for him).

Bolero sat apprehensively on the other side of the room from Fernandillo, causing Juanito, the Potentate, to call me angrily to one side and state in his impeccable Arabic while gesticulating wildly:

"Uh whah ah uh whah a mah ha fla ba da ba *cabrón!*"

I got the picture, and went over to Bolero and told him that the emir was getting mighty angry that Bolero did not seem to think his favorite good enough for him, and that if he knew what was good for him he would go sit next to her again. At this urging Bolero's eyes bulged further out even as a sort of crafty horniness seemed to creep into them, and he did indeed go sit next to Fernandillo.

Fernandillo's face filled with delight when Bolero reseated himself at his side, and he began to converse mutely with Bolero, moving his lips and hands delicately in emphasis of his silent conversation.

"Pori, what the hell is she saying?" Bolero asked, as if I would be able to read the lady's lip in Arabic.

"She says that you are her big handsome hero and if you are as good a lover as you look she wants to take you home with her and make you rich. She says your golden voice reminds her of Arabic fountains at dusk. And so forth."

While I explained this, Fernandillo laid her head on Bolero's shoulder and pressed his hand to her lips. By now, everyone in

138

the room was near hysterics, not only from the extreme comedy going on but from trying to suppress the laughter welling up inside. We were all shaking with mirth but doing our best to keep straight faces, and when someone could contain it no longer he/she rushed from the room and roared with laughter at a safe distance. Bolero, of course, knew that something was going on but as yet had no idea what.

Before too long the scene came to a climax. Fernandillo gestured and made his mouth move Arabicly, indicating he wanted Bolero to sing him a love song. Bolero, by now afraid this strong, sex-crazed woman would rape him in front of everybody, took the opportunity to leap to his feet and theatrically sing to her from the safety of the middle of the floor. While Bolero sang Fernandillo was enraptured, closing his eyes in ecstasy, blowing Bolero delicate kisses, edging up his skirt to well above a decent level. Bolero would glance at the leg cleavage occasionally, blush and quickly glance away.

The end of the scene was a surprise even to those of us who knew to what extremes Fernandillo would go for an effect. Just as Bolero was finishing singing his moving love song, Fernandillo let escape a heartfelt "ayyyyyy," leapt to his feet and embraced Bolero, lifting him clear off the floor, and planted a resounding smooch smack on Bolero's mouth. This brought the house down (except for a couple of the guests who had not as yet gotten used to the sometimes quite unique gypsy-Andalusian sense of humor). The gypsies went wild, rolling around on the floor, tearing at their clothing, beating their heads against the wooden bar, beside themselves with laughter. Fernandillo ripped off his wig, and after his initial shock Bolero also joined in the uproar. Although the joke was on him, being a natural comedian himself he well appreciated its excellent execution.

That year, 1970, was Fernadillo's finest as an artist. His dance, bulerías in the style of the country gypsy, was full of innovation, his singing wildly gypsy. Most important of all, however, were the situations he unfailingly dreamed up, assuring us that dullness and repetition could never creep into our lives as long as he was around. He unhesitatingly invaded new artistic fields in order to carry off some of his ideas, becomoming an excellent mime in the process, often livening up a juerga by riotous imitations of other artists. One of his favourite victims was Manolo el Poeta, more familiarly known as *"Papas Fritas"* (Fried Potatoes), a nickname which has followed Manolo since childhood and which he hates with a passion. Fernandillo's version of El Poeta's recitations were so clever and full of insight into the man and his idiosyncrasies that even Papas Fritas had to end up laughing. An outcome of this was that poetry recitation found its way into Fernandillo's repertoire, usually comical improvisation, occasionally in a serious vein. Like everything else he tried, he did it well.

Along with new flamenco dimensions, now that Fernandillo was making money regularly his standard of living crept up. He and his family united with Diego in sharing a nice apartment near Casa Pepe, and they all started eating and dressing better. Through his performances at Morón's annual *"gazpacho"*, and other nearby flamenco festivals, Fernandillo's artistic reputation was extending beyond Morón. None of these signs of success, however, went to his head any more than they had gone to Diego's. Knowing all conceit to be base, Fernandillo remained unchanged, brimming with life, gaiety and cachondeo.

Then one warm July night we were all sitting under the stars outside Casa Pepe, chatting and sipping our drinks, when one of those present decided he wanted to run down to the flamenco festival at Lebrija, a town some fifty miles southwest. Anzonini and Juanito jumped at the opportunity, and they all convinced a reluctant Fernandillo to go. On the way back from the festival they had an auto accident, and Fernandillo was killed instantly. It was in July of 1970. He was thirty-three.

Fernandillo's death impressed me deeply. I could not imagine Morón, and flamenco, without him, and even today still expect to see him around each corner when I return to Morón. From a personal point of view, Manolito de María, Fernandillo and Diego were so intrinsic a part of the art and life I loved that something in me died with each of them. From an overall point of view, flamenco was badly depleted by each of their deaths. There are simply not many like them left, and soon flamenco will be completely in the hands of the slick professionals, a big city art without soul or meaning.

But life, and the finca operation, went on, and Fernandillo's young understudy in the art of living every moment, his cousin Juanito, stepped in to attempt to fill the huge void left by Fernandillo's death.

JUANITO

When we opened the finca, in 1966, Juanito, sixth eldest of Diego's nephews, was just nineteen. Throughout his childhood he had suffered from hemophilia, as a result of which he had led a confined and rather dull existence that had only one positive consequence: he developed an unusual sensitivity, and sense of fantasy, which led him into poetry. His poems, mainly about his hero figure, Uncle Diego, were most effective in their simplicity. This quiet life style was soon to change, however. In his late teens the disease seemed to ease up, and Juanito felt much like a convict in for life who had been granted a pardon. His reaction was to break loose in several directions. He transferred his talent for poetry to his guitar, which he began taking far more seriously and was soon, in the minds of many, second only to Diego in the art of sensitive accompaniment of the song forms predominent in the Morón area: soleares, seguiriyas and bulerías. Women entered his life, as did drink, horseplay, and whatever else a healthy young boy desires. Most noticeable, though, was his development as an extremely entertaining and imaginative fiestero. His sense of fun was superb, and by the time of Fernandillo's death he was ready to step into the breach.

But Juanito was a mainstay of finca life long before Fernandillo died. By the second year of finca activity this young celibate had already been singled out for a long, sporadic romance by one of the finca guests, an attractive woman who, although ten years Juanito's elder, was only slightly less innocent than himself. True, she had been married and had a child, but it was one of those teenage marriages that lasted all of two months and left her with a fear, and deep distrust, of men. To such an extent, as a matter of fact, that even a mistaken or friendly tap on the arm would often draw a snarl and a "Don't touch me!" Why, then, was Juanito taken under her wing? No doubt because he was only a boy, obviously sensitive, gentle, and innocent. As such, he qualified for her complete confidence and a resultant lowering of barriers.

Juanito is a Spanish gypsy, however, and the combination

of instinct and guidance from his older brothers, relatives and friends quickly produced a noticeable change in him. Their courtship, which started by her leading him around by the nose, quickly developed into a normal Spanish relationship, to be repeated more or less identically by all the gypsies who came into intimate contact with foreign girls. It went like this. The girls fell for the gypsy flamencos for three basic reasons: one, because they were gypsies; two, because they were flamenco artists; and three, because they were exciting, fun-loving types who lived a round-the-clock, wild life that was overwhelmingly appealing to young women looking for adventure. Initially, the looks or character of the gypsy was largely irrelevant. What the girls were after was participation in this exciting life, which the gypsies sensed immediately. Thus, throughout the beginning weeks the flamencos deeply involved their new loves in their life style, until the girls were truly and obviously hooked. Then operation number two began: the jealousy bit.

"Look, sweetheart, I love you so much I can't stand anyone else to be near you, or even to see you. I go crazy each time you go to a juerga and have all the other men eyeing you, or to a bar, even if you're with me."

And on and on. As we have seen in Diego's chapter, the girl of course, was profoundly flattered by this display of true love. Certainly no man from her home country had ever cared so possessively about her. So from then on the girl stayed home and waited for her man to appear, accepting her being almost entirely shut off from the exciting life that attracted her to him in the first place.

Once things had reached this stage, more often than not money entered the picture. The girl had been given ample opportunity to observe in just what primitive conditions the gypsies were living, and was invariably shocked. These people knew none of the amenities that were considered necessities in her culture! During this period of observation the gypsy boyfriend would bemoan his family's poverty (egged on incessantly, of course, by the family) and assert all he would do to alleviate it if only he had the money.

The next step was a matter of course. The girls contacted their banks, or more often their parents, and before long money was finding its way into eager gypsy hands. How gainfully the money was employed would depend entirely upon into whose hands it fell. A good gypsy son wanted very little for himself and did indeed channel most of it into improving the standard of living of his family.

This is what happened in the case of the gypsy Federico and

his American girl Peggy. Peggy came to the finca one of the first years, fell for Federico, and was duly shocked at what seemed to her the dire poverty in which Federico and his family lived. After a period at the finca she moved into town and was soon investing all her savings into a bar for Federico and his family. When she ran out of money, she borrowed from her parents. Nor did she neglect the more immediate "needs" of the family, going so far as to provide it with a TV set, which to her seemed a family necessity (at that time in Spain only a few bars and the well-to-do owned TVs). When the bar was ready for opening, I understand she put it solely in Federico's name, thereby disclaiming all her rights to bar ownership and its proceeds.

As was to be expected, as soon as the legal proceedings had been completed Federico's family tried to get him to dump her. After all, she was now penniless and only a drain on his (the family's) income, and their getting married, as far as the family was concerned, was out of the question. They must think of the purity of blood and race above personal desires. His older brother had already married a "castellana" (non-gypsy Spaniard), and that was enough blood mixing in one family!

What other ending could this story have than Peggy's returning home, heartbroken and penniless? Amazingly, this did not happen. The family had overlooked three basic factors: one, Federico possessed a wide streak of decency; two, he truly loved Peggy; and three, perhaps most important of all, Peggy had character. She was strong enough to withstand the increasing antagonism and unpleasantness of the family (in a town like Morón, where it is impossible to avoid people you do not wish to see, this must have been very trying), and was able to instill into Federico the strength to resist the withering pressure to which the family subjected him. Somehow Peggy and Federico persevered, infuriating the family and puzzling most of the rest of the local gypsies. After such brilliant strategy, why was he blowing it at the last minute?

Federico's (and Peggy's) bar, dedicated to flamenco, was located on an out-of-the-way, picturesque side street with only pedestrian traffic. As such, it attracted few casual customers, and had to rely almost exclusively on flamenco aficionados. Before long, it had become the hangout for Morón's foreign flamenco set, many of whom were as scroungy a set of hangers-on and freeloaders as could be found anywhere in the world during those days of hippiedom. Babies were plopped down on tables to have their diapers changed, the soiled diaper often merely tossed into the corner in the parent's doped-up unawareness. Drugs, dirt and distant looks typified most of these people, which perhaps could have been tolerated if they had at least supported the bar operation. But they had no such redeeming feature; they would spend hours sipping a single drink, much to Federico's annoyance.

At first Spanish aficionados dropped in to see what the bar was like. They found that Federico had decorated well, played good flamenco tapes, had reasonable prices, was himself a very affable bartender-owner, and did (at first) attract most of the town's flamencos (his uncle and cousins, as it were). The place was a natural, if only Federico had driven the hippies away. But he didn't, and the Spanish aficionados took one or two looks and rarely returned, as did several of the gypsy flamencos, including Diego and Fernandillo.

To top it off, Federico's family, initially so interested, was little help. The plan was that they were all to alternate working in the bar, helping Federico out. That worked until the family realized that running a bar is hard work. Then the only family representatives who frequented the bar, with rare exceptions, were mama and papa, who would stop by just long enough to raid the cash box. Even Peggy stopped coming in, partly due to Federico's jealousy, partly because she could not tolerate the hippy and parental scenes in too frequent doses.

Eventually Federico had had enough and closed the doors. After a time he and Peggy went to America, got married, and are at last report living happily ever after. The family still came out ahead. They lost a son and a steady income but ended up with the bar, which they converted into their home.

But most love affairs of this type did not have such happy endings. It was common for girls to buy nice little homes in or near town where they could set up housekeeping with the gypsy of their choice. The more worldly had the presence of mind to have the property deeded, if not in her name alone, at least in both their names. The latter course assured that her man could not sell or rent the property without her consent. In such a case, when the girl was replaced by another, or merely dismissed, she could have the satisfaction of knowing that her gypsy "ex" would suffer considerable frustration when he discovered his hands tied in connection with selling or legally renting.

However, these real estate operations were not really so financially deadly as they must sound to outsiders, who think in terms of various thousands of dollars for a town house or country cottage, no matter how small. In Morón in those days such places (of the run-down variety) could be acquired for less than one thousand dollars, and the girls could even rationalize the purchase by calculating all the money it would save them in pensions and restaurants, in addition to the fact that real estate inevitably goes up in value. Were love not involved, such reasoning would have been feasible. However, when the gypsy tires of his girl (rarely vice versa), the girl wanted nothing more than to lose sight of him and mend her broken heart far away from Morón. Good business it was not.

It must be said that there were exceptions among the eligible gypsy bachelors. Not many, to be sure; but exceptions, yes. Federico was not of this breed. Nor was Juanito. In addition, a certain defense could be established by a good court lawyer. After all, here come these hot young things with money, usually Daddy's, popping out of their pockets, just aching to get involved with a gypsy. What sex-starved, hungry young man could be expected to resist such temptation, even if his destitute family were not exerting considerable pressure? To my way of thinking, it has to be considered as merely another method of redistributing the wealth. A little sexy socialism, so to speak.

But back to Juanito. Normally a happy-go-lucky extrovert, Juanito provided many of our more lively moments during the last years of finca operation. Many episodes come to mind, such as his mock wooing of Rocio, Wonder Maid, when he would drop at her feet and sing her some outlandish verse he made up as he went along, Rocio giggling and blushing happily. Or the time on top of the bridge at the Peñon when, spotting some pigs that were specks far below, he delivered what may well be his greatest discourse.

"ESPAÑOLES,' he roared, pumping his hand up and down in finest Franco fashion, 'BELIEVE IN ME AND YOU WILL HAVE DOUBLE GARAGES FOR YOUR SHEEP, WINE IN YOUR BOTAS, LEAD IN YOUR PENCILS, NO INCOME OR BANK ACCOUNTS TO WORRY ABOUT..." and on and on. The pigs stared up at this raving dot and occasionally seemed to nod their assent. He finished with a hearty "VIVA ESPAÑA! VIVA YO!" and goose-stepped to the other side of the bridge and hurled another barrage of nonsense at a cluster of goats that could be vaguely discerned near the top of the cliff.

Like Fernandillo, Juanito was accomplished at dreaming up bizarre juergas, one of which particularly appealed to the local Spaniards, but was viewed with mixed feelings by attending foreigners.

One day Juanito and I were sipping in Casa Pepe when three or four of Morón's "tontos" (mentally retarded or deranged) entered the bar. Juanito immediately perked up, quickly explained to me that these were all flamenco types, and called out to one of them:

"Torito, I'll buy you a drink if you sing and dance a little for us."

"E, e, e, *eso* e, *está* he, he, *hecho* j, *ja*! R, r, r, right n, n, n, now!" Torito replied in his slurring stammer, and launched into a most comical song and dance that was not without artistry. The others, sniffing free drinks, also pitched in, and we soon had a unique display of retarded flamenco roaring away in Casa Pepe.

I know this sounds completely unreal to most non-Spaniards, and even to big-city Spaniards. It must be considered from the viewpoint of the provincial town and village, where the defective (except for dangerous or completely incompetent cases) are not hidden away as they are in industrial countries and in larger Spanish cities. To the contrary, they remain an active part of the community. The blind and the maimed earn their own livings, primarily by selling the local blind and/or national lotteries. They are most noticeably in the streets and bars chatting it up with everyone while selling, proud members of the community like everyone else. The retarded likewise support themselves, or at least attempt to, working at tasks within their abilities, such as loading and unloading around the marketplace, running errands, whatever. They too are contributing members of the community, and are invariably aware and proud of it. How much better and more humane than stashing them behind the walls of institutions and treating them as if they were different and incapable!

After observing the performance of the retarded for awhile, I turned to Juanito and said:

"*Oye,* Juanito..."

"Ah, just what I was thinking," he immediately replied without even letting me begin, "we round up seven or eight of Morón's best tonto flamencos and have a fiesta at the finca. Give them each food, drink and a little money. They'll be delighted, and it'll be one of the funniest fiestas ever!"

So one night we did just that. The "tontos" were indeed delighted as we drove around town, explained the situation to them and loaded them into the Rover. Only one refused – he was offended at being compared with the rest, and it turns out he was right: he was completely insane, but by no means retarded, as I found out when I got to know him better. In fact, we had such success rounding up tontos that we had to reject several who wished to pass as such for the fun, food, drink and monetary remuneration involved.

The fiesta was a riot, second only to the Fernandillo masquerade party for uniqueness and hilarity, and there was a lot more artistry involved than one might think possible. Their

146

flamenco must be called innovative. One dancer kept throwing himself to the floor and bouncing up again in one motion in a most astounding fashion that would turn many a flashy theatrical flamenco dancer green with envy. The words to song forms were hammered about quite impulsively and often quite colorfully. It was, in short, a fiesta of big children performing for the applause and recognition of their elders. If viewed in this light, it was quite touching.

The tontos had a fine time. Torito presumed to take over the artistic direction of the fiesta, and it went along smoothly enough. The flamencos who accompanied the tontos out to the finca — Juanito, Agustín, and several local friends such as Juan Cala and Manuel de las Alhajas — had the time of their lives as did, I thought, all the rest of us. Such was not the case, however. A small group of French girls made it clear the next day that they did not approve. They seemed to think we were exploiting, or making fun of, the tontos, and no amount of explanation would convince them otherwise. Of course, I should have known better. How could anyone not thoroughly intimate with Andalusian life possibly understand? However, the tontos themselves kept after me for months and years afterwards to throw another fiesta for them. It had been the highlight of their year, and perhaps of their lifetimes, for they had been paid artists at a place so renowned for good flamenco as the finca. Very few around town could say the same thing. It was a feather in their caps, and they never let anyone forget it.

All was not fun and games with Juanito, however. It took a lot to make him serious, but when achieved he was as memorable as at his wildest best. Juanito, as a matter of fact, played a major role in the two most seriously emotional juergas I have witnessed. These were the juergas that followed the respective deaths of Fernandillo and Diego.

Although gypsy protocol does not favorably view the participation in juergas by the immediate relations of a recently deceased person, and in addition no one really felt like juerga-ing after either Fernandillo's or Diego's death, chance had it that in each case we were full of guests who had expressly come to the finca from as far afield as half a world away to live a few days of flamenco, including the promised three or four juergas. It was simply not practical or just to call the whole thing off, nor did the artists who were asked to participate in the juergas want us to. They too felt that the show must go on and besides, they were far enough removed from strict gypsy tradition so that they were able to reason that neither Fernandillo nor Diego would vant each mourner sitting in solitude thinking black thoughts.

After all, the philosophy of each had been that life is but a fleeting moment and must be lived to the hilt without succumbing to such detractors as depression and sorrow.

Therefore, we decided not only to have the juergas but to dedicate them to the recently departed. After Fernandillo's death Diego, as undeclared chief of the Morón gypsies, was the only one who felt he must observe the mourning protocol, at least for two or three weeks. Thus Juanito ended un playing on both occassions.

The juerga following Fernandillo's death was held out of town, arranged by Manuel Gerena, a singer from nearby Puebla de Cazalla who has since become famous as a singer of flamenco protest songs. He arranged for all of us to visit a well-known bull ranch near his town (where it turned out, forlornly enough, that the son of the owner of the ranch was dying at the time), after which we repaired to a little country inn for the juerga.

This fiesta was the opposite of a normal juerga. Usually everyone is in far too good spirits to want to get involved with the mournful and serious. In this instance, the merriment we could work up was fleeting and insincere at best, and the juerga soon lapsed into a most serious and soul-searching business. Fernandillo's death had caught him in his prime, and none of us could get used to the idea that he was no longer with us. When a voice hoarse and raucous like his rang out in the adjacent bar, we all glanced up sharply, fully expecting to see Fernandillo knocking down some wine while telling a joke or setting up a con situation.

This juerga was far more traumatic than that following Diego's death. We all knew that Diego's days were numbered, and his death was not a shock. His fiesta was paying homage to a great man. Fernandillo's was more like a wake, in the most depressing sense of the word. Juanito's youth and inexperience with death did not help him get through the juerga. Nor did the fact that he had been with Fernandillo when he was killed. He broke down several times during the juerga, and at others had tears streaming down his face while accompanying Luisa, Gerena and Joselero in appropiate siguiriyas and soleares.

> *I climbed to the top of the wall,*
> *and the wind said to me:*
> *what is the use of sighing*
> *if there is no longer a remedy?*

When it appeared that Juanito could bear no more, I told him that enough was enough and that we should pack up and go home. He would not hear of it, but rather insisted that he wanted to play for Fernandillo, just the guitar. Everyone hushed up, and Juanito's playing, first por soleares, then por siguiriyas, must have continued without interruption for half-an-hour or more.

Up until now we had all considered Juanito an excellent fiestero and accomplished accompanist, but did not think him capable of a great deal of profundity as a soloist. It is very likely, in fact, that until now he had not possessed such emotion, for how can one express death and profound sadness unless one has observed the first at close quarters and been immersed in the second? Be this as it may, that night Juanito played with such emotion as to be nearly unbearable. We sat transfixed, letting his emotion wash over us, note by note, chord by chord. I had the eerie feeling that Juanito was in part a receiver from some other plane of consciousness. I knew his playing well, and that night he played many passages that were not part of his repertoire and that previously I had not heard anyone play. In fact, I'd swear that Juanito's command expanded for the occasion in order to articulate these strange, highly emotional passages that drifted away from his guitar, many of them never to be heard again.

When he finally stopped, like nearly all the rest I too had eyes brimming with tears as well as the distant feeling that Fernandillo had been mourned most creatively, emotionally, sincerely and appropriately.

PART IV

THE GUESTS

THE GUESTS

If the flamencos in this book seem eccentric, so were many of the finca guests. This was desirable — there was rarely a dull moment — and I would say natural, for the finca did not attract the run-of-the-mill plodder. To the contrary, it attracted the imaginative, the romantic, the adventurous, the artistic.

Nearly all walks of life were represented, The scene held a strong appeal for professional people — lawyers, doctors, scientists, two judges over the years. They came and visibly unwound from the tensions of their professions. For instance, the cancer specialist arrived each year all atwitch, a nervous wreck from helplessly watching many terminal patients-become-friends die during the year. By the end of his stay he would be like a different person, unfortunately fated to return to try desperate, if scientific, cures on still more terminal patients who would become friends, many of whom would die before his next finca visit. The doctor in question, like most of the professional types, was a guitar student, the guitar having a particularly calming effect on people, seemingly offering them almost immediate release from tension.

Many of our guests were of senior high school and college age, while housewives on vacation and lonely divorcees and widows comprised another sector. Still another was composed of the artistically inclined: writers, poets, music buffs. And so forth. Very few just plain business people came. My theory is that the typical business mind could not even conceive of the finca and its operation, much less spend a vacation there when the conventional (Acapulco, Torremolinos, Miami, Palm Springs) beckoned.

Many of the guests became our excellent friends and returned year after year, or as often as they could. The finca became a second home to these people, resulting in a very amicable atmosphere like that of a happy family reunion with a frequent enough turnover so that its members rarely got on each others' nerves to an excessive degree.

Although mental well-balance was certainly prevalent, there were enough of the quirky and the downright unhinged to cause

153

the teeter to tooter occasionally. For instance, over the years we had two suicide attempts, one very nearly successful (nighttime rush to the hospital, stomach pumping and strong caffeine injections, stopped heart repeatedly massaged back to life, finally the passing of the danger with the morning sunshine), and still another woman who was fascinated by the idea but fortunately never quite worked herself up to it.

There were, of course, moments of aggression, most often when wine amongst those unaccustomed to drink caused frustrations to surface. Possibly because they knew they could get away with it, most overt aggression was feminine, when tipsy young girls tended to be too quick with slaps and scratches, One male, however, was obviously the most potentially dangerous crater of violence, his whole attitude continuously emitting warning signals. Fortunately, his only eruptions came during juergas, when he would jump up and incongruously stomp and leap through the wildest "dances" one can ever expect to see. He would then slump back into his chair, purged of violence for the time being.

But in reality, aggressiveness was far more the exception than the rule. Most finca anecdotes tend to be gentle and amusing. Such as those involving Rocio the Wonder Maid, so innately curious and full of bubbling life and fun. Rocio was everywhere on that finca, and made a definite point of sniffing out each and every potential scandal and happening, all of which she would duly rush to report to our usually reluctant ears amidst much giggling and wide-eyed wonderment.

One day she came full of praise for a young man from Harvard who had just moved in, because of his respect and love for his father. "Wouldn't every father like to have a son who puts his picture on the shelf and lights candles to him every day?" We became quite intrigued with this, and I decided to investigate by visiting the young fellow in his room. Sure enough, he had candles lit on either side of a framed photograph, but his father turned out to be his current Indian guru. We never enlightened Rocio, and to this day the Harvard boy remains her idea of the ideal son.

Another guest, an elderly gentleman with a touching childlike naiveté, calculated that because Rocio was Spanish she would be knowledgeable about all things Spanish, and took to following her around asking her a wide variety of questions about topics of which she had no understanding whatsoever. Who was her favorite Spanish painter (the only ones she knew anything about were the two locals), her favorite Spanish writer (she could neither read nor write), her favorite Spanish composer

(Diego), her favorite guitarist (Diego), and so forth. At first she thought it all very funny, for she was without pretentions, well quessing the extent of her ignorance, but eventually the kindly old man began getting in her way and interfering with her daily housekeeping routines. That was going too far, for Rocio liked to zip and zap here and there, never letting down until the work was done to her satisfaction. So she became less and less polite, and soon we witnessed the spectacle of Rocio flashing through the finca dusting, cleaning, mopping, making beds, with the elderly gentleman hard on her heels popping question after question. Fortunately, the gentleman left the finca before Rocio completely lost her patience.

I don't believe that even our hardest critics could deny that the finca crowd brightened considerably Morón's normally quiet existence. Particularly on certain animated occasions, such as the time a Spanish dance instructress came down from Paris with a bevy of her dance students, some ten females and one male. Now this was back when Morón was still living its dark ages (1967, I believe it was), when most town folks dressed soberly and somberly, and any act only slightly out of the ordinary caused eyebrows to rise and tongue to wag.

The French girls, however, all Paris residents, were unconcerned about such antiquated mores and came on, you might say, like gangbusters. Miniskirts and halters revealed shapely, firm dancers' bodies, and the town came alive in a dither. Casa Pepe was suddenly inundated by new customers waiting for us to make our appearances, and visitors appeared at the finca gates on any farfetched pretext, hoping to catch a glimpse of bikini-clad girls around pool's edge.

Like other liberated girls who visited us at that time, the French girls were not a bit intimidated by the puritanical Morón scene. They carried on exactly as if in Paris, with lots of horseplay, much laughter and joking, and an innocent annoyance at the groups of young men who followed them around the streets, some in silent wonderment, others calling out comments and suggestions. As far as the local yokels were concerned, girls who dressed and behaved in such a fashion were asking for some action. This belief combined with the young men's natural don Juanian conceit and arrogance to make it even more crushing to their pride when they were curtly rebuked by the offended girls.

Even out at the Peñon and the Charco – our picnic spots miles removed from the nearest village – there was no escape for the girls, not, I might add, for the poor frustrated shepherds who some- how sniffed out the situation and appeared as silhouettes on the surrounding hilltops. There they would remain observing until they had either satiated their curiosity or could no longer stand it. (It should be pointed out here that very few rural men, including the men of fairly good-sized towns like Morón, had ever seen a nude female body except perhaps that of a whore. Their wives never disrobed in front of them, and even to make love would merely lift their skirts, or undress and cuddle up in the darkest dark. After all, the Church reasoned, procreation was the goal, and visual and physical pleasures were definitely discouraged as sinful. Thus, to these men girls in bikinis or miniskirts were wildly and erotically attractive, tempting, and, no doubt, evil).

I made a point to climb up the hills and make friends with some of these lonely country men. A few were itinerant shepherds and slept under the stars at night, but most lived in little adobe farm houses with their families within two or three kilometers of the picnic spots. One such family invited us all over to its little house to partake of homemade bread and sausage. Although it is doubtful that the family could afford such generosity, I found it difficult to refuse. These people had very little contact with the outside world and almost no social life, and having us as guests was an exciting event for them indeed. Invariably their friendship and hospitality were overwhelming and authentic, and their sense of dignity, regardless of the conditions in which they lived, impeccable.

Though the female guests at the finca inspired romantic notions in the heads of many of the locals, the finca guests' romances were confined pretty well to other guests – except, of course, for the quite numerous finca girls who became caught up in the gypsy-flamenco web of charm. Much to Rocio's delight there were few dull moments romance-wise at the finca, and she loved to keep tabs on all the little giveaways: sex stains, beds unslept in, clothing left behind in wrong rooms.... Her curiosity was so great, in fact, that she acquired the rather dubious habit of knocking on a guest's door and then bursting in before the guest could even mutter a reply, immediately followed by a thousand stammered apologies (while surveying the scene) and insisting that as no one answered she thought the room empty.

This practice did not bother most of the guests. Rocio was loved by all and they did not begrudge her these opportunities to brighten her rather drab existence, and besides, the guests were there for only a short time and really couldn't care less what Rocio thought of their sexual habits (if they did, they could always bolt their doors from the inside). Thus Rocio was a fountain of unsolicited information about who was sleeping with whom, which she insisted on revealing to us, bubbling and giggling, each morning (it would obviously be no fun if she had to keep it to herself). One morning she was particularly enthralled after stumbling upon two girls and a fellow in a room and ran around sophisticatedly whispering about round beds for days afterwards, her eyes sparkling with mischief.

One of the more picturesque anecdotes of a romantic nature involved a young man who kept turning up at the finca with a different girl on his arm each time. One time he arrived unexpectedly with a girl friend and three of her friends. We had a juerga that night, at the end of which it had to be computed just where the new guests were to sleep, for there were not enough rooms to go around. Some regular guests, alone in double rooms, volunteered to share their rooms. That took care of the three friends but still left Tom and his girl, who wanted the privacy of their own room if possible. Finally a girl was talked into giving up her double room and rooming with someone else for the night. Or so we thought, but she apparently thought better of it and decided to stay in her original room.

Tom lingered on over a nightcap or two, little suspecting that both beds in the allotted room held girls. He finished his drink and entered the dark room, threw off his clothing, felt a body in the first bed he came to and jumped in, fully amorous, raring to go. As luck would have it, he got the wrong girl, who was trying to stifle her laughter, thinking the whole scene terribly funny. Tom, however, could not figure out why his love was shaking with suppressed mirth until a very irritated voice issued forth from the other bed:

"Tommmmm!!!"

It is said that Tom went sexless that night. It seems he should have known the difference immediately and not lingered so long in bed No. 1.

During another night of grand juerga in the big house, one of our young bachelor guests lured a young married girl up to his room. Both, of course, were tipsy. Her husband noticed her absence almost immediately and began inquiring around after his Sally. Upon hearing this, Luisa noticed that bachelor Jim was also missing, and went directly to his room to forewarn them before the husband arrived at the same conclusion. She knocked on the door and heard scampering of feet and other commotion before Jim nonchalantly opened the door.

"Is Sally here? Pete is looking for her, and quite upset!"

"Oh no. I was just resting a bit, but I'm on my way back down now."

At this point irate husband Pete had reached the top of the

stairs enroute to Jim's room. He was, however, thrown off the scent by seeing Luisa and Jim coming down the hall alone, chatting casually, and followed them downstairs. Luisa suggested to Pete that Sally was probably in the juerga room. Pete went tearing off there, upon which Luisa rushed back to bachelor Jim's room, together with another woman who had sensed the scene, to search for Sally. Not under the bed. The closet door was flung open, and there was Sally, petrified and speechless, unable to move. Luisa yanked her out of the closet and the room and into the nearby bathroom, where they were all three safely ensconced when husband Pete came roaring upstairs for another look. Lurking violence had been nipped in the bud.

Backelor Jim, an arduous young man if ever there was one, was more successful on another occasion, in a manury kind of way. This time the fiesta took place in the little juerga house in back, and the girl was single. Now Jim's long stay at the finca happened to coincide with a dearth of available girls, and he was desperately sex starved. This particular night he had also consumed a goodly quantity of spirits, and was feeling no pain. Thus, when the pact between male and female had been established, Jim was too eager and confused to be wise in his choice of spots, and hustled her directly to the darkest part of the back patio, which was the far corner where our horse Palomo was hobbled. "Ah ha," thought Jim cunningly, "no one will ever think of looking behind Palomo."

He did not think of Palomo's droppings, however, except to note vaguely that the concrete floor was not so uncomfortable as he would have thought, had he thought about it.

Strangely enough, one thing that put off a few of our more serious guests was that finca life was fun. These deceived individuals seemed to have expected a crash course of intensive study so as to learn all about flamenco in ten days or two weeks, culminated by penetration into its most profound and emotional undercurrents. My viewpoint was that concrete knowledge could be gleaned from books and records (most of the guests had read my books, and in addition the finca had a sizeable flamenco-Spanish library), and the second objective, penetrating flamenco's depths, was next to impossible in so short a time, no matter how sensitive the individual. The chances are that until one is truly immersed in flamenco and has a quite complete understanding of it, one may not even recognize the great moments, much less appreciate them to the fullest. After all, in all my years of experience amongst the flamencos I witnessed the genuinely profound relatively few times, and arrived at the naked crux of the matter only twice: with the deaths of Fernandillo and

Diego, in which the actual and immediate (not make-believe or time-softened) Grim Reaper presided over the tragic events. What the finca could, and did, offer was an involvement in the flamenco life style, that all-important factor that cannot be learned from books and without which the art in flamenco cannot be truly understood. That the flamenco life style was a constant whirlwind of fun and diversion delighted most; only a few were disillusioned.

The finca contributed its own unique addition to these pleasurable activities with our futbolín table, which is an oversized wooden table simulating a soccer field, with two offensive and two defensive lines of players for each team. The game is played by two or four people, the object being to knock a little white ball into the opponent's goal. Contrary to the small tables seen in the game parlors outside Spain, the large Andalusian variety necessitates a great deal of practice and skill to play properly. Very little luck is involved.

Futbolín at the finca served for purposes other than diversion. It proved to be an effective ice-breaker, causing even the shyest and most reticent guests soon to be jumping about excitedly and opening up with little curses when they slipped up. It also served as an excellent character gauge. The bad sports and those with other personality problems, such as an excess of potential violence, were quickly discerned, information that could be useful in future dealings. (The younger gypsy flamencos proved very adept at futbolín, displaying lightening reflexes, and heated tournaments between payos and gypsies were staged in which the losers had to fetch the next round.)

The waterfights that broke out sporadically during finca life also served as excellent character gauges. These will be remembered by finca guests as great fun or dastardly outbusrts of immaturity, depending on one's bent. At mealtime the temptation was always present, in form of four or five siphon (gasified) water bottles that were used to sparkle up the wine by those who wished. It was so easy, when wine had made one playful, to direct a jolly little spurt at a victim across the table, who might welcome it in the summer heat, or become angry and sulk, or grab another bottle and squirt back. The matter would usually end there, but occasionally others would feel like entering into the fun and then would ensue the spectacle of guests chasing each other around squirting wildly with siphon water. Those who could not obtain a siphon bottle had no choice but to repair to the nearest water faucet with glass in hand and flail out from there. Rocío, of course, had to mop up the spillage, so she figured she might as well add to it and also got in her licks.

Once in a while such frolicing would erupt in back during a juerga break. Most of the flamencos had well-developed senses of fun and thrived on it, when not actually responsible for starting it. Those who did not were respected and left alone. The same was true of the guests, of course, and so the only hard feelings such happenings generated came about with the occasional guest who enjoyed giving but not receiving. One woman comes to mind, who during a free-for-all was instinctively being left alone until she opened up with a gleeful laugh and a glassful. Being doused in return, however, was another story. She hurled her glass at the offending party and stormed out of the room, refusing to talk to any of us for the next couple of days. (It was this same lady whom Enrique, Rocio's son, observed being photographed in the buff by her boyfriend early one morning down by the pool.) She also took delight in breaking up the late night tippling and bull sessions that sometimes took place in the upstairs kitchen, near her room. Instead of participating in them and enjoying finca life to the fullest, she would send her boyfriend out to harrass the group in a most offensive manner, when all it ever took was a friendly appeal for quiet. Approached in that manner, the group automatically moved on to a more remote spot and continued the session.

Ironically, the previous year the Boyfriend had come to the finca alone, and had been one of the social ringleaders and principal womanizers. No hour had been too late, no discussion was missed. Did he recognize the vast change in himself, from bon vivant to kill-joy in just one year, and feel as foolish as he should have? I think not.

This commonplace phenomenon, that of mate inhibiting mate, was certainly a frequent occurrence in finca life, but never to such a hypocritical degree as displayed by the Boyfriend. At its most serious it was not caused by such vulgarity as mere bitchiness, as in the case just reviewed, but rather by a self-defense mechanism awakened in one side of the matrimony (usually the female) when the partner fell hard for the whole scene and began talking about escaping the rat race, quitting his job, selling their possessions, and immersing himself full-time in flamenco life. Upon hearing or even sensing this attitude, the little woman understandably rose to the threat in a most formidable manner. The finca, flamenco, myself and everything I stood for became her enemies in a bitter battle to preserve her comfort, security and identity. In a surprisingly short time the very fellow who had just yesterday praised the scene to high heaven suddenly had to cut his stay short and rush off to an important meeting that had somehow slipped his mind. Fortunately, such cases were

160

definitely in the minority. Most married couples enjoyed their week or two at the finca and then easily readjusted to their habitual lives back home. Many such couples came year after year, signifiing that the pull of flamenco and finca life was strong for them, but not so strong as to threaten their normal life flow.

I, of course, identified strongly with (although never encouraged) those who felt the overwhelming tug, because it had happened to me. At one point in my youth I had had to make the choice between marriage to a beautiful (if neurotic) rich girl that embodied gifts of a house, car and excellent job with an assured future (if one toed the line), or Adventure in Flamenco-land on the GI Bill. What choice? Off to Spain! There was no choice to make because there has never been any doubt in my mind that the time to do "romantic" things is during the romantic age. The accepted process of securing one's entire existence *before* adventuring is not valid, for by then the senses of adventure and romance have in most cases been destroyed by age and wisdom. Who feels at ages fifty or sixty as does a youth of twenty, thirty or even forty? The retired, well-heeled ages are fine for cautious, thoughtful, knowledge-seeking, comfortable journeys and mini-experiences, but are not at all appropriate for the ballsy blast of youth.

In fact, in my opinion the entire system is mistaken. Just after high school youths should be given a number of years to sow their wild oats and contemplate just what they want to make of themselves, for who can truly know at ages seventeen or eighteen? This is the peak period of idealism and romantic and adventurous longing, all of which combine to impede clear thought amidst the roar of surging sperm and adrenalin. This is also the period of life in which one gets by happily on next to no money; in fact, tends to scorn money, and is happy bumming around where impulse takes him or her.

Then, at age twenty-five or so, those who want go to college. By now they have a pretty good idea of their objectives and will be much more prepared to throw themselves maturely into their studies and truly assimilate knowledge. Others can go straight into sundry endeavours, for they have found out they really have no need for college training. They all have several presumably wild years behind them and are ready to settle down and put their noses to grindstones for the next twenty or thirty years (shudder). Many will even welcome it.

A humane, even efficient dream, if perhaps impossible, for the brain-washing of an entire world would have to be eliminated, a world which advocates that the energies of youth should be spent in the uninterrupted battle for money, success, power, and future security.

In an artistic sense, the finca guests varied enormously. Many were not aspiring artists, but were there to observe, listen and enjoy, or were learning to play/dance/sing a little strictly for their own relaxation and amusement. Many others labored away amidst dreams of one day becoming professionals, or at least beguiling their friends with their art. Still others were already quite competent, and were there to polish up, or learn new, routines. The latter group caused the most friction, for many of them were very fixed in their artistic ways and tended to resent advice afforded them by their instructors. How many dancers came from incompetent teachers doing nearly everything wrong, who greatly admired Luisa's dancing but could not get it into their heads that they did not look like her when they danced. (It was through observing many of the dance and guitar students that I realized that one sees, understands, and assimilates only what one wishes.) And how many guitarists who systematically destroyed, by adding complexity and/or speed, what they were taught by Diego. True, many did so unwittingly; they simply could not hear the difference. Others, cocksure of their razzle-dazzle (after all, it drew applause), overlooked the fact that they had only scratched flamenco's surface, that technique is just one of flamenco's facets. They refused to recognize that more important, if one wants to play meaningfully, is a knowledge of flamenco's traditions, of its dances and songs, emotions and life style. Otherwise, such guitarists end up playing a shallow, showy, emotionless type of flamenco of only superficial interest and value.

The Over-sized Ego was a major obstacle for some students. Three examples come to mind, all young American guitarrists who, in theory, came to Morón to learn. I shall state their cases briefly, for I believe there is much to be learned from their mistakes.

The first, an excellent technician on his instrument, arranged for a lesson with Diego and then proceeded to play straight through the class without so much as handing Diego the guitar. I imagine Diego was supposed to be impressed, but he only commented that he wished all lessons were so easy and chuckled over it for weeks afterwards.

The second was a young greenhorn who came to a finca juerga one night convinced that he was one of flamenco's top guitarists. At the first opportunity he began playing for us. And he played for us. And he continued. And more. An aficionado hogging the guitar at a juerga is sin enough, but to make matters worse, he was only mediocre at best. His idea of flamenco was hammering and tearing at the strings, producing raucously loud music underscored by buzzing and rattling sounds. This, he must have felt, was "gutsy" playing. Moreover, his beat (compás) was faulty, another important flaw in the eyes of aficionados. After a time his audience quietly stepped outside for a breath of fresh air, and he found himself playing to an empty room. This infuriated him, but instead of a little self-examination he crossed us all off as a bunch of insensitive ignoramuses.

In truth it was not all the fault of the blundering young guitarist, for he was the protegé of a wealthy chap who kept insisting, in no uncertain terms, that his boy was among the world's greatest. I suspect that if one is told that often enough, it is human nature to begin believing it.

The third young fellow possessed a curious mixture of comprehension and blindness. His main obstacle was an overly technical mind, better suited to engineering or computer programming than flamenco, that caused him to dissect and systematize the very music he loved when the gypsies played it. But not only for his own usage; his zeal would bubble over to such a point that one would encounter him attempting to instruct the gypsies how to better their own creations. After awhile Diego and the others began shying away from this young pedant. This hurt him and he asked me, in a roundabout way, why he was being avoided. I could only tell him to intellectualize less, have a few relaxing drinks more, and sit back and enjoy. He did, and improved considerably. (I knew about this, for I was born with the same analytical tendency and had had to suppress it in the field of flamenco. This occurred when I was researching the third book of my proposed trilogy, which was to have been a highly technical study of flamenco's songs, dances and guitar. The further I delved into it the more the idea repelled me as it became clear that flamenco's true claim to greatness, its emotional profundity, is a very delicate element only too easily destroyed by an excess of intellectualization. Far more important than flamenco's technicalities, I came to realize, is its life style. Thus, there is no doubt in my mind that this book completes the flamenco trilogy much more logically and appropriately.)

I could continue at great length about the finca guests but feel that further expansion on this subject would lie outside the scope of this book. So we shall leave the guests by saying, in summation, that the finca community was composed of an exciting mixture of the delightful and the difficult, the well-balanced and the neurotic. Conflicts occasionally arose, as they will in any close-knit communal life. At times chaos seemed just around the corner, but it was always thwarted by that common demoninator which was able effectively to reconcile most differences: our shared love of flamenco.

"Big men play big guitars." This photo shows some Capa Pepe regulars around 1965. Diego and Juanito are fourth and fifth from left, respectively, Gregorio is handling the big guitar, and Pepe of Casa Pepe (right) sports his favorite apron. Photo by the author.

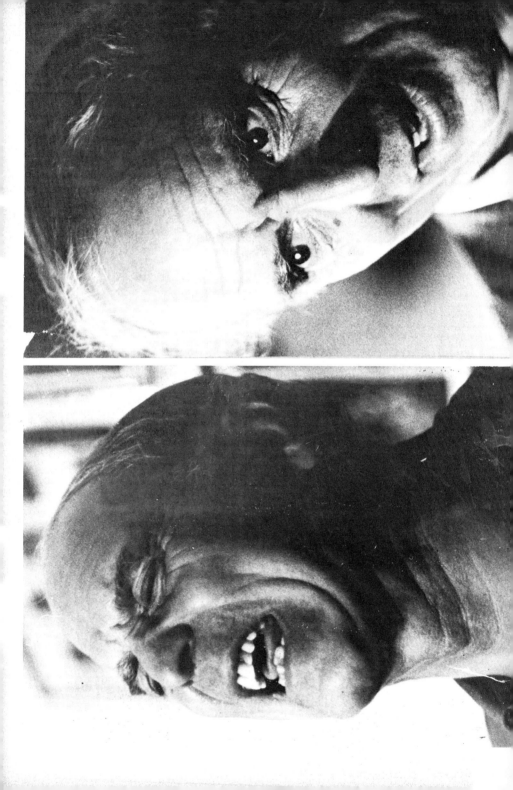

Five studies of Diego. Above, singing the *soleá* of his mother, and being Diego. Below, L. to R.: tranquilly making a point in Casa Pepe: "What the hell is he saying?"; "Now you listen to me...!" Photos by Dick Frisell.

Diego with his mother shortly before her death. Casa Pepe is on the left. Above, Diego's brother, Mellizo. Photos by Gómez Teruel, Sr.

Above: Diego playing. Below: Juanito and Juan Cala jamming upstairs at Casa Pepe. Photos by Ira Gavrin.

Above, L. to R.: Juan Cala, Juanito, Tina, Luisa, Fernandillo (in drag) at emir's *juerga* (as described in the Fernandillo section). Left: Fernandillo cooking something up (side-down). Right: Fernandillo strikes a pose on the pedestrian walk now officially named the *"calle* Diego del Gastor." Photos by the author, Dick Frisell, and unknown, respectively.

Above: Joselero sings with *duende,* Anzonini accompanies. Below: Joselero laughs, Fernandillo schemes ... Photos by Dick Frisell.

Above: Paco de Valdepeñas (dancing) and Anzonini at the finca. Below, L. to R.: Bernardo de los Lobitos, Paco de Valdepeñas, Manolito de María and Paco del Gastor at a 1964 juerga in our club in Madrid. Photos by Carol Whitney and Phil Slight, respectively.

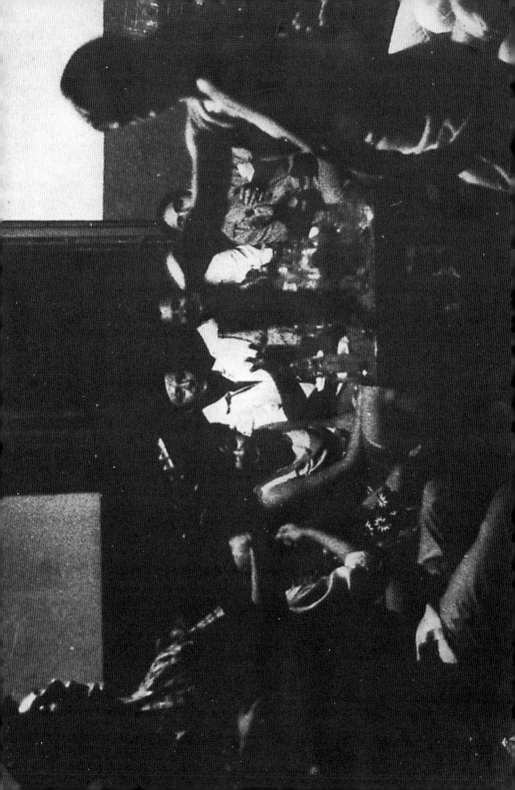

Left: another moment of *duende* as Luisa dances to Agustín's singing and playing upstairs at Casa Pepe. Above: Bolero sings, Rocio the Wonder Maid sniffs scandals, Juanito and Tina horseplay, the author observes a frog in his drink. At the Charco Charcal. Photos by Dick Frisell, and unknown, respectively.

Above: view of the finca from across the river. Below: the finca, the Land Rover awaiting its next mission, and boxer. Photos by Luisa Pohren.

The gypsies from Alcalá de Guadaira dance and sing the Tangos Flamencos. Left to right: the author on the guitar. Manolito de Maria sings. Algodón. Manolo el Poeta. Snow-white dances with the young girl.

Andorrano delights Diego with his singing. c.1968.

PART V

THE JUERGA

THE JUERGA

I am sure it has been made quite evident in this book that the juerga, or flamenco jam session, is the only group vehicle for true flamenco expression. This is so because choreography and sophistication enter the picture as soon as a stage is involved, factors that are deadly to emotional folk arts. Flamenco on stage is almost invariably commercialized, often even by artists who may be purists offstage. Such artists are convinced, often correctly, that the public prefers it this way; and they bend over backwards (way backwards, in the case of commercial flamenco dancers) to provide it, frequently with ludicrous results.

Even a juerga situation does not necessarily insure pure flamenco. It depends on the caliber of the artists involved, needless to say. But there is a built-in guarantee in the paid juerga for those in search of the authentic – if the purist knows he is being hired for purity of expression, purity of expression he will usually deliver. And that brings us to the basic difference between the stage and the private juerga. On stage the artist is getting paid to entertain. In a serious juerga, to express.

Juergas were the most important aspect of finca life. The operation was built around them and catered to them. But we soon learned that successful juergas were not so simple to organize. The juerga situation – the seating of four or five artists in a room and waiting for them to turn on – was oftentimes not enough. As we have seen in another section (over the next couple of pages I sum up some already discussed material), before each juerga it had to be ascertained whether the artists chosen for the occasion were at least on speaking terms with each other at the moment and, preferably, enjoyed a certain friendship that permitted them to relax in each other's presence and at the same time sparked them on to greater efforts. This factor alone was frustratingly evasive. Other than this, we learned that diversification of juerga themes and settings was extremely important, for it had the effect of igniting the imaginations of artists and spectators alike and of producing more inspired juergas. Diversification was also calculated to maintain the interest of long-term guests, as well as my own interest and that of Luisa. No

167

matter how immersed one is in a performing art, two or three sessions a week, each lasting an average of six to eight hours, can get to be old hat unless the utmost imagination is employed.

The abstemious will be shocked to read that alcohol plays an extremely important role in bringing off a good juerga. (14) It was common practice to warm up the artists with a few drinks in town before bringing them to the juerga (if they had not already warmed themselves up). In addition, there were times when I and/or the guests had a heck of a time working up the proper enthusiasm for a forthcoming juerga – when after dinner, at about 11:30 p.m. or midnight a little card playing and quiet music seemed far more fetching – so that we had to rely on alcohol to get the juices flowing. I must say it rarely failed to achieve the desired effect, and often those initially uninviting fiestas turned out to be among the most memorable.

As stated, diversification of artists was of maximum importance and is what most complicated my life. Our Morón artists were like part of the Finca Family, and of course expected (or at least hoped) to be involved in each finca happening. Some of the guests backed them up on this if they were particularly enthralled by a certain artist, or with the group as a whole. So at least once a week I had to explain to local artists and certain guests alike the need for variety – to convince both that if rotation of artists was neglected, even those guests most insistent on repetition would go away saying that the finca used the same six or seven artists all the time and that the art accordingly became stale.

However, achieving variety was a lot easier said than done. The flamencos were extremely reluctant to venture into another territory, even to a neighboring village, where they generally feel out of place and ill at ease away from their cronies and habitual surroundings. Thus, when they did consent to come to the finca they often brought a piece of their surroundings with them, in the form of two or three of their friends, which sometimes worked out well and sometimes did not. In addition, visiting artists had the tendency to demand much more remuneration than they normally received and to put on airs, requesting whiskey and the like (to no avail at the finca; we could not afford to be *espléndidos* in our juerga presentations) when the rest of us were drinking wine or beer. Worst of all, however, was having to pick the visiting artists up and take them home, or otherwise pay exorbitant cab fares. They would rarely deign to utilize public transport, no matter how badly the needed the juerga money, even if I were willing to schedule the juerga to fit the bus schedule and invited them to stay over at the finca during the period of waiting to return home, if any. (15)

In lieu of these considerations, we took to having guest artists at the finca less and less, and more to going, en masse, to them. Jerez de la Frontera was a favorite excursion. Not only is Jerez teeming with excellent flamencos – more so than any other place in Spain – but there was also the attraction of the many sherry wineries as well as that of the nearby beaches and *manzanilla* vineyards of Sanlúcar de Barrameda.

An oftenrepeated plan was to reach Sanlúcar, some two-and-one-half hours from the finca, by eleven in the morning, visit a winery, then head for the beach. Touch football was a favorite beach diversion, not only for us but for the group of fishermen we invariably attracted who would watch with wide smiles and bulging eyes the bouncy-wouncy of the females in their brief bikinis. A meal of fresh seafood and a nap on the beach would precede our covering the twenty-four kilometers to Jerez, where I would drop everyone off at the juerga site and drive into the Barrio de Santiago to pick up the artists for the occasion.

At the best of times in Jerez we hired four crusty old-timers, all gypsies who exuded gracia and good humor and never failed to produce memorable juergas. Foremost among them was Tía Anica la Piriñaca, whose primitive renditions of siguiryas, soleares and tangos carry an incredible impact, (16) and who also dances and sings exciting bulerías despite her obesity and advanced age (in her early eighties when we were frequenting Jerez). Pepa la Chicharrona, a delightful, bubbling woman who in appearance represented everyone's concept of the ideal sweet old grand-mother, followed Tía Anica in longevity (late seventies at the time). The third female of the group was an enormously fat and cuttingly witty woman named Juana la Pipa, relatively young then at middle age. Both La Chicharrona (Crisply Fried Bacon Fat) and La Pipa (Sunflower Seed) were respected fiesteras, and as such concentrated their artistry on the fiesteros' favorite flamenco form, the bulerías. The fourth of the picturesque quartet was a gentle little fellow in his late sixties nicknamed El Choza (The Hut), who sang and danced his absolutely unique creations of bulerías and who would sometimes get a gleam in his eye at the height of a juerga and provoke La Chicharrona to dance his most original "rooster" dance with him. In truth, it didn't take much provoking to get these old gals into a scandalously off-color mood, for their normal language was enough to make the devil blush. Being of flamenco's old school, it is likely that they had lived life with the throttle wide open, and austere innocence had gone by the wayside long ago. At any rate, as often as not it would be La Chicharrona, after a half bottle of sherry, who would jump up, with turn-of-the-century knee-length bloomers showing whenever she pulled her skirt up a tad, and coquettishly waggle her bottom at El Choza. Zip went Choza's zipper, zap went his hand into his bottomless righ† pocket and zam, out flopped his index finger through the open fly, which stiffened as he rose slow-motion from his chair. Once he and everything else was up, however, the slow motion ended and Choza took off after Chicharrona like any cock after his hen. And they would feint and circle and dodge and merge in a most artful and frolicsome fashion, singing double-duty verses at each other, causing the Spaniards to laugh uproariously and shocking many of the foreign element, not accustomed to such openly lascivious old folks.

There are various excellent guitarists in Jerez as well, but we found them conceited and aloof, not types that blend well into juerga situations. In addition, they had an exaggerated sense of their monetary value, demanding more payment than even La Piriñaca was receiving. Thus, we quickly took to bringing our own guitarists along from Morón, varying them each trip so as to give all an opportunity. The reactions of the Jerez artists were interesting to observe. They all fell for Diego as a person and loved his accompanying. They had heard much about him and found he lived up to his reputation. Nephew Paco was too dynamically fancy and modern for them, while Juanito was rated second only to Diego in the accompaniment of the old-time bulerías sung and danced in Jerez as well as in the profound forms sung by La Piriñaca. Agustín played well but lacked experience in accompanying the Jerez style of flamenco, and his playing was somewhat confused then due to his experimenting with various styles of playing. Dieguito, the youngest of Diego's nephews then playing, was very inexperienced at accompaying at that time and had a very tough night of it.

Luisa often did not accompany us on these excursions, preferring to stay back and do long neglected things around the finca, or merely recoup strength, but the first time she did and jumped up to dance, the old artists' eyes nearly bugged out. "Coño," they exclaimed, "who is this young thing, dancing better than the professionals?" Then it had to be explained that, regardless of her foreign husband and friends, she was Spanish, with ancestors from Ronda, and then they understood and embraced her with new interest and affection.

When the venta closed, at 1:00 a.m., we often loaded everyone into the Rover and moved on to another one, further out in the country, that was allowed open until three a.m. "Loading" was literally the word, for I and perhaps another hearty type would have to hoist the two heaviest ladies into the high front seat, where they insisted on sitting, while La Chicharrona carried on in the back seat like any gum-popping teenager.

"Oye," she cried out to me once as we covered a particularly bad stretch of road, "you're going to deflower me if this thing doesn't stop bouncing around!"

To which another of the gals responded.

"The only flowers you've ever seen have been sticking out of the front of pants!"

And they would break into peals of laughter, having a great time, enjoying life right up to their last day. This, I believe, is called aging gracefully.

Our last juerga in Jerez with these artists was in 1973. Since then both the Hen and the Rooster have died, La Chicharrona in her native Barrio de Santiago, El Choza in an old people's asylum in Lebrija. La Piriñaca and La Pipa, however, carry on undaunted, as we had the great fortune of seeing for ourselves just before midnight of New Year's Eve, 1977. Our TV, playing to an empty room, suddenly broke forth por bulerías, sung by the unmistakable voice of Tía Anica la Piriñaca and backed up by much handclapping and shouts of encouragement. We all quickly converged to catch the show, and were rewarded by some excellent old-time Jerez juerga flamenco, highlighted by Tía Anica's singing and the dancing of both Tía Anica and La Pipa. Tía Anica, now nearing ninety, danced last in a surprisingly agile fashion, after which she walked off stage in a far more cumbersome and clumsy manner. To us it seemed entirely appropriate that in her last years the old gypsy should dance better than she walks.

The show made our night, although we could not help being wounded by a touch of melancholy: the group was just not complete for us without the Cock and the Hen.

Another group well along in age to whom we used to travel lived in Triana, the flamenco neighborhood of Sevilla. They were all artists that had enjoyed renown thirty to fifty years ago, when they were young and cafés cantantes still existed in Sevilla, but had been forgotten in flamenco's decline of the 1930's, 40's and 50's. Flamenco's sudden surge to new popularity in the 60's and 70's had helped them but little, for by then they were too old and their flamenco too dated for the modern aficionado's tastes. However, as the Spanish saying goes, there is no bad from which some good does not come, and we happened to be around to reap that good. These artists had remained pure, true to the style of their youth, and as such presented a rare opportunity to experience at firsthand the café cantante flamenco of the

171

first thirty years of this century.

It is of interest to point out that while both the Triana and Jerez groups of old-timers can be considered purists, in that they never commercialized their art, there was still a significant difference between them, which boils down to one factor: the degree of sophistication in their art. Probably because Jerez was more of a backwater town than Sevilla, the Jerez flamencos in question had not ventured beyond their own local flamenco forms. They were happy with these forms, which fulfilled their complete expression, so why bother with outside forms? In Triana, too, the artists in question specialized in the forms from their area; but they also embraced certain forms of other areas as well, thus broadening their flamenco horizons. This no doubt came about because the outside forms were demanded of them in the cafes cantantes of sophisticated Sevilla, leaving them no choice. Nonetheless, the Triana group remained far more at ease with the forms inherent in their region, using the imported forms chiefly as changes of pace or fillers.

Two of this little group of Triana purists, inseparable companions, were La Perla de Triana and Rosalía de Triana. As their names indicate, both hailed from Triana and sang the song styles of Triana with utmost purity of expression, although by now with cracking, failing voices. And they were amiable, charming women, ideal in juergas, happy and flattered to be remembered and listened to with the reverence we displayed. Unfortunately, our contact with these women was cut short by an accident unusual even in flamenco circles. It happened that Rosalía and Perla's mode of transportation was, of all things, a motor scooter. Picture the scene, two septuagenarians racing along, Perla a very black gypsy, Rosalia less dark but also noticeably gypsy, skirts flying, dodging in and out of traffic, laughing and chatting happily. One day they didn't dodge quickly enough, were knocked down, and were lost to us the rest of that season. Rosalia reappeared the following year, but La Perla's hip did not mend properly and she disappeared permanently from our juergas, much to our disappointment.

Then there was the dancer, Pastora la Posaera (La Posaera and Rosalia are included in a group photo of flamenco artists, dated 1925, that I have published in my book "Lives and Legends of Flamenco"), in her mid-sixties the youngest of the girls. She used to sit quietly in her old-style cotton dancing dress until she had soaked up an entire bottle of Tío Pepe, at which time her palmas would ring out overloud and her bulerías would gain a special zing. Not long after she would search her memory bag of old dance and come up with her *alegrías,* traditionally flamenco's basic dance for the female, danced in exactly the style that had been popular fifty and even one hundred years earlier. She would then be transformed for a few minutes from an awkward, overweight old hag into the picture of grace, a young girl again, moving her arms majestically, her carriage proud and youthful, her face once more coquettish and full of expectation. I never tired of witnessing this astonishing and beautiful transformation. Afterwards she quickly reverted to her cunning old self, attempting to browbeat me out of more fee than stipulated, to work her very mediocre young nieces into our juergas, and so forth.

The excellent and knowledgeable accompaniment of guitarist Antonio Sanlúcar (brother of the well-known guitarist, Esteban) helped make the singing and dancing of these old styles possible. In his late sixties at the time, he would hunch over his guitar looking every inch the ferocious bulldog, a smile flitting across his face and his eyes lighting up briefly when he or another of the artists accomplished something particularly worthy. His playing style was straight from the past, much like what one hears on the old 78s from the 1920's and 30's.

Sometimes we tried combining younger artists with the old-timers. On the surface this seemed to work well, but upon closer inspection one could discern that neither generation was comfortable with the other. The old-timers did not understand or appreciate the endless *rumbas* and other youthful nonsense, nor were the youngsters happy with the flamenco of the old fogies; the young guitarists accompanied the older artists badly, and the older flamenco was not the type in which the modern dancer, with all his or her razzle-dazzle, could shine regardless of the fact that the forms were identical, as was the compás. What had changed was the feeling. Much as the horse and buggy has given way to ever newer and faster automobiles, so flamenco had ceded to the frantic age.

One combination that turned out well was Antonio el Farruco, Luisa and the old-timers. Both El Farruco, the outstanding male flamenco dancer of the past twenty years in the minds of most aficionados, and Luisa have a tendency towards the traditional style, which the old folks well appreciated. (17) Sanlúcar had no trouble accompanying them, nor the singer singing to them, and their dances came out well. When they danced together it was sensational, especially considering it was all spur-of-the-momento improvisation. They had danced together once or twice previously at finca juergas but had by no means ever worked anything out. A flamenco adage states that if two artists of the same generation know their art well they should have no

173

problems performing together. El Farruco and Luisa proved this to be true, as did Luisa and Andorrano de Morón a couple of times at finca juergas when a driving bulerías inspired them simultaneously and they leapt up and started dancing together in a manner that could hardly have been improved upon by choreography and rehearsal. Such spontaneously creative performing, to my mind, is the peak of achievement in a performing art, far overshadowing even the most perfect choreography.

The colorful cave area of Alcalá de Guadaira also attracted us for many juergas, above all when Manolito de María was still alive. The caves in their rusticity gave one the impression of experiencing flamenco in its truly natural habitat, by candle or oil lamp, amid a stark but somehow not so malignant poverty (if compared with the misery of big city slums). Flamenco, above all gypsy flamenco, had been born and reared in such surroundings, and only in such an ambiance did many of the more primitive flamenco verses become poignantly significant.

Two such cave fiestas particularly stand out in my mind, one for its artistry, the other for its unusualness.

On the first occasion a reduced number of us — only three or four — picked up Diego at Casa Pepe and Francisco (Curro) Mairena at his favorite bar in Mairena del Alcor, then drove to Alcalá de Guadaira to find Manolito and an adequate cave for the session, a session still memorable for its incredible profundity of expression. After a beginning sparkling with bulerías all three got down to the nitty gritty, Manolito por soleares, Mairena por siguiriyas, and Diego with beautiful, sensitive accompaniments and an occasional moving solo. It was one of the rare juergas in which very little horseplay occurred. Despite all the wine consumed, we returned home at dawn sober and somewhat somber, with a heightened awareness of the darker side of life that lies just below the surface of good health and good fortune.

The other memorable juerga occurred after Manolito's death. (18) I mention this because, had he been alive, the event I am about to recount would not have happened; Manolito's influence was too great over the people of his neighborhood. At this particular juerga there were too many of us to crowd into one of the run-of-the-mill small caves, and we were offered a special cave with a large, walled-in patio in front where we could all gather comfortably this warm summer night. The cave owners wanted five hundred pesetas for their trouble, to which we agreed, much to their delight. (Five hundred pesetas was a considerable sum then for such poor people, and in addition they could drink and enjoy the juerga!) Everyone was happy with the arrangement except the son of the owners, a man in his mid-thirties, alcoholic by

174

trade, whose pickled brain would not listen to reason. He refused to grant us permission, although his reasons were never made clear; I suppose pride was at the bottom of it. His parents, however, were having none of his smart talk. After all, they were the owners of the cave, not their son; and they thought they had solved the problem by making him leave home for the night. But no sooner had we all gotten settled down and the first bulerías cranked up when we heard SMASH CRASH CRUNCH and the wooden door leading into the patio began rattling and shaking and finally burst inwards on top of one of our party (who had had his chair comfortably tilted against the door). In rushed the son (appropriately nicknamed "Spark"), wildly drunk, and roared that we must all leave. His mother, in her late sixties if a day, marched right up to Spark and began calling him every name in the book while applying open-handed rights and lefts across his face with all her might. He stood there taking it, undoubtedly not feeling. a thing. When this became tiresome and Spark kept insisting we leave, his father swung into action, picking up an enormous club and telling his son in no uncertain terms that he had better get out. Spark's foggy brain did catch the significance of this and he decided to retreat, but only temporarily. He kept roaring he'd be back with reinforcements, and we'd better be gone!

By that time the local artists were imploring us to get the hell out of there, for they knew by experience that a drunken Spark was capable of anything and was likely to return with the most lethal weapon he could find.

So we left, leaving the parents two hundred pesetas for their good will and the fine boxing exhibition the mother had staged, and transported everyone out to a nearby stand of pines where we built a fire and had our juerga amidst pine fragrance and moon beams. Nothing lost, and a colorful episode gained.

Then there were those change-of-pace juergas we held on our own grounds, at the far point of the finca where the river converged with our eucalyptus and olive groves. This was an ideal spot when going to the Peñón or the Charco seemed like too much work; and besides, it held certain advantages over the distant picnic places: guests could come and go by foot as they pleased, it was more accessible for desirable friends from town to drop by, and the juerga could be continued up at the house if we deemed it desirable, which was usually the case sometime during the night. As we have seen, a change of location always sparks up a juerga, and in addition the smooth floor of the juerga room was better suited for dancing than the rough ground of the picnic area.

The problem of logistics was overwhelmingly simple at our

picnic area – load up the Rover with the foods, water, wine, beer, sometimes *sangría* (finca fruit, red wine, a little sparkling water, no sugar), sometimes gin and lemon for openers, and drive down the one hundred or so meters along the path lined with brambleberry bushes to the clearing in the trees. There we would set things up, and the chef-of-the-day would begin preparing the fire and the meal. The flamencos nearly fought for the opportunity of cooking over an open fire. They all seemed to consider themselves excellent cooks, and by Morón standards some really were. Fernando and Juanito were passable if erratic; Anzonini was consistently the best; while Juan Cala, the mason with the perpetual hat, was the most colorful. Juan would somehow get the spectators to do most of the peeling, chopping and cutting while he threw instructions around like the best from the Ritz. When everything was prepared he would place it all in the big stew pot, usually on second thought adding more white wine, bay leaves, pepper corns, garlic and onion, and perhaps hot peppers, depending on how his ulcer and kidney (only one of each at that time) were behaving. Then it was time for a bit of witchcraft. Juan would dance around the stew Macbeth-witches-style, intoning mystic chants while the firelight flickered against the black of the surrounding trees. When the spell had been cast, assuring us of a fine witches brew, he would just as deftly break it by challenging Manuel de las Alhajas to a dance contest, winner take all. Manuel would leap to his feet, challenge accepted. Juanito would quickly proceed to collect a *duro* (five pesetas) from each of the spectators, to be given the winner. Judges were chosen. Someone was delegated to watch the stew. One of the guitarists would start up por bulerías, and off they would go. First Juan Cala, singing at the top of his voice whatever silly verse occurred to him while executing some highly original dance, shouting *olés* and other encouragement to himself, spurring himself on to a supreme effort. When spent, he would give way to Alhajas, who with simulated artistic pretensions and cool would sing and dance por bulerías with true gypsy gracia. When he finished they would both clamorously demand the prize money. However, the jury would insist they were both so bad the prize had to be declared void, fully intending to split up the money for beer in town later on. But they had not reckoned with Juanito, collector and holder of the seventy-five or eighty pesetas, who in turn declared the jury as crooked as the dancers were bad and decided to keep the money himself, "in trustworthy hands," until the next contest. *Adiós* money.

And so it went, the juergas and the artistry and the good times clicking away the years until suddenly it was all over.

Things had changed; the mood was different. Fun for fun's sake and art for art's sake fell largely by the wayside, and a lust for materialism took over. While previously the flamencos had been happy with basic sustenance and plenty of time to pursue their life style, now they caught the sickness of the times, the irrational urge to compete with the Joneses today and, even worse, the constant gnawing, life-sucking worry over tomorrow and the need to amass a bundle in preparation for it. I will tell you and the old-style flamencos will tell you they were far happier before, but the process is irreversible. There is no going back (unless forced to do so by widespread economic depression). (19)

The combination of this development and Diego's death decided us to close down the operation at the end of the 1973 season. We were urged to commercialize as a sort of rural tablao, but that would have been intolerable. Once one has been immersed in the real thing, one cannot settle for distant second best, not even for the sake of *Don Dinero* (Mr. Money).

Four years later we sold the finca and took up full-time residence in Madrid. All that is left are the memories, and the consoling knowledge that we have lived as few have had the opportunity to do.

That must suffice.

EPILOGUE

I reopen this book with a depressing, even spooky, incident. When it came time to turn the manuscript over to the printer — when it would be irretrievably out of my hands for further additions, corrections, changes — I could not bring myself to do it. Although this is always a difficult step to take, this time something truly important seemed lacking, although I had no idea what it might be. So I decided to wait a few days, and in the meantime pay Morón our first visit in a year-and-a-half. En route, Luisa had a premonition: "What if we arrive at Morón and Pepe (of Casa Pepe) has just died?" This chilling thought was entirely out of the blue. Although Pepe had been ailing for some years with diabetes, to our knowledge his condition was not at all grave, so I laughed it off as one of her witchlike presentiments which, fortunately, are generally unfounded, and we forgot about it. But not for long. Upon entering Morón we stopped for a minute at a store before continuing up to Casa Pepe for a joyous homecoming, and were informed that Pepe had died that very morning!

We were stunned. Other than the significant parapsychological implications of it all, including my not having been able to complete the manuscript, Pepe was one of our great favorites. The all-afternoon and night wake was already underway when we arrived, the men in the bar (for reasons of space only — nothing was served), the women in Pepe's apartment across the street. The consensus of opinion in both sectors was to the effect that Pepe for years had been benefactor to Morón's poor and needy, a soft touch whose earnings flowed out in loans (too frequently not repaid) and acts of mercy nearly as fast as his (and his family's) hard work and long hours garnered them.

Another sad prospect surfaced during that long night of January 3, 1979. Casa Pepe would likely be closed down permanently, and probably even be put on the demolition block in order to pave the way for new construction on that corner.

What the hell, I found myself thinking, if it is going to

179

end, let it be thorough! For the passing of Pepe and his bar concluded an epoch. Flamenco in Morón as we mourners at the wake had known it had received its final blow. Fernandillo's death had badly disturbed the scene, Diego's death, coupled with the simultaneous rise of materialism, signified the end was near, and now Pepe's death and the closing of Casa Pepe were the finishing touches.

May they all, and it all, rest in peace.

EPILOGUE TO THE NEW EDITION
Translated from the 1998 Spanish Edition

This book must be alive, for I feel compelled to open it again for this second edition to tell of a surprising event that took place just last June (1997), which was a homage given my wife and me by the town of Morón for our part in "the most glorious flamenco epoch in Morón's history."

I say "surprising" because when we closed the finca and left Morón it appeared that materialism in the life style and soph-istication/bastardization in the art would kill true flamenco nearly overnight. Which it appeared to do. Juergas became a thing of the past. True afición amongst the artists became rare – when they do get together their conversation more often than not avoids flamenco, just the opposite from before. The name of the game has become money; those not in it basically for just that are considered "bichos raros" (strange beings, definitely stated in a derogatory sense).

However, today a tiny current of counter revolution can be detected, of nostalgia for the flamenco and its way of life that existed so few years ago. The movement is growing – many aficionados are frankly fed up with the theatricality they are being fed, and are seeking something basic and substantial to counter the superficiality of staged flamenco. The people once had a true art of their own that far surpassed common folklore; it has been taken away from them and launched into the sphere of sophistication and make-believe. The revolutionary current of which I speak is attempting, in its small way, to take it back to where it belongs.

Our homage in Morón was part of this movement. (A major reason for the homage was the series of articles I have written in Spanish for the flamenco magazine "El Candil", entitled "the Golden Age", many of which have been reprinted in the local Morón magazine "El Mauror.") Highlights of the homage: the presentation to my wife and me of a plaque consisting of nine hand-painted tiles framed in wood. In addition, I was surprised by the revelation that the Fundación Fernando Villalón had nearly completed the translation into Spanish of this very book and will soon be publishing it.

It was great embracing the attending survivors of our heyday. Gregorio, now 84, and Bernabé Coronado are doing well (see page 27); Juan Cala (page 176 and elsewhere plus photos) is better than ever;

181

This plaque was presented to the Pohrens at a homage given to them by the town of Morón de la Frontera in 1997. Depicted on it are the famous Gypsy artists (now deceased), Diego del Gastor, guitarist, and Joselero de Móron, singer, two of the stalwarts of the Pohrens flamenco centre, which in turn is shown at right. The guitar in the foreground represents the spirit of the endeavour. The inscription reads "Móron a Don E. Pohren".

Some of the protagonists for the book three decades later (photograph taken on the 29 June 1997). Standing: Juan del Gastor. Seated from left: Luisa embraces Pepi, daughter of Pepe de Casa Pepe and her husband Pepe, who worked alongside his father-in-law in the bar; the author and Juan Cala.

Juan and Paco del Gastor are thriving, artistically and in their private lives; Rocio the Wonder Maid still works at the air base and would be content were it not for the recent loss of her son Enrique to cancer; illness has confined live-wire Manuel de las Alajas (page 176 and elsewhere) to a wheelchair, hopefully only temporarily; Anita, wife of Pepe of Casa Pepe, is still going strong at age 84, and her offspring all do well – Casa Pepe, however, closed down long ago and no bar even remotely similar has taken its place; Finca Espartero lies on its majestic site in complete ruin – everything of the slightest value has been removed from it and its few remaining roofless and floorless walls can in no way remind the observer of the grand things that went on there.

In summation, although many of the people who made the Golden Age shine are still with us, the spark has been extinguished. Flamenco is now respectably costumed, perfumed and up on stage, on TV and on the radio and in books and magazines, but barely survives where it was at its best, in the bars and ventas and backrooms and fincas and marketplaces and picnic spots and the back of Landrovers and spilling out into the streets when its practitioners could no longer contain themselves. In these last thirty or forty years it has passed over from the natural expression of a very special breed to a choreographed, rehearsed and staged show. Ayyyyy …

But what about that tiny current of counter revolution, that nostalgic desire for the return of truth and naturalness?

We can only hope.

Don Pohren
November 1997

PART VI

EXPLANATORY
NOTES
AND
GLOSSARY

EXPLANATORY NOTES

(1) From P. 27. This development represented great progress in this area, for Morón had been a republican stronghold during the Civil War, and afterwards its citizens had suffered accordingly. Those considered dangerous had been given long jail sentences, and the area had been closely observed for years after the war as a possible hotbed of rebellion. The facist authorities had been correct in their suspicions, which came to light with Spain's 1976 liberalization, at which time Morón's numerous communists and socialists surfaced, a communist newspaper was founded, and Morón, along with most of the rest of Andalusia, voted for the communist or socialist parties. This is not surprising in view of the fact that Andalusia ranks high among the least advanced regions of Spain and is today called "the land of unemployment." Morón alone has declined in population from some forty thousand after the war to a mere twenty thousand today. People are leaving by the busloads for more prosperous areas because Morón simply cannot provide enough work for them at present. Those who are left are demanding equal opportunities with the rest of Spain, which the communist and socialist parties promise. The people are fed up with a few big landowners holding most of the wealth, and things could come to a bad head unless the present democratic congress (the majority of congressional seats are held by the Center, followed by the Socialists) quickly alleviates the unemployment problem (it claims it is doing its best to do so, but that it will take time).

(2) From P. 32. On two occasions we nearly ran into brave bulls in the last tunnel before reaching the Peñón. The Land Rover's headlights picked up the eyes of the otherwise black bulls in the even blacker tunnel. They were coming towards us, undoubtedly pondering just what to do about this diesel monster with the shining eyes rattling towards them. Fortunately, before they decided on a course of action I put the Rover into reverse and backed slowly out, leaving the bulls plenty of space to leave the tunnel, and trail, without feeling threatened. As soon as they emerged they headed for open spaces, and the danger was over. They didn't want a confrontation any more than we did.

(3) From P. 42. This type of malicious activity is most prevalent in Andalusia, although by no means unknown in other parts of Spain. A type of humor more universally Spanish pokes fun at the traits, idiosyncrasies, failures, and even accomplishments of the wealthy and powerful. For instance, when Franco built a series of very beneficial dams throughout Spain he became known as "Paquito Rana," or "Frankie Frog." Many,

187

many jokes concerned themselves with Franco and his regime, which Franco apparantly enjoyed as much as anyone else if it is true that he used to urge his close associates to recount even the most critical jokes to him and laugh uproariously if they were cleverly conceived (they invariably are).

But the most popular humor throughout Spain is black humor. A rash of ingenious jokes pops up seemingly simultaneously with almost all major events of a nature tragic to some. Now famous examples of such black humor deal with the death of Carrero Blanco, longtime President of Spain under Franco, who was murdered while on his way to church some five years ago. Terrorists had placed a bomb under a Madrid street that Carrero Blanco habitually used, and when his car reached the precise spot, the car and its occupants (Carrero Blanco, a secret service man and the chauffeur) were blown clear over a six-story building and into the inner courtyard of a monastery. All the car's occupants, of course, were killed. Now, regardless of the fact that Carrero Blanco was not a popular figure, this does not seem like joking material to most non-Spaniards. But to the Spaniard, with his professed disregard for death, this is the stuff of instant humor. Two jokes in particular spread like wildfire:

Background, Joke 1: Carrero Blanco was extremely religious, and was on his way to take communion. In the communion ceremony, the host (wafer) is called "hostia" in Spanish, which also happens to be a very irreverent swear word.

Joke 1: Just after the bomb exploded, when the car was at about second story level and rising rapidly, Carrero Blanco exclaimed:

"¡Hostia, qué bache!" "Hostia, what a bump!"

Background, Joke 2: As already stated, the car landed in the inner courtyard of a monastery after having been blown some seventy or eighty feet high.

Joke 2: "Carrero Blanco must have been a saint."

"Why?"

"He was given a Holy Ascension."

(Yes, the jokes suffer in translation.)

As we have seen, Franco got a big kick out of Franco jokes, but would he have enjoyed this one, that circulated immediately after his death?

Joke: Franco had been hanging on at death's door for an agonizingly long period. His team of doctors finally decided there was nothing more they could do, and decided to take him to Lourdes and pray for a miracle. Upon arrival, they immersed him in the Holy Water. He died instantly, at which the doctors all joyously exclaimed:

"MIRACLE!"

(4) From P. 52.· As may have been observed in the past two paragraphs, Fernandillo could not exactly be considered the ideal family man. Ladies, start appreciating your husbands, for there is more to come. True to gypsy tradition, Fernandillo's wife never sat down to eat until Fernandillo had finished and had left the table. Even when there were guests, she limited herself to cooking and serving until we had all finished, then ate her meal (or, more often, she ate it standing up while bustling about). This surprised us and I once asked Fernandillo why this was so. He replied that other than

gypsy tradition (he did not know the source or cause of the tradition) it was only practical. If she also sat down, who would do the cooking and serving? (There is something to this; the kitchens of the poor usually have only one burner, and certainly no stove for keeping dishes hot, so one dish must be eaten while the next is cooking.) In addition, he claimed that she was much too shy to eat with the rest of us, and one day asked her if she would like to. She blushed and refused.

(5) From P. 66. Fortunately, our boxer dynasty lives on with us today, in form of one of Willie's daughters (Simba) and grandsons (Oscar). They are just as loving as Willie was and far more civilized, as befits big city apartment living.

(6) From P. 79. Andaluz anger rises to a quick head and is often long lasting. Feuds develop over the most trivial matters, time-hardened by pig-headedness. I was personally involved in three such situations during the Morón years, much to my regret, for they were all with good and respected friends. Two were with local flamencos, who were lost to our juergas for about a year each, and another with a local mason, a man of high intelligence of whom I was very fond (we didn't speak for about three years). All the feuds were eventually dissolved over a few drinks and much laughter at our ridiculous behavior and excessive pride. Everyone had been longing to resume friendship but had not known how to do so without losing face.

(7) From P. 82. In Spain, the drug laws, when enforced, are severely enforced. At best, foreign offenders are given twenty-four hours to leave Spain permanently; at worst, several years in prison.

(8) From P. 85. "Mesón Arni" is now open and doing well in Estepona, a Costa del Sol town near Marbella. (Calle Mondéjar 15. Tel.: 952-800731.)

(9) From P. 107. "Chimney" and "Owl," respectively. Nearly everyone in Spanish towns has a nickname, frequently used much more often than the person's true name. Nicknames are usually a direct reflection of a person's profession or major physical or mental characteristic, but also can merely be inherited from a parent or even grandparent. The nature of the nickname and sensitivity of the bearer determine whether or not it can be used in the bearer's presence.

(10) From P. 119. The featherless *gallo* (rooster or cock) is revered in Morón, to the extent that a bronze replica is mounted on a soaring pedestal in the center of Morón's highest square (up a series of steep steps from Casa Pepe). The square in question affords a sweeping view of Morón and environs, and the impression is given that the featherless bird is in constant vigilance against purveyors of evil (above all after one knows the legend; beforehand, the statue appears rather ludicrous).

There are several accounts attempting to explain this phenomenon, by far the most widely supported being as follows:

Back in the 15th Century Morón was plagued by a bald (featherless) tax collector nicknamed "El Gallo." This man was extremely heavy-handed in his collections of the King's taxes, having no mercy whatsoever even on the poor and needy. Besides, it was common knowledge that he collected far more than the King's quota and pocketed the surplus, which practice permitted him to live in a grand manner. As human nature will have it, El Gallo became more and more greedy as the years passed, until the tax payers would take no more. They then turned on him with a vengeance, giving El Gallo a sound beating followed by tarring and feathering, tying him on a donkey, and steering him in a northerly direction, towards Madrid.

El Gallo was never seen or heard from again, nor was any retribution initiated by the authorities. The defiant act had been successful, and from then on the featherless rooster has symbolized liberty and justice in Morón de la Frontera.

(11) From P. 120. In those days funeral processions were comprised solely of men. Women *were* allowed to attend the church service, but then repaired directly to the house of the widow to mourn and give comfort. Thus, custom dictated that only men take part in Diego's funeral procession, plus the few women who dared defy tradition. Today, women's lib has reached even towns like Morón, and such customs are being discarded rapidly. (Including another that forbade mothers to attend the christenings of their own babies; mothers stayed home preparing for the post-baptismal festivities, while the godmother represented the mother at the ceremony.)

(12) From P. 123. One of the ridiculous feuds to which I refer in a previous footnote began this night, and with no less a friend than Fernandillo. Just as the juerga was beginning, all the booze Fernandillo had consumed the previous days started making him feel ill, and he asked me to take him home. I told him I couldn't leave right then but would run him home once the juerga was properly underway. Meantime, he could lie down in one of the bedrooms. In his stubborn drunkenness he demanded to be taken home instantly. I reiterated my position, and much to my surprise he stomped off in great anger and apparently walked home. I was even more surprised when he followed up by refusing subsequent finca juergas, for I figured that once he sobered up the matter would be forgotten. He let the grapevine know he was waiting for me to apologize and beg him to return. I wasn't about to, for I considered the whole thing entirely his fault, and a long stalemate developed. He finally decided his course of inaction was not very clever and one day invited me to a drink in Casa Pepe as if nothing had happened (previous to this he had made friendly overtures to Luisa and Tina, so we knew he was coming around). Nearly a year had been lost by the foolishness.

(13) From P. 127. In reality, Sr. Stern, being a countryman of advanced age, calculated money in *reales*. A "real" is worth twenty-five centimos, or a quarter of a peseta, which in his youth had been a significant monetary value. (Twenty-five centimo coins disappeared some years ago.) Thus, Sr. Stern articulated his initial offer as two thousand reales instead of five hundred pesetas, which Fernandillo automatically translated into *duros*,

the more realistic monetary shortcut of a new generation (one duro = five pesetas = twenty reales; thus the initial offer of 500 pesetas = 2000 reales = 100 duros). Ironically, the Watch Boaster, an educated gentleman who seemingly would be far more capable than his nearly illiterate counterparts at making these rapid calculations, thought in terms of pesetas, although he had to be able to handle with ease the other values.

So Fernandillo's and Sr. Stern's final price of 1100 pesetas was considered by Fernandillo as 220 duros and by Sr. Stern as 4400 reales. Complicated? Absolutely.

(14) From P. 168. Science tells us that a certain amount of alcohol deadens the intellect and releases the emotions. As flamenco is basically an emotional art, it is thus enhanced by a reasonable amount of alcohol, which amount varies with each person. Spacy drugs such as pot, however, have an opposite effect, that of inhibiting the emotional part of the brain and intensifying the intellect. This is not desirable for flamenco. The whole emotive force of flamenco, its very reason for being, is lost when viewed by an aloof, overblown intellect.

(15) From P. 169. The flamencos had another highly valid reason for not being too eager to attend juergas out of town. Occasionally the hiring señorito would somehow be short of cash at the time of payment and would casually remark to the flamencos that they could drop by in two or three days for their money. Such a turn of events upset even the local artists, for they lived by the day and had planned immediate use of the money, but really inconvenienced the out-of-town artists, who would have to make at least one extra trip to collect their share. *If* they collected, I might add, for class distinctions were (and still are) so immense in Andalusia that the flamencos didn't dare become too insistent, and it sometimes came to pass that after two or three visits to a neighboring town, bumming rides when they could to avoid expenses and humbly approaching the señorito about the payment (when he could he found), they would give up. Strangely enough, the flamencos took these non-payment juergas in stride. The "guasa" system came to their rescue, for as much as they needed the money and were truly disappointed at the loss (sometimes working themselves up to a high pitch of frustration during the doubtful period), if ultimately not paid they were able to joke about how cleverly they had been duped and grudgingly admire the duper. What else could they do? The law would have laughed at them and told them to be more careful next time.

Then there were the señorito "guasones" who played more complex jokes, toying, as it were, with human greed. One such "joke" went like this. At juerga's end the hiring señorito slipped an unstipulated wad of bills into one of the artist's pockets, which the artists were to divvy up amongst themselves as they saw fit. The immediate reaction was that all the other artists stuck to the money-bearer like glue, just in case he tried to hide part of it or pass some of it to an accomplice, or even slip away with all of it. (This has actually happened, is indeed considered the highest form of guasa if one gets away with it; however, such a blatant guasón of the same class — that is to say, without the privileges of the señorito — could also end up with

191

a knife in his guts.) Thus, in order to avoid suspicion and the almost certain accusations, the entrusted artist more often than not insisted that another of the artists carry the money. Everyone usually refused. They all preferred to suspect than be suspected. But finally someone agreed to take the risk, and they all repaired to some private spot to begin the divvying-up process.

I was present at one such affair, upstairs at Casa Pepe. Some ten artists were involved, including Diego, who suggested I come up to observe the procedure as part of my education in Andalusian life. (I had been downstairs in Casa Pepe when they all appeared.) Diego was an old hand at such proceedings, and just sat back and enjoyed them. So, in this case, did I.

The first trauma came when the money-carrier laid the loot out on the table. There was considerably less of it than this señorito normally paid, and the carrier was under immediate suspicion. Fortunately it was soon agreed, after he had emptied all his pockets and revealed all possible hiding places, that he could not possibly have cheated them – nine pairs of eyes had followed his every move since he received the money. Therefore, that "hijo de puta" señorito had deceived them! (As Diego knew all along, this particular señorito was really quite a decent type. Part of his guasa, of course, had been to pay far less in this case than he normally did, which he made up for at the next juerga.) The next fifteen or twenty minutes were devoted to slandering the fellow, as well as all of his ancestors. When this became tiresome, the artists reasoned realistically that they had to make do with the sum they had, and might as well get down to the business of splitting it up.

Now is when it hit the fan. Great shouting, stomping and pounding on the table ensued, for the señorito's major triumph had been leaving it up to the flamencos themselves to decide how the money was to be divided. Before, they had all been united, fellow victims of adversity. Now it was a pitched battle of egos, every man for himself. Insults filled the air like artillery fire, picaresque pronouncements attacking everything from each other's artistry to his manhood. As the battle raged alarming crescendos climaxed, when it seemed there had to be enormous free-for-alls, at which moments someone always broke the tension with bits of inspired humor, making the group laugh in spite of itself. After this happened a few times it dawned on me that these people were having the time of their lives, taking the affair only half seriously at most. The money didn't really matter that much. The important thing was to carry on and have fun.

The "negotiations" began in the morning and continued until closing time, some fourteen hours. In the interim the artists drank up a storm, beginning with *fino* and soon switching to whiskey, all of which greatly depleted the artists' treasure pot and which Pepe downstairs raked in with bubbling good humor, enjoying the scene upstairs as much as the profits (for the insults, *cachondeo* and raucousness could distinctly be heard downstairs, and a good ways down the street as well). Actually, the negotiating didn't really last the full fourteen hours, for in the late afternoon the artists burst into juerga, during the course of which they invited everyone up from downstairs to share in the juerga, the huge stew they had Pepe's wife Anita make, and the endless wine and whiskey. By closing time the little that was left of the juerga money was split up evenly, and everyone staggered off happily into the night (the out-of-towners having to share a cab home, which took up nearly all their remaining earnings).

Diego and I had a last nightcap with Pepe. They asked me how I had enjoyed the show. I could only grin and mutter "unbeatable."

Although the flamencos well appreciated the fine guasa involved in all of the above — in fact, felt rather helpless before it, for only bad sports do not appreciate well-conceived guasa — they far preferred the finca method of payment, which was consistently immediate for out-of-towners, and at worst no later than the following day for the locals.

(16) From P. 169. This "primitive" way of singing avoids usage of adornment and ostentation of any kind. The verses are short and direct, arriving straight to the point without wordiness, doubling back, warbles or wobbles. As sung by La Piriñaca, the *Cante* is not so much an art of singing as a direct cry from the soul.

(17) From P. 173. El Farruco is not only gypsy traditional in his dance (within the framework of having become sufficiently commercial artistically to make his living in tablaos, night clubs and flamenco festivals) but even more so in other ways. No doubt thinking that Luisa and I could prove very useful to him in the flamenco world (and believing us rich, what with the finca and all the fanfare), he began suggesting that his dancing son and our dancing daughter should get married. The fact that the young people had not even met made no difference to him; plenty of time for that after the marriage. At first we laughed, thinking he was joking, but soon saw he was completely in earnest. We tried explaining that in our culture sons and daughters marry whom they please. This sounded like weakness to him, and he exclaimed that gypsy offspring marry whom their parents choose, the only practical way!

Once he saw his plan was to no avail, he turned off on us. Our potential usefulness to him had dissipated, and in addition I suppose he was wounded, most likely thinking that we considered our daughter above marriage with a gypsy. It was useless to reiterate that she could marry whom she chooses, gypsy or otherwise.

(18) From P. 174. Manolito's death, in 1968, was as unusual as his life had been. A variety of illnesses suddenly ganged up on him when in his mid-sixties and Manolito was interned in Sevilla's general hospital where, according to patients and staff with whom we talked, he liked to wander around at all hours of the day or night singing flamenco to his new friends. He did not recognize us when we visited him shortly before he died, but he seemed content. His funeral, regardless of the fact that Manolito died penniless, was grandiose. Half of Alcalá turned out to pay homage to his fiercely independent bohemian, including the local authorities and the region's most prominent flamenco artists and aficionados.

(19) From P. 177. My experience in pre-industrial Andalusia was that not only were the flamencos happier, the people in general were more

content than they are in today's industrial democracy. Excepting the politically minded, that is, for creeds other than Franco's were not tolerated. Franco's regime was also very tough on wrongdoers. Almost no delinquency existed, a condition remembered today with nostalgia, for with the democratic liberalization of police policy malefactors are, predictably enough, crawling out of the woodwork in alarming quantities. But other than those two exceptions, Franco's rule had become relatively benevolent by the mid-fifties.Though the people did not have much in the way of material possessions, they did have the basic needs, as well as jobs or trades in which they could take pride (assembly lines were still in the future) and an easy-going life style that was absolutely captivating to one like myself, precisely in Spain to escape the extreme materialism of the USA. The fact that very little ambition existed among a great percentage of the population (because it was so difficult at that time for the masses to move beyond their traditional niches, due to their lack of education, training and culture, that the possibility rarely even entered their minds) also furthered the relaxed life of the Andalusian. He had no pressure on him to better his position, was instead respected for being exactly what he was. In short, he did his job at a leisurely pace, and then was able to sit back and enjoy life to the fullest, which habitually included dropping into his favorite bar after work, as well as on and off during the day, for some wine (cleverly kept by the government at an extremely low price), conversation and joking, and perhaps a game or two of dominos or cards involving just enough low-key gambling to retain one's interest. And for those of a flamenco bent there was the nearly continual singing, dancing and/or guitar playing in certain bars, such as Casa Pepe *(before* the invasion of television, that is, for the noise and distraction of the Box effectively cut down and eventually killed the flamenco initiative in bars even as it peddled materialism).

Oh yes, and one other extremely important factor existed that contributed enormously to the contentment of the Spaniard: a nearly complete ignorance of, and isolation from, the rest of the world, brought about in Spain's case by a particular set of circumstances over the last century-and-a-half (no foreign invasion of Spain since Napoleon's of the early 1800's, extremely limited tourism into Spain until the middle 1950's, and the fact that few Spaniards had the means to travel outside of Spain until just recently). This isolationism made it possible for the propaganda efforts of two dictatorships in this century to effectively create the belief in Spaniards that their country was a sort of paradise populated by chosen people (for with whom and what was the Spaniard to compare himself and his condition?) Primo de Rivero made a point of increasing his people's happiness by dwelling upon their superiority, and then Franco's all-out propaganda effort along the same lines swept away remaining doubts in all but the most worldly Spaniards.

Thus, when I arrived in Spain in 1953 I was constantly being told (by people who had neither been out of Spain nor had contact with non-Spaniards) that Spanish women were the world's most lovely, Spanish food the best, Spanish men the most macho, Spanish scenery the most beautiful, Spanish wine the most outstanding, Spaniards the most spiritual (the were extremely smug in their Catholocism; all non-catholics were believed heretics or heathens who would not be permitted into heaven), and even the sky was different: it was thought to be more blue over Spain. These and many other ignorant beliefs were deeply imbedded, giving each Spaniard a complacency and self-assurance wonderful to behold (if a bit maddening at times).

This age of innocence and naiveté was abruptly swept away by the progress of the industrial age. Hollywood instilled the first vague doubts, making these folks realize there was something else, but it all seemed so distant and far-fetched they could not take the movies too seriously. Then came the American air bases in the early 1950's, populated by thousands of American servicemen with their oversized American cars and their Big Bucks, gobbling up everything in sight. Simultaneously the hordes of tourists began sweeping through Spain, also flaunting their gadgets, extravagant clothing and stacks of money. TV was the finishing touch. By the late sixties television had invaded all Spanish bars and many homes. The people could no longer escape the outside world even if they had so desired.

And down tumbled the Spanish myth of superiority. It didn't take long for the folks in even the most remote villages to realize that they were only too obviously "backward" compared with much of the rest of the world, and they (unfortunately) felt ashamed of it. They now realized that their former contentment had been based on lies, misconceptions, ignorance and economic under-development, and they felt deceived and foolish. A smoldering discontentment set in, and the people eagerly embraced the Twentieth Century Gods: Progress and Consumer Goods, vastly inadequate deities shown by experience in industrial countries to corrode insidiously our mental well-being even as they increase our physical comforts. Complacency and religion, the keys to former happiness, became outmoded concepts, as they have in all progressive societies, replaced by driving ambition. Bicycles were discarded for motorcycles, for faster motorcycles, for automobiles, for faster automobiles. TV and a thousand other contrivances became "necessities." More and more people began leaving their proud trades and quiet lives for big city factory jobs in which no one can take pride. And *pluriempleo,* the holding of more than one job at a time, became commonplace (how else to pay for the latest "necessities" and the big city cost of living). The Spanish people had embarked on a one way road from which there is no turning back.

That the end of Spanish complacency occurred simultaneously with the end of the flamenco way of life is no coincidence. Both were struck down by the same inevitable causes.

GLOSSARY

aficionado(a) — enthusiast; in this book, flamenco enthusiast.

alhaja — jewel.

alegrías — alegría = gaiety; the alegrías are a joyful flamenco form from the province of Cádiz, basically gypsy in nature.

Andalusia — the southernmost region of Spain, consisting of eight provinces: Huelva, Sevilla, Cádiz, Córdoba, Málaga, Granada, Jaén and Almería.

Andalusian-style flamenco — a melodic, lyrical, often free-form style of flamenco, favored by most non-gypsy Andalusians over the more down-to-earth gypsy variety.

andaluz — Andalusian

artista — artist; in this book, performer of flamenco.

barbaridades — barbarity; rashness.

bulerías — flamenco's most lively and driving form, decidedly gypsy in nature.

cabrón — billygoat; in slang, a cuckold.

cachondeo — hell-raising, reveling, good times (modern, and this book's, usage; literally has a sexual connotation).

cacique — town influential who controls the local situation; he may or may not hold a political office.

café cantante — the name given commercial flamenco establishments in the XIX century.

calle — street.

Cante — flamenco singing.

cante — a particular flamenco song form.

caseta — cottage or hut; also a temporary edifice constructed by groups for the enjoyment of Andalusian fairs.

castellana — gypsy term for a non-gypsy Spanish woman; literally, a woman from Castile.

charco — pool, water hole.

colmado — archaic Andalusian term for tavern or cabaret.

coño — literally, "cunt," but quite meaningless when used as an exclamation, as is popularly done.

compás — rhythm, beat.

cursi — pretentious, putting on airs to an unnatural extent.

de — of.

duende — feeling, emotion.

ese gitano — that gypsy.

espléndido — splendid, big spender, grand acting.

fandangos — the favorite non-gypsy flamenco form, which can be lively (fandangos de Huelva, fandanguillos) or serious (fandangos grandes). The "grandes," although conceived by non-gypsies, are also favorites among the gypsies.

fiesta — party; also a substitute word for "juerga" in flamenco jargon.

fiestero(a) — an all-round artist who usually both dances and sings as well as being an accomplished jaleador(a). He/she may also play the guitar, recite poetry, have a gift for humorous stories... in short, whatever it takes to liven up a juerga.

finca — a farm, ranch, country house or estate of relatively small extension if compared with an hacienda (larger) or cortijo (largest).

finca de recreo — pleasure finca equipped more for comfortable living than for farming or ranching.

fino — elegant; also, a type of strong white Andalusian wine.

fui — I went.

Fulano(a) de Tal — a symbolic name, like John or Jane Doe.

fonda — village boarding house.

gazpacho — a cold Andalusian salad soup, made from tomatoes/bread/olive oil/garlic/water, often garnished with minced tomato, onion, green pepper and/or hard-boiled egg.

gracia — charm, wit.

gracioso — funny, witty, pleasing.

Guardia Civil — Civil Guard.

guasa, guasón — consult P. 41.

gypsy-style flamenco — flamenco developed by the gypsies, more straight-forward and earthily emotional than the flamenco of the non-gypsies.

hola — hi.

hombre — man.

hijo de puta — son-of-a-whore, a term more often used in jest than seriously.

jaleador(a) — a person who animates another's performance by hand-clapping, finger-snapping, tongue-clacking, shouts of encouragement, and/or foot-stomping.

joder — literally, "fuck," or "to fuck," but largely meaningless when used as an exclamation, as is popularly done.

juerga — live flamenco jam session.

macho — traditionaly, "real man," or "stud." Today macho has a derogatory ring to it, above all on the lips of women libbers.

malagueñas — Andalusian, rhythmless sòng form from the province of Málaga.

mamá — mama, mamma.

martinetes — song form that developed in the gypsy forges to the ring of hammers. Traditionally without instrumental accompaniment, nor danced.

me cago en la mar -- popular Andalusian expression meaning "I shit in the sea."

mierda — shit; a turd.

muy simpático — very charming, congenial, pleasant.

¡ojú ¡ — an Andalusian manner of exclaiming "Jesus!"

¡olé! — shout of approval.

one thousand pesetas varies in value according to the monetary exchange, was worth in those days some $17-$20.

oye, oiga — listen.

palmas — hand-clapping; palms of the hands.

payo(a) – non-gypsy; also, *gachó(í)*.

peñón – cliff.

Pepe Marchena – most famous recent exponent of a commercialized version of the Andalusian style of song.

pesetas – Spanish currency.

por – for, through.

¡Por Dios! – For God's sake!

pueblo – town, village, hamlet.

rumba – a flamenco form, derived from the Cuban rumba, that has caught on in modern times due to its simple and catchy rhythm.

sangría – a drink comprising red wine and fruit.

señorito – traditionally "young gentleman, master"; today more often than not used derogatorily as the ruling class loses its grip.

sevillanas – a lively folkloric song and dance from Sevilla that is not truly a part of flamenco.

sierra – mountain range.

siesta – afternoon nap.

seguiriyas – a gypsy-conceived flamenco form that is flamenco's most despondent.

simpático – charming, congenial, pleasant.

soleá – shortened form of saying "soleares."

soleares – a gypsy-conceived flamenco form considered flamenco's main embodiment of love.

tablao – name given to present-day commercial flamenco establishments; literally, "tablado," meaning platform or stage.

tangos – gypsy-conceived flamenco form that originated in the province of Cádiz.

tanguillos – a lighter, gaier little brother of the tangos.

tapas – small portions of food traditionally served with alcoholic beverages in both bars and homes. Besides being gastronomically exciting, they are excellent insulation against drunkenness. In Andalusia, where the men, particularly the flamencos, spend a good share of their time in bars, tapas make up a major portion of their diet. Today tapas are slowly disappearing from the scene, above all in the big cities. They are time-consuming and therefore costly to prepare, not giving a large enough profit margin. "Raciones," or "rations," are taking over, far larger and costlier portions of food which do allow substantial profits.

venga ya – come off it.

venta – a country inn serving drinks and food, rarely large and auspicious enough to have guest rooms.

vino – wine.

viva – long live.

¡Ya está! – That does it!